THE SMALL WORLD OF
ANTIQUE DOLLS' HOUSES

THE SMALL WORLD OF ANTIQUE DOLLS' HOUSES

SIX DECADES OF COLLECTING MANSIONS, COTTAGES, SHOPS, STABLES, THEATERS, CHURCHES—EVEN A ZOO!

BY FLORA GILL JACOBS

LAKE ISLE PRESS, INC.
NEW YORK

Grateful acknowledgment is made to the following for permission to reprint
previously published material: (See Source Notes, page 430)

Published by:
Lake Isle Press, Inc.
16 West 32nd Street, Suite 10-B
New York, NY 10001
(212) 273-0796
E-mail: lakeisle@earthlink.net

Distributed to the trade by:
National Book Network (NBN), Inc.
4501 Forbes Boulevard, Suite 200
Landham, MD 20706
1 (800) 462-6420
www.nbnbooks.com

Library of Congress Control Number: 2005929922

ISBN: 1-891105-07-8

Book Design: Clover Archer

Cover Design: Ellen Swandiak

First Edition

Printed in China

10 9 8 7 6 5 4 3 2 1

*For Sadie and her feline predecessors, Annie, Gumbie,
Pandora, and Patty, who brought a note of grace—and a
bit of fun—to every project, including this one.*

ACKNOWLEDGMENTS

Special thanks are owing to Marianne and Jürgen Cieslik
who gave permission to reproduce photos from their remarkable
Gottschalk archive, to Matthew Ward who came twice
from England to do much of the major photography, and to my
publisher, Hiroko Kiiffner, who arranged for him to come.
Most especially, I wish to thank James Reus, a restorer, dealer and
scholar of dolls' houses, who photographed most of the
innumerable detail illustrations, and patiently waited for the fussy
author to peer into his lens before each shot. He also
provided infinitely helpful technical assistance. Thanks as well to
those members of my staff at The Washington Dolls'
House & Toy Museum★ who initially helped to transfer untidy
typed pages to the essential computer. And, finally, (all too
finally), to my friend Faith Eaton, recently deceased, and, therefore,
no longer present to receive my gratitude. At a time when
she was under pressure to complete a book of her own, she
graciously provided the preface for this one.

★*Which reluctantly closed its doors on May 1, 2004.*

TABLE OF CONTENTS

FOREWORD *Page 2*

PREFACE *Page 5*

PART I

American Houses, Handcrafted

Page 7

PART II

American Houses, Commercially Made

Page 95

PART III

English Houses, Both Stately and Modest

Page 155

PART IV

European Houses: Mansions, Villas, and Cottages

Page 211

PART V

Chambers, Salons, and Such

Page 247

PART VI

Kitchens, Plumbing, and a Dentist's Office

Page 287

PART VII

Shops: Mercantile History in Miniature

Page 315

PART VIII

Assorted Structures: Churches, Stables, Firehouses, Etc.

Page 355

PART IX

Arts & Leisure: Theaters, Zoos—Even a Houseboat

Page 385

PART X

The Mexican Mansion: An Extravaganza

Page 411

INDEX

Page 423

A RATHER AUTOBIOGRAPHICAL FOREWORD

The collection to be seen in these pages assuredly is related to a personal preoccupation with the architecture and the decorative arts of the past—and with the past itself—both in full-size and in miniature.

I was overtaken by the miniature aspect of this preoccupation in 1945 when antique dolls' houses and related miniaturiana hadn't quite been discovered and, as a result, were more affordable—when they could be found. In any case, the collecting of such objects became an irresistible disease.

What follows is a rather personal tour of the resulting collection. This was begun more than half a century ago, in 1945, by happenstance. It began as an attempt to write a book for children, one which was part story and part "how-to," how to make a dolls' house out of a cardboard box, and furnishings from spools and match boxes and such. The latter was at least partially inspired by a dolls' house-making project for my fourth grade class at John Eaton School in Washington, D.C. (I remember that my creation was fashioned from a square hat box for which I provided striped awnings.)

A few years later, further inspiration was undoubtedly supplied by the arrival of a marvelous dolls' house next door when a military family moved in. The thoroughly furnished house of my late friend, Laura Ellis Mulligan, was fashioned by her remarkable mother from an improbable source—gas mask boxes, when the Ellis family was stationed in Nuremberg after World War II. It was crammed with many of the early furnishings now sought by collectors. I did not have a dolls' house, (only some furniture which I arranged and re-arranged) but, during the three years the Ellises were stationed in Washington, there was ample time for inspiration from Laura's house.

As a young writer, I was advised to query an editor rather than to send a completed manuscript. The New York editor I queried agreed to see the manuscript but mentioned that she had reservations about combining story and how-to. Needless to say, I forwarded this simple project promptly and received the amazing response that she was coming to Washington and would like to take me to lunch. It was a heady response! Decades later, I don't recall another editor coming to Washington to take me to lunch.

She was a wonderful lady—the late Siri Andrews of Henry Holt & Co., later head of the Children's Division of the New York Public Library. At lunch she told me that, as she thought, she did not care for the combination of story and how-to, and suggested removing the story. I declined and that manuscript is in the attic somewhere.

However, she further suggested that I think

A HOUSE FROM HOVE
GLAZED CASE: HEIGHT: 9" WIDTH: 10"

about possibilities for the twelve to sixteen age group (there was such an age group in those days.) I was not about to let such an opportunity go by, and I came up with the not especially brilliant idea of doing a book about a celebrated dolls' house in terms of interior decoration for children. I mentioned Colleen Moore's castle which I had not seen at the time and which, with its chandeliers made from the silent screen star's diamond jewelry, would have been totally inappropriate for such a purpose. Siri Andrews liked the idea but proposed a book about several famous dolls' houses she mentioned Queen Mary's at Windsor and suggested some preliminary research.

Fortuitously, the Library of Congress is in my town, and when I began a happy year of delving there, I discovered that there had never been a history of dolls' houses[1] and didn't realize that I was about to write the first. When I submitted, as suggested, four chapters and a synopsis, and it was decided that the book should be for collectors rather than children, I lost Siri Andrews to a series of editors. Finally it fell into the hands of a gentleman who was not interested in dolls' houses and it was locked up in the publisher's safe for a few years, before it was taken by Scribner's. When I started writing about dolls' houses in 1945, I started to collect almost immediately. The chicken, as I've often said, came first, not the egg.

During the course of the first quarter century of The Washington Dolls' House & Toy Museum, I've often been asked how the collection evolved, and that is why I've gone into the "whole story." I've also been asked how the museum came into being, and the answer there is simpler: There were so many requests to see the collection at home from friends, friends' friends, and from friends' Brownie troops, that the tours became inordinately time-consuming. Usually tea and cookies were offered (on the antique china.) I'd fall behind—and when weeks would go by with assorted requests unacknowledged, a museum, open to the public, seemed a logical alternative.

The result is often referred to as the "doll museum," but it is more accurately, per its rather ungainly name, a dolls' *house* and toy museum, the pioneer of such museums. (There have been many doll museums, in the past, with dolls sitting in rows on shelves.) The Museum was given, in 1981, a small, splendid collection of large dolls by a remarkable California woman (page 180). With those, the museum was splendidly enhanced. I had always collected small dolls—dolls' house dolls to occupy the houses and related structures, the dolls which looked like little people and were suitably dressed as cooks, mothers, fathers, chauffeurs, children, nannies and such. I'd included a few "large" dolls and increasingly became involved with antique toys and games, but that is another story.

Strewn through these opening paragraphs are illustrations of miniature structures made for other purposes. There is a quite spectacular Victorian Gothic Martin house (which resides on a sizeable screened porch.) There is a diminutive residence, under a glass dome, of Bristol board (the perforated cardboard on which Berlin-work and other types of wool-work were often embroidered.) This is sufficiently ancient that one of the early Victorian

A VICTORIAN GOTHIC MARTIN HOUSE
WIDTH (AT BASE): 34" HEIGHT: 21 1/2" (PLUS SPIRE)

1. There was a scholarly work published in 1909 in Dutch and German, about the celebrated Dutch Patrizienhauser of the seventeenth and eighteenth centuries. And there was *The Book of the Queen's Dolls' House* published in England in 1924.

columns on its portico has disappeared. Another similarly petite but highly detailed English residence is sealed into a glazed case. This, of heavy card, and realistic with garden and conservatory, is complete with smoke rising from a few of its numerous chimney-pots. It is from Hove, near Brighton, and is a house, I was told, associated with Princess Louise.[1] Such representations as these, along with watercolors and assorted graphics of houses are fulfilling to an amateur of architecture.

As for the furnishings of the structures, I longed to include here, as I did in an earlier book, groupings of objects in miniature ("Heating and Lighting," "Pastimes and Pleasures"). When I did this in 1967 in *A Book of Dolls and Dolls' Houses* (and later in *Victorian Dolls' Houses*) most were necessarily in black and white, and this collection was considerably smaller. Alas, that will have to await a book about furnishings—if time is willing. (There were more than 200 chairs in (poor) color in *Dolls' Houses in America*. If chairs were to be photographed now, from the collection in the museum and at home, it might be possible to illustrate 500—antique and each different.)

Here, numerous furnishings are shown and described. Many of the houses shown in these pages when found were devoid of their original contents. It has been my pleasure to furnish the empty chambers. After more than six decades of collecting and studying interiors, both full-sized and miniature, one learns—or should have learned—what style and what vintage a chair or candlestick should represent before it is placed in a room.

If this collector sees an object in miniature, she tends to want it in full-size. If she has it in full-size, she tends to want it in miniature. There is, for instance, the miniature chatelaine which has been collected along with the full-sized chatelaine, and the miniature transitional chandelier to represent the full-sized specimen. The latter, now completely electrified, still contains its six gas globes facing up and its six electric bulb shades facing down in our full-sized dining room.

Perhaps the state of such a collector's mind should be referred to not as a preoccupation with the structures of the past and its lares and penates, but as an addiction to *all of the above*.

It has always been my great regret that all of the collection shown in the following pages could not be displayed under one roof. Even here, much has been omitted. In any case, the portion to be seen during nearly three decades at The Washington Dolls' House & Toy Museum, and the balance on display at home, are herewith, for the first time, united under "one roof."

★★★

A Postscript: In its thirtieth year, The Washington Dolls' House & Toy Museum closed its doors in May of 2004.

Many kind words were spoken at its demise, but my favorite tribute came during the course of the final weeks, from a tiny girl for whom I was signing one of my juvenile mysteries. She could not have been more than four or five and seemed no higher than my knee. She looked up at me and said something so softly that I had to ask her to repeat it. When I still could not catch what she said, her mother repeated it for her.

She said, "You are a very good finder." I hope the following pages which illustrate many pieces in the Museum along with many in the collection at home, will serve to confirm her charming words.

BRISTOL BOARD HOUSE UNDER DOME
DIAMETER OF BASE: 5 3/4"

1. By the late John Noble, former toy curator of The Museum of the City of New York, from whom I acquired it many long years ago.

PREFACE
BY FAITH EATON

To find one's self able to carry a tea set in a teaspoon, pick up a wardrobe with one hand or sit comfortably in a chair whilst cleaning flights of stair-carpets with a toothbrush...well, as Humpty Dumpty remarked to Alice in another wonderland, "There's glory for you."

In her enchanting museum and in her home Flora Gill Jacobs has assembled with care and painstaking research over a period of more than six decades, a breathtaking assortment of diminutive dwellings, a microcosm of our domestic world, along with assorted shops, stables, zoos, and other miniature buildings.

For this amazing array of miniature, fully-furnished mansions, townhouses, and cottages does not only encapsulate the domestic architecture and interior design of past centuries, it also illustrates social history and the customs and the ways of living over many decades.

The value of such a vast collection is incalculable, for it has the power to educate as well as enchant; to satisfy those who want to escape for a little while from present everyday worries, and recapture a remembered childhood delight.

Since the first one was published in 1953 collectors have read—and reread—Mrs. Jacobs' books on the history of dolls' houses with appreciation. Despite this feeling I think others have shared my wish for a book, which tells us how, and when and where this dolls' house, or that shop or kitchen, came into her keeping.

Now, at last, in this delightful book, with its superb illustrations which add much to our pleasure and knowledge, we have the longed for guided tour through the author's cherished and enchanted domain.

Though realizing it would need many volumes to cover all the stories about these dolls' houses, their furnishings and inhabitants, and the shops, stables, zoos and related buildings, this most welcome account is waiting to be read, so let us, quickly, turn the page and begin...

PART I

American Houses, Handcrafted

A Mammoth "Classic" from New England

Often in children's storybooks, especially of mid-nineteenth century American origin, when a dolls' house is illustrated, it has a certain "look." Usually it is large, with at least four sizeable rooms. It is open from the front, often with perhaps a pair of drawers beneath, presumably for storing furniture.

Such a classic dolls' house is the mammoth (five-foot tall) example pictured. Some provenance accompanied its acquisition. It was purchased at an auction, at about the turn of the century, by Emma Owens Stearns of Chestnut Hill, Massachusetts. It assuredly originated well before then—perhaps at mid-century.

There are not only four sizeable rooms divided by staircase halls, but two substantial drawers, side by side, below. On the façade, which lifts off, there are five well-designed windows with bracketed lintels and a well-designed door. The latter is glass-paneled with an arched top but, oddly, is no larger than the windows. (There are four matching windows on each of the sides.)

The house is strong as well as mammoth, obviously built by a professional or a truly gifted family member. There is a dentelated molding beneath an imposing cornice, and a strong foundation supports the deep base. At some point in its history it was painted a vivid yellow with green trim. There is evidence that originally it was a more sedate gray.

The substantial stove, an ornate toast rack, shown on page 10, and a few bits of porcelain were the only pieces which accompanied the house when it came to the Museum. However, the original floor coverings and wallpapers remained in all the rooms except for the kitchen. There were shards of a blue paper on the walls, and therefore an antique blue paper was substituted. There are also unusual red silk shades which roll down at a number of the windows.

It was a challenge to go through the Museum's reserve collection for larger-scaled pieces.[1] These

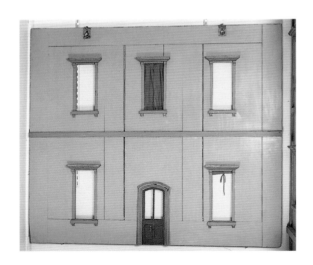

FAÇADE FITS BETWEEN CORNICE AND BASE

1. Herewith a reminder that nineteenth century dolls' house makers and furnishers did not refer to scale (today's one inch to one foot) but pieces were often made in several sizes. (Another small coincidence, one of the sort collectors thrive on, relates to the very elaborate toast rack. I'd never seen another till recently when the identical toast rack complete with the original toast was discovered in the booth of a kindly dealer who agreed to sell two slices for the toast-less example which came with this house!)

included a set of Biedermeier in the parlor and a number of Stevens & Brown iron pieces in kitchen and bedroom.

Long ago, I'd bought a collection of china dolls which had come "out of a Baltimore attic." They were dressed probably to represent a wedding party—including gentlemen in formal black and one lady in white with a long train. (Her veil was

MID-NINETEENTH CENTURY. HEIGHT: 5' WIDTH: 38"

probably removed for the reception!) They were too large for most dolls' houses but they were irresistible. They were tucked away for years, but they look very much at home here.

A fairly recent and proud addition to the house consists of three unusual chandeliers. These were discovered in a case in an antiques mall in Massachusetts. They had come, I was told, from a wonderful dolls' house which, sadly, was gradually being dismantled. In any case, the chandeliers, like the dolls, look very much at home and, like the house, were found in Massachusetts—a proper coincidence.

KITCHEN WITH CRIMSON ROLLER BLINDS

CLOCKWISE FROM TOP LEFT:
TOAST RACK
CHANDELIER
EARLY BISQUE FOOD
SILVER DUCK PIN CUSHION
WAX JACK

RARE FIREPLACE WITH GRIFFONS

IRON STEVENS & BROWN CHEST

A Somerville, Massachusetts Mansion

The idiosyncrasies of old dolls' houses are end-lessly fascinating to those who study them. This example from New England offers more than its share of possibilities, especially when it is compared to the Tiffany-Platt (page 23) from New York.

When it was offered, it was described as a copy of "an existing house"[1] in Somerville, Massachusetts. When it arrived, it was clear that its plans, its proportions, and even its very dimensions bore a striking resemblance to the Tiffany-Platt. "It is almost," I once wrote, "as though a cousin in Massachusetts had sent a sketch to a cousin in New York." And I might have added that there is always the possibility that a dolls' house plan was published in a periodical of the day, inspiring sub-scribers in different regions to reach for their hammers (or to send for their carpenters).

In both houses, there is the same arrangement of rooms and, with minor differences, of windows, and such details as bracketed cornices under the eaves. Double chimneys on the pitched rooftops are common to both. The two houses also diverge in striking ways.

Where the Tiffany-Platt has its charmingly over-scaled stoop (with sitting-room for owner and friend), Somerville substitutes a practical fea-ture of another sort: a storage drawer which flanks each side of the well-scaled stairs and double doors. Despite their paneled perfection, these doors are no more operable than the gray-green trompe l'oeil entrance door of the Tiffany, but there is a red glass toplight above them and there is a doorbell. The windows, as well as these doors, are made with more elaboration than those of the Tiffany-Platt, on which the sash bars are painted. Here the framework and sash bars are stained with outer frames and pedimented lintels painted dark

Height: 5' Width: 44"

brown as they are on the Tiffany-Platt. Another similarity: both houses are buff with dark brown rooftops to match the trim.

There is an almost mystical coincidence about the red glass toplight. The glass was missing when the house was acquired. Later I bought somewhere a box of stained glass segments. Miraculously, one piece, when inserted into the Tiffany toplight, fit-ted as though cut for it! Collectors, needless to say, thrive on such occurrences.

It is possible however, that the missing piece bore a number—a street number or a year—as American houses of this style and vintage sometimes do. It is to

---

1. With the passage of time, of course, the likelihood of this possibility has diminished.

be lamented if such was the case here, but almost compensated for by the coincidence.

In their interiors, the differences between the Tiffany and Somerville houses are even fewer, though the Tiffany has an English basement while the first floor ceilings of the Somerville are of normal height. The Somerville's rooms are papered. The Tiffany's are painted.

Although this is one of the few houses (in more than half a century of collecting) which have come to the collector purportedly with original furnishings, most of the contents when it arrived were either damaged, or of considerably later vintage than the house itself. The elegant double drawing room[1], with its twin fireplaces, contains several of the most important pieces which were salvaged, including one of a pair of twin Märklin "ormolu" chandeliers and, between the fireplaces, the early Biedermeier marble-topped chest.

ASPHALTUM KEY CABINET

ABOVE LEFT: FROM STEVENS & BROWN 1872 CATALOGUE
ABOVE RIGHT: CHAIR

ABOVE AND BELOW:
HERSEY TABLE WITH ORIGINAL PAPER LABEL

1. This room is shown at left, and the story of the furniture described in detail on page 14.

Two partial sets of Stevens & Brown iron parlor furniture have been added, combined to supply twin sofas, a pair of "easy chairs" (which we now call "gentlemen's chairs"), a pair of ottomans, and a set of side chairs in the popular balloon shape. All these pieces retain their red-flocked "upholstery." The center table with its lyre-shaped pedestal supporting a top "marbled" with paint, and the cheval glass with the patent date of "Feb. 8, 1867" on the back of the frame, are also part of this parlor set.

The pair of looking glasses over the mantels, a square pianoforte (with black and white keys reversed, as they frequently were on full-sized pianos in earlier days), and many pictures and accessories have been added. A number of the furnishings and accessories (framed photos of Danish ancestors among them) came many years ago in a collection from Copenhagen.

One addition, of sentimental value as well as antiquarian interest, is the lovely silver teapot in the upstairs sitting room. Judging by its style, including its straight spout, it is early, and it was given to me more than half a century ago by my gracious editor at Scribner's, Elinor Parker. It was from her mother's dolls' house, and I greatly regret my failure to ask her mother's maiden name and birth date. I recall that she lived to be one hundred. This piece, of course, may predate even her childhood.

The most remarkable piece of furniture which accompanied the house is the unpainted card table with its original label, that of Samuel Hersey of Hingham, Massachusetts. This rare table, placed in the third floor sitting room, may be seen on page 13.

SILVER TEAPOT

EARLY GERMAN SETTEE MADE FOR THE FRENCH MARKET

WALTERSHAUSEN PIANO

A "Colonial" House with a Garden

"Colonial" is a term used advisedly here. This relatively modest structure, believed to be from Philadelphia, is early—from the middle of the nineteenth century[1]—but the style is unmistakable.

The "garden" consists of a green-painted wooden lawn, bisected by a painted wooden path, and surrounded by a neat picket fence. The façade of the house has a proper glazed fanlight over the door and three steps below. The door is flanked by a pair of hand-carved pilasters. The pair of dormers on the deeply pitched roof are decidedly off-hand, with six hand-carved mullions in one, and nine in the other, but somehow this foible seems only to add to the appeal of this small, hand-crafted structure with its twin chimneys.

AMERICAN.
HEIGHT: 19" (PLUS CHIMNEYS)
BASE: 20" X 21 1/4"

1. To judge by the square nails and general construction.

The latter are divided by internal flues, two of which lead logically to deeply projecting fireplaces within, one on each floor. The interior, open at the back, contains two rooms. When a rather drab cream wallpaper is peeled back in the upper room, an attractive rose pattern emerges.

No furnishings came with the house with the exception of a simple wooden ladder. This, with an opening presumably, for hanging on a peg, appears to be an accessory for the inaccessible attic.

The furniture which has been included is a set of four tiny chairs and a table. These came to me in a small, ancient, cloth-hinged wooden box with a hand-written message affixed to the lid: "My little chairs I had when I was six years old. I am 84, November 22, 1940." Alas, the writer did not include her name. The smallest possible polished Waltershausen table accompanied the rather rustic chairs, all of the proper vintage for this elderly treasure.

I have taken the liberty of placing in the garden one of my most cherished possessions: a pair of exquisite, early peg wooden dolls, a lady and gentleman dressed in Quaker clothing. These

came with the provenance that they belonged to Clara Hoopes of Philadelphia, ca. 1845. Because they are of the perfect period and place for this house, even though they are a bit over-scaled, it was irresistible to include them.

QUAKER DOLLS. CA. 1845, FROM PHILADELPHIA

TINY SET. CA. 1862

THE RATHER PLAIN INTERIOR

ARCHITECTURE FROM FREDERICK, MARYLAND

In February of 1954, a letter arrived from Miss Constance Harding of Frederick, Maryland, which began, "I have been interested in doll houses all my life..." Miss Harding mentioned that she'd been collecting dolls' house furnishings for years, as well as houses. "We owned a number," she wrote, "but the one I've kept is like the old houses in Frederick." She alluded to a dolls' house exhibition just concluded at the Baltimore Museum of Art, and the interest it created, and she mentioned the affinity of cats to dolls' houses.[1] She

ended with an invitation: "If you ever come to Frederick, I wish you would drop in and see mine. I think you would like it."

When I thanked Miss Harding for her invitation, I invited her and her sister to see my collection, then quite small. Frederick was only forty miles away, but somehow the years passed without my visiting Miss Harding's dolls' house, or her visiting Chevy Chase.

However, as one often notes, the dolls' house world is small, figuratively as well as literally, and in

MID-NINETEENTH CENTURY. HEIGHT: 41" (PLUS CHIMNEYS) WIDTH: 39" (INCLUDING EAVES)

1. "I noticed in the article about your book," Miss Harding wrote, "about the Siamese cat's interest. Cats of ours always loved to play in the doll houses, and never broke anything." This charming footnote is included in deference to an association often observed by dolls' house owners.

1969, Mrs. John Hanna of Frederick notified me of a Victorian dolls' house to be sold as part of an estate. It was, as may be guessed, Miss Harding's. Mrs. Hanna who, as executrix, had come across the few letters I'd exchanged with Miss Harding fourteen years before, hoped to have the Harding house remain in the Maryland area, and she liked the idea of its eventual display in a museum where it would be seen by the public. At long last I went to see the house and furnishings I'd been invited to visit so many years before and, ultimately, acquired it.

The roofline of the house with its dormered central gable is certainly typical of rural houses built in the Frederick area, and in other parts of Maryland during the nineteenth century; the lovely old row houses which line the residential streets of Frederick are mostly narrow and deep. Many are Federal or earlier and most, happily, have survived. When Miss Harding referred to "the old houses of Frederick," perhaps she was picturing houses remembered from her youth, which eventually gave way to commercialization or demolition.

Without documentation, one is faced with the dilemma of when the dolls' house, obviously Victorian, may have been copied or adapted from existing architecture. Its sheer bulk suggests a reasonably early date, a time when nurseries were still sufficiently sizeable to accommodate such gargantuan toys. The care with which the house was built—the raised-panel double-doors, the clapboarding and coigning, the rows of shaped shingles under the side gables (a double-rowed variation embellishes the roof), even the rather shallow dentelated cornice suggests a mid-century origin— and a skillful carpenter.

The style of the few bits of hardware on the house help to reinforce this dating, although some expertise on Victorian latches would be welcome.[1] A large flat hook fastens the façade, which

---

1. A dolls' house historian should, ideally, have information about every aspect of architecture and antiques. Willy-nilly, laborers in this miniature vineyard acquire a little knowledge about many things. As this one has remarked more than once: "If a little knowledge is a dangerous thing, I am a very dangerous person."

MÄRKLIN FIREPLACE

FURNITURE MARKED "CLD"

swings open in one huge section. The double front doors may also be opened, and small hooks, one at the top of the right-hand door, and one at the center of the left-hand one, secure them. There is a neat porcelain knob inside as well as outside on these.

A pleasant-looking, china-headed lady has been lashed (literally!) to the wall which bisects the central window. The builder, who lavished such professionalism on the exterior of this house, went to little trouble for the interior, which he divided into four well-proportioned chambers and let them go at that. The fact that the middle window on the second floor was bisected by a wall didn't seem to bother him at all. The china-headed lady helps to conceal this lapse. (On the first floor, a solid pair of doors avoid the problem.)

When the house came to me, the interior was painted white—as mid-century American hous-

es often were. However, there was a great deal of pencil scribbling on the walls, and taking an unpardonable liberty, I supplied antique wallpapers.[1] (The kitchen was left pristine.) One other liberty was taken: as a self-described purist (admitting no reproductions to my small world), I should be reluctant to confess that the single dormer, resembling the Black Hole of Calcutta, was opened long enough to insert lighting, a bit of wallpaper, curtains, and (whatever else!) a cat.

Old furnishings came with the house, and although they were an amalgamation rather than pieces original to it (and though many of them had been "restored" by Miss Harding and her sister in a manner not entirely acceptable to a fanatical antiquarian), some of them have been placed in the house.

In the first-floor parlor, a Waltershausen suite in somewhat larger scale than the furniture in the

1. These are of miniature patterns which were available when a sizable cache of early wallpapers was discovered in an old store in Wisconsin.

UPSTAIRS SITTING ROOM

other rooms relates to the generous proportions of the chambers with their high ceilings. In the upstairs sitting room, a Märklin fireplace looks at home in a space dominated by two rare pieces—a tall and splendid display cabinet and a matching tufted chair. These feature highly ornamental pressed-wood detailing. The tall cabinet contains numerous niches for the bric-a-brac so essential to the Victorian spirit (page 19).

There's a turkey in the oven of the very American (possibly Hubley) iron stove, but some German accessories have been permitted. There are several hard-to-find Märklin chairs, one of them a rocker. Inasmuch as a faux-grained tin rack is labeled for "Handtuch," "Tellertuch," and "Glasertuch," one could not possibly confuse the hand-towel with the dishcloth. In late-nineteenth century Germany, there appears to be a carefully labeled accessory for every

purpose: the barrel-like container next to the stove is for "Kehricht"— "shavings."[1]

Old laces curtain the windows. Old velvets carpet the floors. On two of the carpets, squares of Victorian needlepoint are placed, a useful device for adding atmosphere to a room.

SHAVINGS BARREL

MÄRKLIN ROCKER

---

1. A dolls' house historian who speaks no German is highly dependent on a German dictionary.

AN ELDERLY BROWNSTONE FROM PENNSYLVANIA

This brownstone residence is not large, but it is exquisitely designed and executed. The interior is modest, but the builder dedicated considerable expertise to its shell. Arched windows on the façade and sides have well-defined projecting lintels and sills. A strong cornice and the small columned portico are similarly accomplished. All of this is well coated with brownstone (sandstone) so perfectly applied as to be almost palpable.

The house was found many years ago in an antiques shop alongside the Susquehanna River, near Columbia, Pennsylvania, and, of course, its origin may have been neighboring New Jersey, or anywhere the proprietor may have ventured. It doesn't really matter. It is an exquisite example of its genre, and we are grateful for its survival.

The arched windows on the projecting bay on the right-hand side are outlined in green, the only other color to be seen on the exterior, although the lace curtains to be seen through the windows also add a contrast to the brownstone surface.

The back opens in two simple, hinged sections, and there are two rooms, one up and one down. At first glance, these appear to be unadorned, and a flashlight is required to disclose, on the floors, an unusual paper so faded that the eye needs time to discern a pattern which includes peach dots (possibly once red) at intervals. Owing to the numerous windows, it is even more difficult to perceive the bits of faded, patterned wallpaper between them, and even some gilt strips which have lost much of their glitter over the years. There are scorch marks on the white-papered ceiling on the second story, with two round openings, the size of a small orange, on the floor below. Perhaps at a later point in its history, this became a house for a Christmas garden, for use under a tree.[1] If so, we must be grateful that candles which may have been lighted below, did not engulf this small treasure.

MID-NINETEENTH CENTURY. HEIGHT: 16" (PLUS CHIMNEY) WIDTH: 15" (PLUS BAY)

1. With its numerous German communities, Pennsylvania was well supplied with Christmas gardens.

THE TIFFANY-PLATT RESIDENCE

When this mid-nineteenth century mansion was acquired in 1957 from a New Jersey antiques dealer, it was accompanied by the information that it had been made for a member of New York's Tiffany family. There was no doubt that, with its English basement and Italianate details, it resembled a New York townhouse, and that with its windows on three sides, it was no row house, however imposing, such as those which lined Fifth Avenue for blocks even before the Civil War.

Even with its wildly over-scaled front steps, clearly provided as seating for a young owner and her companion, and its absurdly under-scaled front door, on a façade of otherwise noble proportions, this was clearly a toy house worthy of a family as illustrious as the Tiffanys.

The New Jersey dealer who had sold the house, which had been in her own collection, cooperatively furnished the name of the Kingston, New York antiques dealer from whom she'd acquired it about eight years before. This dealer promptly replied to an inquiry, verifying his belief that the house had indeed been made for a Tiffany, and offering to seek information from the original source.

No further word was received and an indirect inquiry, some years later (through a family connection) to two venerable Tiffany ladies who might have been supposed to recall such an heirloom, withal long departed, was also fruitless.

In the early 'seventies, the 1957 letter of the Kingston antiques dealer surfaced and inspired a phone call. Remarkably, the dealer was at the same address and new information resulted.

In light of this conversation, it appeared that the provenance relating to the house was, at best, possible, and at worst, hearsay. The Tiffany name had been "dropped" at a sale of possessions of the

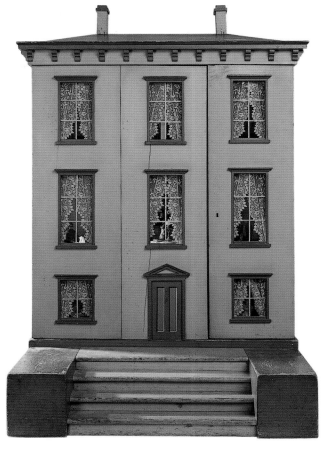

AMERICAN. MID-NINETEENTH CENTURY.
EXTERIOR HEIGHT: 54" WIDTH: 40"

Platt family, from New Hamburg, New York, "an old Hudson River family," in the words of the dealer. He believed the owner's uncle had been a United States Senator in the 1880's. He added the seemingly gratuitous detail that the family "had an account at Tiffany's for about forty years, buying such things as Russian porcelains and Russian enamels."[1] He did not mention family heirlooms. An attempt to reach a Platt descendant whose name and town he provided proved fruitless. Investigation revealed that there had indeed been a Senator Thomas Platt, born in 1833 in Oswego, New York, and first elected to the Senate in 1881. A biographical summary relates that his mother

---

1. This detail proved to be corroborative rather than gratuitous when it was learned that Senator Platt and his family moved to New York City in 1880, making Tiffany purchases convenient and a Tiffany-Platt acquaintance possible.

ANNIE GETTING IN TROUBLE

CLOCKWISE LEFT TO RIGHT: STUDENT LAMP,
TRANSITIONAL LAMP, PARLOR LAMP

was a member of "a Long Island family represented in the Colonial and Revolutionary wars," but unfortunately this fails to mention any Hudson River connections.

Although even a rationalization for the acquisition by the Platts of a dolls' house belonging to the Tiffanys is by no means clear, it seems appropriate to continue to refer to the dolls' house as the "Tiffany-Platt."

So much for the history of the dolls' house, which is arresting but vague. (It is presented in full in the hope that, in future, some Tiffany or Platt will come forward and clarify it.)[1]

Two-thirds of the hinged façade swing open to the left, the remaining third to the right. In addition to the eight windows on the front, double windows on both sides of each story make the window total impressive and the curtain problem formidable.[2]

Although its key is missing, the lock on the façade remains, suggesting that the original own-

ers held the furnishings in some esteem.

Happily, some of these remain (page 26). The New Jersey dealer had been told that five of the pieces were original, and they are of the mid-nineteenth century Biedermeier, the imitation rosewood one would associate with a house of this vintage and quality. These include the tester bed with its original gossamer pink silk bed curtains, and a marble-topped dresser with the printed gilt inlay (in imitation of the gilt metal inlay of Boule), on mirror frame, doors, and drawer. Age has taken its toll of the green silk curtain on the commode where it no longer quite conceals the article of convenience within. The same green silk has met a similar fate on the sofa. The secretaire, to be found in many sizes and variations throughout the nineteenth century, contains the customary drop-front writing compartment with three miniscule drawers at each side of a bit of mirror. Above this compartment there is one wide drawer and there are three below, and since the lowest, unlike the

1. Robert Pierce, a Pennsylvania collector, in recent years acquired an elegant dolls' house known to be from the Tiffany family. This, though more elaborate than the Museum's "Tiffany," bears a striking resemblance to the latter, hereby suggesting a Tiffany connection, after all. (Mr. Pierce's house, [shown on page 26], opens at the back.)
2. The curtains were present when the house was acquired in 1957. Although clearly not original, the lace is old and decorative and the twenty (!) pairs have been left intact.

RARE
TESTER BED

KESTNER BUREAU

CHINESE TABLE AND CHAIR

ROBERT PIERCE TIFFANY HOUSE

others, has no embossed pewter knob, it may be intended as a secret drawer.

It is not possible to know how much of the other furniture which came with the house was with it originally. Most of the turn-of-the-century electric fixtures, obviously a later addition, have been replaced by gasoliers. A rare, three-branch lamp on the parlor table has a Bristol shade pretending to shield an old oil font; early pointed electric bulbs sheathed by fluted Bristol shades complete a type of transitional fixture which was essential at the turn of the century: when the early electricity failed, one had a built-in alternative. Similar transitional lighting, of course, was available in both ceiling and wall fixtures.

A most unusual dining-room set, consisting of a sideboard, oval table and four chairs, lavishly carved in a black wood meant to represent teak, is clearly Chinese, and since I have never seen another set (only a chair or two), it may be presumed rare and early, and therefore possibly original to the house. When the "Tiffany" was acquired, this dining room

had been placed on the top floor, and since it was too elegant to install in the English basement, it has been left in this improbable location.

Built-in black mantels, probably meant to represent marble, in the drawing room and the two upper rooms, are unquestionably original. Although there are no other interior architectural details, the abundant windows and the noble proportions of the rooms, and of the house itself, contribute to the splendor of the Tiffany-Platt.

"ORMOLU" CHAISE

PENNSYLVANIA CUPBOARD HOUSE

"Owing to the sad economic fact that dealers can profit more by selling off the contents piecemeal, it has become increasingly difficult to find an old dolls' house with its original furnish- ings. Much household history has been dispersed along with these miniature lares and penates, and collectors and historians must bow to the inex- orable law of (very) small business."

CA. 1870. HEIGHT: 50" WIDTH: 42"

I wrote that paragraph more than thirty years ago, and true then, sadly, it is even truer now. The Cupboard House, found in Pennsylvania in 1945, escaped such pillaging. Its furnishings, an assortment in several scales, were jumbled in boxes when found, but they made a splendid miscellany to represent a Victorian household quite thoroughly.

With a deferential bow to the elaborate cabinet houses of the Netherlands in the seventeenth and eighteenth centuries, this rather austere cupboard was probably run up by the local carpenter. Other than a pitched roof and a doorbell, the façade, to distinguish it, consists of only four, square paneled doors, one to each room, but the rooms are of noble, high-ceilinged proportions with correspondingly tall windows and with the original draperies, cornices, and wallpapers.

There were many treasures among the furnishings, especially a gilded-lead chandelier with white Bristol globes and workable wicks. Of particular interest is the black and gold japanned-tin bedroom suite with a hinged lift-top table (a supply of linen inside), a dresser with looking-glass (vintage

undergarments in the drawers), and a tester bed resembling one shown in an early Hull & Stafford (Clinton, Connecticut) catalogue. The table appears to be identical to one pictured by Francis,

BEDROOM WITH HULL AND STAFFORD TOLE FURNITURE
DOLL ORIGINAL TO HOUSE

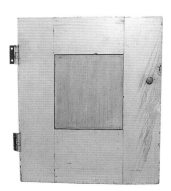

ONE OF FOUR
SECTIONS OF FAÇADE

PARLOR WITH
ORIGINAL DRAPERIES

Field & Francis, also known as the Philadelphia Tin Toy Mfg. Co., and since the Cupboard House and its contents were found near Philadelphia, perhaps this is the most likely source. Some of the bits of linen are marked "Bethel," which Welsh name may be a clue to the lost identity of the long-ago owner. "The bits of linen" suggest that this owner, or perhaps her mother or nanny, was a talented needlewoman. To the many young girls of the period who worked samplers, many of them elaborate, supplying such items as the undergarments in the bureau drawers, the curtains and draperies at the windows, and the original, obviously handmade bed curtains and coverings, would have been a simple matter. The most striking survivor, however, of the anonymous artist is the macramé lambrequin on the parlor mantel, a small work of art.

The doll in the bedroom wearing pantalettes is original to the house. The other dolls are additions.

ABOVE: FRANCIS, FIELD & FRANCIS LIFT-TOP TABLE
RIGHT: ÉTAGÈRE WITH JENNY LIND BOX

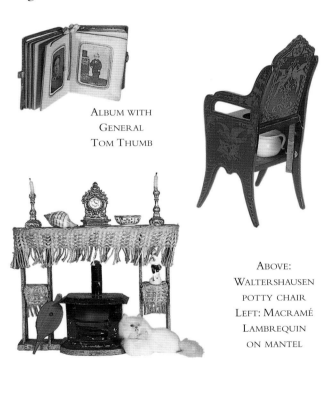

ALBUM WITH GENERAL TOM THUMB

ABOVE: WALTERSHAUSEN POTTY CHAIR
LEFT: MACRAMÉ LAMBREQUIN ON MANTEL

KITCHEN ALL ORIGINAL: DOLLS ADDED

THREE TIN DRESSERS. LEFT TO RIGHT: HULL & STAFFORD; ELLIS, BRITTON & EATON; THIRD IS UNCERTAIN

A New Hampshire House

All that was known about this well-built house when it was acquired was that it was from New Hampshire, but it is clear that it was created by a superior craftsman.

There is no façade, but there are embellishments which provide an attractive alternative—bay windows at the sides, an imposing pair of chimneys, proper coigning, a majestic cornice, and door frame (though there is no door).

Within, the most impressive feature is the handsome winding staircase with its elegantly-turned newel post and balustrade. There are

HEIGHT: 28 1/2" WIDTH: 42" (PLUS BAYS)

windows on the back wall, and I was unable to resist placing a light to illuminate a gentleman (?) who is peering through the one in the kitchen.

Inside, there are two unusual floor-to-ceiling alcoves, one in the parlor and the other in the bedchamber above it. The latter is covered by a pair of curtains, in what appears to be an early fabric. The lower contains a set of old shelves which just happened to be at hand, and which popped into the space as though made for it.

Although this house arrived, as is usually the case, with no furniture, but with its early wallpapers, it seemed to be the perfect setting for the rare, early American furniture, mostly from New England, which now fills the rooms.

There are two bedchambers upstairs. The one at left features the tin "oak-grained chamber set" shown in the 1872 catalogue of Stevens & Brown of Cromwell, Connecticut. The bed is occupied by porcelain twins of the correct vintage, warmed by an antique quilt. When the set was acquired the towel rail was missing and, with one of those bits of collector's luck which collectors cherish, I found this essential member a few years later at an antique show. Oddly enough, it was the only furnishing the dealer had. The lift-top commode is an especially endearing period piece.[1]

The other bed chamber is furnished with pieces to be found in the 1874 catalogue of Althof, Bergmann & Co. of "30, 32, 34, 36 Park Place at the corner of Church Street in New York City." Although the firm, which began in 1867, referred to itself as "importers of toys and fancy goods," they also alluded with some pride, to "toys of our own manufacture." These included tin toys to which they promised to "pay particular attention to avoid all sharp edges and corners."

The rare sets, when they can be found, are to be seen in blue or green with black stenciling. The green set shown, lacks a "towel stand" mentioned in the catalogue, but contains washstands in two

COIN SILVER TEASET, AMERICAN.

AMERICA'S CUP

ELLIS, BRITTON & EATON CLOCK

TOWEL RACK

widths, with a variation in the knob on the drawer below each, suggesting a different year or possibly a different maker for one of these. In the bed are an early mother and baby, nicely dressed in vintage garments. An unusual pierced cardboard wall pocket embroidered in crimson from a long-ago craft set is hung above the dresser. A faux-grained Gothic clock is on the mantel.

Tin seems an unlikely material in which to interpret a "rosewood parlor set with velvet upholstery," as described by Ellis, Britton & Eaton in their 1869 catalogue, but as the set in the photograph suggests, this feat was successfully accomplished. (Confusingly enough, this set was also

1. See dolls' house made from a person-size lift-top commode on page 38.

shown in Stevens & Brown's catalogue of 1872.)[1]

The green-flocked tin upholstery[2] is remarkably true to the ubiquitous tufted furniture of the period. There is a sofa, a gentleman's chair, an ottoman, and three side chairs. The faux marble top on the parlor table may not be quite as successful as the tufted pieces, but the intention is unmistakable. Also in the room, a mantelpiece with a built-in mirror-and-candlesticks has been placed. This mantelpiece features a metal urn at either side, each with the remains of a wick. These are unmistakably original to the piece, and may well have been capped with globes, but I cannot say, having never seen another. A framed portrait of Abraham Lincoln may be seen on the mantel, not surprisingly, in a New England residence. On the parlor table, there is a coin silver tea service, assuredly American and not especially rare, but never found, to my knowledge, outside the U.S. (These simply-shaped pieces are always seen with an ornate tray and sugar tongs, possibly added from another source by the maker.)

On one of the shelves in the parlor alcove, there is a miniscule wood and paper model of an American yacht, possibly related to America's Cup. A silver replica of the cup itself may be seen on a Stevens & Brown iron table in the downstairs hall.

There is more Stevens & Brown iron furniture in the kitchen, a rocker in which a pair of bisque twins are seated, and a rectangular table and two chairs (one gold and green, and one in the more familiar red and black). However, the rare furniture in the kitchen is of tin, again a product of Althof, Bergmann, to judge by the presence of stenciled green chairs similar to those in the bedroom, plus a matching rectangular table and step-back cupboard with shelves above and doors below. The latter, again, is the only one I have ever encountered. There are also a wooden spinning wheel and related yarn winder with unusual metal embellishments, and a pair of snowshoes on the kitchen wall, in deference to New England weather. Hazeltine's Almanac for 1881, on a chair, may be about right for this mid-Victorian household.

FROM ELLIS, BRITTON & EATON
1869 CATALOGUE

AMERICAN TIN CHAIRS FROM LEFT TO RIGHT:
ELLIS, BRITTON & EATON; ALTHOF, BERGMANN

1. I reported this small mystery in 1974 *Dolls' Houses in America* along with the fact that the chairs from the faux oak-grained tin chamber set shown in the Stevens & Brown catalogue were also to be seen in the "office set" illustrated by Ellis, Britton & Eaton in 1869. I have yet to solve this puzzle. The McClintocks, in their comprehensive *Toys in America*, wrote that the George W. Brown Co. of Forestville, Connecticut combined with J. & E. Stevens, from about 1868 through 1872, to form The American Toy Company." Since Stevens made iron toys and Brown tin toys" they wrote, "their lines complemented each other." This is confirmed by the 1872 Stevens & Brown "Illustrated Price List" in which not only their own Connecticut address is featured on the cover, but "Warehouse in New York, The American Toy Company, 17 Park Place," is given equal "billing."
2. A pair of gentleman's chairs in rose may be seen in the "Lift-Top Commode" house, on page 38.

THE SOUTH JERSEY MANSION

I n 1945, I began to write *A History of Dolls' Houses* and then, almost immediately, to collect. As I've often said: "The chicken came first, not the egg."

The South Jersey house was beginner's luck. Driving through Southern New Jersey, we came upon a very good antique shop in Malaga, a place with a name and a few buildings—it wasn't even a village. The proprietor, a Mr. Jackson, was showing us some dolls' house furniture when he mentioned that he had a dolls' house in his barn.

We went at once to the barn. (To my regret, I never saw the furniture again!) There stood an ancient dolls' house—a derelict if ever there was one. It had been there for "about eight years," the support of rickety chairs and several layers of other

CA. 1870. EXTERIOR HEIGHT: 44" WIDTH: 40" (PLUS BAYS)

CHAIRS WITH "ORMOLU"
TRIM AND SIMILAR
UPHOLSTERY;
IN TWO SIZES

HARPSICHORD,
STOOL TURNS

CHEST IN SHADOW BOX; PART OF
DRAWING ROOM SET

unsold antiques, a great credit to its strength. It was cobwebbed and dirty, with a discouraging number of broken windows, and was known to its new owner—(who promptly accepted it in exchange for $35) as "The Haunted House."[1] Nevertheless it is a splendid example of post-Civil War sandstone architecture. It is, as its portrait suggests, a stately town house spangled with windows of every description—bay, casement, sash, and dormer.

With its maroon and spinach green sandstone façade[2] its paneled double doors with crimson stained-glass sidelights, and blue-patterned top-light, and with its convex "tiled" mansard roof painted with black and gray checkerboard squares (interspersed with floral medallions), it seems the very essence of a mid-nineteenth century residence—a diminutive version of such faded relics now usually to be seen on the wrong side of the tracks, often glimpsed from train windows on the Eastern seaboard. The detail suggests that this was a faithful copy of an actual house. One longs to find the original, but more than half a century of inquiries have been fruitless.

Restoration related to more than broken windows. The foundation (which adds greatly to a dolls' house but is often omitted by latter-day builders), was missing, but fortuitously, one section, well detailed to resemble stone, was present, indicating the depth and style. The stairs to the imposing front entrance were also absent and the surviving segment of the foundation was divided

DRAWING-ROOM DESK
AND ITS OWNER

to support proper stairs.

Pictures were taken of building entrances of similar style and vintage. The one chosen is an approximation of the entrance to St. John's Parish House in Lafayette Square, Washington, D.C. French toy-train street lamps (marked DÉPOSÉ JS PARIS") with workable wicks, were luckily found in time to be mounted at either side of the stairs.

The segment of the roof above the mansard was also missing. This was replaced by one with an unobtrusive pitch. It is tempting to imagine that the original roofline included a central turret.

Iron deer, per tradition, guard the front lawn which is further protected by an old green and gilt Christmas tree fence.

Unlike Hunca Munca and Tom Thumb,[3] the mice who once inhabited the South Jersey house weren't left so much as a plaster ham.

Nevertheless, even though the floors were warped and not even a shred of drapery remained when the house was found, evidence lingered of the children (as well as the mice), whose house it had been. A few of the ten small, paneled, hand-carved doors were missing and had to be replaced. Small scrap pictures had been stuck on the ceilings, covering parts of the original, beguiling, hand-painted medallions. Smudge marks on walls and ceilings suggested that the young owners had actually lighted long-departed sconces and chandeliers.

A staircase with a landing, and two small fireplaces were the only other surviving built-in features. Access to the eight rooms, four large and four small, including hallways, is through three hinged, windowed panels at the rear. These of course, have been carefully preserved but replaced by plexiglas panels for viewing ease. The front hall, too small to be readily entered through its rear (kitchen) door by a full-sized hand, lends easier admittance through the double front door. The deep rooms,

---

1. This was prophetic. The house later inspired *The Doll House Mystery.* Coward-McCann, New York, 1958, now in its 16th printing. Recent printings by *The Washington Dolls' House & Toy Museum.*
2. Made possibly by dripping sand onto a surface of wet glue.
3. *A Tale of Two Bad Mice.* Beatrix Potter.

fifteen by twenty-four inches, offer the same imposing impression given by full-sized, high ceiling chambers of their day. A large garret, another typical feature, is formed by the mansard roof. Early in my collecting days, I took the liberty of adding a bathroom to the rear upstairs hall where probably none existed before. Such a rash addition, I might, in more mature years, have resisted.

Because the South Jersey house was the first house I found when I started to collect in 1945, the furnishing became a mélange of early, "mid," and late Victorian pieces. Inasmuch as many of these furnishings are described in *The Doll House Mystery,* these have been left in the house with very few modifications.

A relatively unexciting set of "yellow cherry" (the Schneegass catalogue description) occupies the dining room. A considerably earlier and more elegant suite ornaments the drawing room. With its charming bird and flower upholstery and its metal mounts—actual metal "ormolu" embellishments—its discovery, more than half a century ago,

was beginner's luck, like the South Jersey house. This magnificent group was the first antique dolls' house furniture I found and placed in the remarkable South Jersey. (The furniture was discovered at a Washington, D.C. antique show in 1945, before there were lines at antiques show doors.) A rare, matching three-drawer chest which was included in the set—one piece too many even for the sizable South Jersey drawing room—is displayed elsewhere. (page 35)

Because the style was French, naively I assumed that this elegant suite was made in France. It wasn't until years later, when my friend Vivien Greene visited me, that I learned she had seen it in the Waltershausen sample books when she visited East Germany.

(An almost identical suite may be seen in the Graddon family parlor (page 248), upholstered in a simple blue silk. A magnificent set of larger scale with the bird and flower upholstery, and a different "ormolu" pattern, from Baltimore's Abell family, may be seen on page 183.)

THE "LIFT-TOP COMMODE" HOUSE

At some point during the second half of the nineteenth century, a practical carpenter converted a popular Victorian furnishing, the lift-top commode, into this dolls' house.

Hinges remain where the front of the commode was removed, four windows were added, one for each room, and the lift-top is still liftable. The approximate time of the transformation is suggested by the early wallpapers and the built-in, faux-grained fireplaces. Like the New Hampshire House on page 30,[1] this one, probably also from New England, has been provided with American furnishings of the period, all of them relatively rare.

The kitchen, like the other rooms, contains a built-in fireplace, reinforcing an early date for the house, and an early tin stove with an open hearth

AMERICAN. CA. 1870. HEIGHT: 33" WIDTH: 33"

1. A miniature version of the lift-top commode is part of the oak-grained bedroom set in the 1872 Stevens & Brown catalogue—and it is to be seen in the New Hampshire house on page 30. This perhaps more appropriately should be displayed in this house. (See detail, above.)

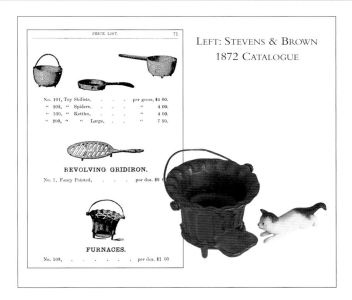

LEFT: STEVENS & BROWN 1872 CATALOGUE

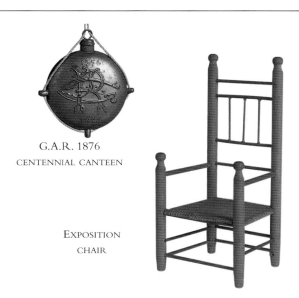

G.A.R. 1876
CENTENNIAL CANTEEN

EXPOSITION
CHAIR

bearing the name of "Gypsy" in stenciled letters,[1] has been placed in front of this as, later, these often were. Another heating device in this kitchen is a low iron "furnace," so described in the Stevens & Brown 1872 catalogue.[2] There are other Stevens & Brown iron pieces—kitchen chairs, tables, and benches plus stoneware jugs, iron trivets—assorted kitchen accessories.

There is more Stevens & Brown in the dining room. The "dining-table" was made in two sizes, and probably this is the larger. (Unfortunately the price rather than the size is listed in the catalogue.) There is gold stenciling on the black, scalloped oval table-top, not shown in the catalogue illustration. This iron piece is surprisingly effective surrounded by chairs pictured in the catalogue as "parlor chairs."

Brass chandeliers with candles hang in the bedroom and parlor. The latter is elegant with wallpaper in a subtle diaper pattern applied in panels edged with narrow gilt paper strips. A pair of Ellis, Britton & Eaton (and/or Stevens & Brown) tin gentleman's chairs with rose tufting are placed at either side of the mantel, with the

matching tin faux marble center table in, of course, the center.

An imposing china personage with pierced ears presides over the bedroom which contains American tin furniture from two sources. The green tin bed and matching stenciled chair may be seen in the Althof, Bergmann 1874 catalogue.[3] Recently tin bedroom pieces were acquired in the same shade of green. Though there was no bed, there was a washstand a bedside table, and three chairs in a style never seen by me before. And, most unusual, a three-drawer chest with faux drawers and a removable top![4]

A photograph of two young boys, the writer's cousins, long deceased, is hung above the bedroom mantel. The older was born in 1883 and is about the right vintage for this house.

Other accessories include a brass canteen in perfect scale, hanging on the parlor wall. This is a centennial piece dated "1776" and "1876" on one side, with the entwined initials of the Grand Army of the Republic on the other, suitable amongst the New England furniture.

1. One with all the time in the world might compile a learned list of the names on toy stoves, both of tin and iron, relating these to their makers.
2. See detail picture, above.
3. See the New Hampshire House, on page 30.
4. Shortly after this set was discovered, I saw a similar chest in blue with operable drawers and, more logically, a fixed top.

BEVERLY HOUSE

Although this unusual house from Beverly, Massachusetts is not large, its slender façade, erect and prim as an ancestor in a New England portrait, stands tall. There is evidence that a chimney once crowned the pleasing exterior, making it taller still.

A dozen glazed windows, six to a side, light the rooms within, but the hinged façade surprises with matching panes on the wood, beneath bracketed lintels identical to those under the glass windows. The arched, double front doors are also hand-painted rather than three-dimensional, but all the painting, of folk art flavor, is done with style and charm, including appealing decor on the inside of the façade.

What is most intriguing of all is what appears to be an address: "46 HUNT" painted on the doors. However, the dealer from whom the house was purchased in 1963, wrote that the inscription was thought to relate to the Hunt sisters who had a large waterfront estate on Ober Street in Beverly. The number may be related to the address, but a more logical possibility is that the "46" refers to 1846, a quite logical date for this piece of miniature architecture.

This house somehow appeared to require a central chimney, not only with respect to its style, but with respect to its built-in fireplaces. One does not wish to second-guess a deceased architect, but, willy-nilly, a chimney has been added.

Inasmuch as a key now missing once turned a lock next to the second-story windows, it is clear that this house was a prized possession. Unfortunately, except for the white, dotted-swiss curtains, a few pictures and a gilt-rimmed "ogee" mirror, the original contents had been dispersed, but the three rooms, one to a floor, have their original papers. Even these, along with the pictures and curtains, may have been early replacements and/or additions in the long life of the house.

As in a number of houses in the collection, the scale of the rooms requires furniture similarly diminutive. Among pieces which have been supplied, notable is an "ormolu" fireplace, probably late for the house, but rare with its built-in clock. The iron "Bay State" stove with open hearth is properly American, by Stevens & Brown of Cromwell, Connecticut, and illustrated in their 1872 catalogue. There were four sizes.

HEIGHT: 39" WIDTH: 18" (PLUS CHIMNEY)

ASPHALTUM PIANO

"ORMOLU" FIREPLACE WITH CLOCK

WAMPUM COTTAGE

When I first saw this house, it was on a table facing the bay in an Annapolis antiques shop. For me, its array of windows, the first and second story ones alight with frosted patterns, and the mansard ones bright with green glass, will always seem to be shimmering with water.

The Annapolis dealer had found it in Pennsylvania, which has no coastline, but certain dolls' houses, like certain houses, have a way of evoking identical responses in a variety of people. More than one viewer, gazing upon this lively façade exclaimed, "It's a seaside cottage!" (Possibly it originated in neighboring New Jersey.) In any case,

when I first wrote about it more than thirty years ago, I dubbed it "A Victorian Seaside Cottage."

In recent years it has had a name change. It was discovered that this handcrafted, yellow clapboard, mansard-roofed residence was fashioned from a wooden Wampum crate. Stamped on the bottom was "Stone-Orlean-Wells" plus "Wampum" and "Duluth, Minnesota." This led to some correspondence on the part of the writer who had been aware of "Wampum" only as an early form of Indian currency used for barter. An inquiry disclosed that at the turn of the century and before, the Minnesota firm dispensed canned goods!

CA. 1875. EXTERIOR HEIGHT: 22" WIDTH: 29"

An "indiscrète" (for three)

Asphaltum high chair

Table with opaline
tea set

Because the house opened at the back, and therefore required (always) limited space for interior viewing, it for years had been relegated to an upper display shelf in the Museum. It remained unfurnished till The National Trust for Historic Preservation featured it on a Christmas card, whereupon it was furnished and placed in a central area.

It is clear that a sure and patient hand fashioned the shingled roof, the ornate bays, the dentelated moldings and the workable pierced-tin shutters. No detail is omitted, from the blue-and-white stained glass over-door panel to the metal rain gutters and downspouts—one of only a few dolls' house examples I've ever encountered.

The mansard roof is open which causes one to wonder wistfully if the missing segment might have included a cupola.

The back of the house opens with two hinged wooden doors, and within the four rooms and the two beguiling bays, the original wallpapers survive. Having provided such a detailed exterior, the maker stopped short of absolute realism by using the same warm, figured maroon-and-cream paper in each of the rooms—including the kitchen! Somehow the paper is not as intrusive in the kitchen as one might have supposed it would be. The suspension of disbelief which certain types of dolls' houses provide is evident in this kitchen.

The latter contains a winding staircase to the second floor and has been supplied with furnishings of a smaller scale—perhaps 2/3 inch to one foot—than the modern, customary "inch to the foot."[1]

Antique furnishings of large scale are more readily found, and it is always a challenge to furnish such rooms as these, but gratifying when the project is completed.

GUTTERS AND DOWNSPOUTS

It was particularly satisfying to have two matching German metal fireplaces, with overmantels and filigree trim, for two of the rooms. The small inhabitants include a bisque-headed lady who strongly resembles the Baker's chocolate maiden—by coincidence or design. There are also several of the small charming glass-eyed dolls known as mignonettes.

Other notable furnishings include an opaline tea set so small that it came to me, from France many years ago in a "large" capsule, an asphaltum high chair and an indiscrète. This rare piece seats three. (When it is for two, it is known as a "confidante.") See pictures on previous page.

1. In England, referred to as 1/12th scale. As has been mentioned elsewhere in these pages, makers of antique dolls' house furnishings, both commercial and handcrafted, did not speak of scale. However, mid-nineteenth century German toy catalogues often show a piece of furniture in several sizes.

A "Regional" Massachusetts Victorian

Regional architecture in full-sized structures is readily discerned, but it has been intriguing to discover, upon occasion, regional dolls' house architecture. A striking example of the latter is to be found in a type of Victorian dolls' house from Massachusetts. This features dark-stained wood both inside and out, an open front (with only a suggestion of façade), an attic room or two, and even an incised block foundation.

The house pictured is of this persuasion, with the exception of the interior walls, papered later—I think—in lush Victorian patterns. When it was acquired, many long years ago, the Massachusetts dealer who sold it alluded to "a Mrs. Sheldon of Sheldonville" (Mass.) who "brought back" such antique dolls' houses, (presumably to their former glory).

If "Mrs. Sheldon" did indeed bring this house

CA. 1880. EXTERIOR HEIGHT: 46" WIDTH: 49"

HALF-TESTER METAL BED

"back," she clearly knew what she was doing. Although one's own preference is always to leave these treasures from the past as they were, none of these alterations is disfiguring, or even irremovable. There are, as can be seen, lush Victorian wallpapers, draperies, carpets, and beaded chandeliers in each of the four principal rooms and even in the attic. (The kitchen has been unceremoniously abolished.) This decor seemingly has been superimposed on walls, floors, and ceilings which, for decades, may have been as unadorned as those, for instance, in the Bessie Lincoln house in Salem,[1] a larger dolls' house with a number of resemblances to this one.

It is impossible to tell because old materials were used and the artful designer was either of the period, or had such a feeling for it, along with taste and style, that high Victoriana emerges.

Here the pitched roof is crowned by a widow's (or captain's) walk where Bessie Lincoln's roof is a

mansard with two chimneys, but each contains an attic room. This one features a lift-out dormer with a stained glass panel where Bessie Lincoln, poor thing, had to make do with a mere unadorned opening.

An emphasis on crimson and gold in the wallpapers (blue and silver in the nursery) with suitable borders, and on velvets, laces, braids, tassels, bows, and fringes for the curtains and draperies, illuminate an era of interior decoration that was popular decades before it became fashionable to refer to "interior design." The beaded chandeliers are themselves a minor art form—a triumph of tiny beads and bangles in intricately composed patterns. There are proper portières in two of the interior doorways. (One liberty has been taken—a supplement in the form of stair carpet cut from old paisley.)

The same gifted hand that fashioned these adornments was clearly responsible for some of the furnishings. Among them is a crimson velvet-draped

1. The Essex Institute, Salem, MA,

table, fringed at the base and swagged near the top with garnet beads, and garnet and gold silken tassels.

The decorator, who evidently could see no scope for her tassels or her talents in a kitchen, dispensed with the one which the architect probably intended. The latter's (anonymous) fame will have to rest on his prepossessingly reeded newel posts, which match the posts on his captain's walk, and on his fitted stained-glass dormer.

Alas, this is a house which, when it was in the museum, was plundered. Fortunately nothing taken was of the magnitude of the precious pieces snitched in 1831 from the celebrated seventeenth-century Utrecht dolls' house in the Netherlands, and fortunately quite a lot remains.

There is a black and gilt metal half-tester bed of

the genre with twisted posts and gilt ball finials. This is elegantly dressed and be-pillowed, again—dare we say—by the lady in Sheldonville? Of similar elegance, and undoubtedly by the same hand, is the canopied baby's cot.

A glass-eyed Simon & Halbig grandmother is seated in her room with her feet resting on a needlepoint footrest, possibly her own handiwork inasmuch as her accessorized knitting basket is beside her.

A family of pugs[1]—most Victorian of dogs—play in the parlor. Luggage and discarded furniture are visible in the attic. One could continue, but the story of this house is the decor—in which any decorator of a proper Victorian dolls' house may find inspiration.

OCCUPIED OTTOMAN

BEDROOM
NOTE BEADED CHANDELIER

1. The pugs, alas, were kidnapped and have been replaced by spaniels. Sadly, the collection has been plagued by assorted snitchings.

GINGERBREAD FROM BEL AIR

In 1978, a post card came to the museum from Bel Air, Maryland. Pictured on it was the ultimate gingerbread dolls' house, but, regrettably, the card was damaged—folded in half and jammed into an envelope.[1]

Embellished to a fare-thee-well with spindles and balconies and other gimcrackeries, the dolls' house was pictured beneath a huge Christmas tree. It was for sale. When we went to view the house, I was able to see the fourteen-foot ceiling in the

CA.1880. HEIGHT: 40" (INCLUDING CHIMNEYS) BASE: 36" X 25"

1. Luckily another copy was available and it may be seen herewith.

ancient mansion where it—and the mansion— were moldering away.

This was a house with provenance, so marvelous to have and so often lacking. It had been built in the early 'eighties for five little sisters— Lottie, Annie, Naomi, Margaret, and Etta Inez Dibb. It was acquired for the Museum from the latter, Mrs. James Martz of Bel Air.

For many years, we were told, it was part of an elaborate Christmas garden, beneath a fourteen-foot tree, to which neighboring school children were brought during the holiday season. (It seems appropriate that a Christmas card was made of this very festive house by The National Trust for Historic Preservation.)

The early photograph, unfortunately undated, showing the house in situ, reveals an elaborate, fenced garden beneath house and tree, of gazebos, dolls, and other accoutrements. A painted tin cupola, perched on the roof of the house in the early photo, made by Mr. Dibb, a Bel Air tinsmith, did not come with the house, but a wooden fountain and a pair of matching urns accompanied it to its new home. The handsome wooden fence is from the Museum's collection. Though it looks perfectly at home here, one wonders what wonderful lost house it originally surrounded.

Because this is a back-opening house and, owing to space limitations, is presently placed against a wall, it is not maintained fully furnished. (The illustration reveals the house as furnished for the National Trust card.)

REAR OF HOUSE

The eleven windows on the façade and the ten on the sides—for a total of twenty-one windows (!)—offer twenty-one opportunities for viewing. The thirteen (!) balconies—the dolls' house world's largest supply, surely, for one house, supply standing

DOLL COOLING PIE

room for a considerable gathering of dolls. Here a twin brother and sister in brown velvet may be seen on an upper balcony. Below, a cook loiters outside the kitchen, pie in hand, presumably letting it cool.

She has moved back into the kitchen for the interior view. The latter offers a rather humdrum glimpse of the underside of the staircase which the Christmas tree with its miniscule Christmas garden helps to camouflage.

A splendid Märklin gilt "ormolu" fireplace with its matching overmantel mirror lends importance to the upstairs hall. A Stevens & Brown iron stove and chair may be seen in the kitchen, with the ever-reliable Schneegass "yellow cherry" table and chairs in the dining room. The children of the house play with their Christmas toys in the nursery while their parents linger perpetually—with no place to sleep—in the upstairs parlor across the hall. But this is a fantasy house. It defies logic (architectural logic) and exudes charm.

According to the family tradition, two identical houses were built by a Baltimore carpenter. The whereabouts of the twin is unknown.

HOUSE UNDER 14' TREE AS
ORIGINALLY PHOTOGRAPHED
(DATE UNKNOWN)

DR. SATTERLEE'S STATELY HOME

Provenance is a factor which every serious collector longs for. This stately house, even without it, is clearly of importance, but a slip of paper which accompanied its purchase, bore, in neat calligraphy, a message: "Built for Dr. Francis LeRoy Satterlee by a Grateful Patient." The house was also accompanied by a rumor that it had been de-accessioned by a New York State museum.

This was welcome—considerably more provenance than is usually available, and there were two clues to the unknown: The Doctor's unusual name and the New York reference, however vague. A kind acquaintance, who happens to live in Manhattan, did a bit of research. She found "Dr. Francis LeRoy Satterlee, 1847-1912" and "Resided (resident?) at Bellevue Hospital, N.Y. 1867-8" and "graduated University of New York Medical Department, March 1868." There was also an address on West 21st Street with what appear to be office hours.

The grateful builder must, alas, remain anonymous, but it is heartening to have information about the fortunate recipient who shared it with presumably a small daughter or daughters in the

HEIGHT: 48" WIDTH: 36"

RARE IRON FENCE HAS BEEN ADDED

late 70's or early 80's.

In the tradition of a number of substantial American handcrafted houses such as the Somerville and the Tiffany-Platt, the Satterlee house rises three stories with two rooms each on first and third floors, and a wide drawing-room between on the second. Like the Somerville and the Tiffany, it contains no interior staircase, and in all three houses the façade swings open in two hinged sections.

Then the Satterlee diverges. With its pitched roof and Indian-red brick façade, there is a strong

CA. 1880. HEIGHT: 48" WIDTH: 36"

cornice painted gray with a matching pediment. There are wide pilasters at either side of the paneled front door with its pediments matching those on the second-story windows. All woodwork except for the white door, is painted gray, including the two tall red-brick chimneys.

No furniture came with the house but there are chimney-pieces in all five rooms which properly correspond to the position of the chimneys, including one at either end of the drawing-room. The only built-in feature other than these is a set of shelves which almost completely cover the back wall in the kitchen (and permit such fitments as a set of hot dish covers). There is also, in the kitchen, a patterned oilcloth floor, which appears to be original, and there are appealing early wallpapers in all but one of the other rooms. (An antique rosebud paper has been provided for the upper right-hand bedroom.)

One of the most satisfying aspects of the house relates to the drawing-room paper, an unassuming pale rose laid on in formal white-framed panels. With this and the twin fireplaces, the room seemed to call for duplicate pieces. The French set from the turn-of-the-century is a bit over-scaled and a bit late for the house, but it seemed perfect

FILIGREE METAL
DRESSING TABLE
NICELY DRESSED

KESTNER CONCERTINA
TABLE EXTENDED

BUILT-IN SHELVES IN KITCHEN

DINING ROOM

from every other point of view—the delicate floral upholstery in pink and pale green—the pair of glazed cabinets and a pair of settees, all of it cream with gilt trim. A pair of Märklin gilt chandeliers hang above the felicitous grouping. On the center table is one of the rarest of pieces—a metal epergne with original fruits and cakes on each of its three tiers.

Other rare pieces to be seen in this house include a "telescope" or "concertina" table (a reference to the extension mechanism beneath) in the dining-room, an extravagantly metal folding screen in the nursery with exuberantly lithographed nymphs in each panel and, also in the nursery, a metal dressing-table with its early lacy drapery both above the mirror and below.

A postscript: After Matthew Ward came from England and splendidly photographed this house, I came across, in my collection, a rare iron fence which seemed worthy of this remarkable house. Accordingly, it was installed and is shown on page 51 on a Christmas card made for The National Trust for Historic Preservation for Christmas, 2002.

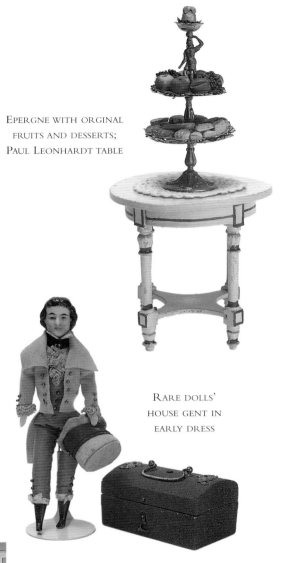

EPERGNE WITH ORGINAL FRUITS AND DESSERTS; PAUL LEONHARDT TABLE

RARE DOLLS' HOUSE GENT IN EARLY DRESS

DRAWING ROOM, LEFT SIDE

RARE SCREEN

A Fretwork Cottage from Nag's Head

The dealer from whom this small house was acquired found it in Nag's Head, North Carolina, which does not, of course, guarantee that it originated in the seaside resort. It seems more a townhouse: the bisque lady, somehow, appears more likely to be surveying a cityscape from her balcony rather than the ocean's waves. On the other hand, the widow's walk atop the deep mansard has its traditional seaside associations. Wilmington, located on a considerably more southerly segment of the North Carolina coastline, with an excellent supply of Victorian (and earlier) architecture, seems a plausible alternative.

A tool which had a busy revival beginning in the 1870's, the fret saw, has given the house much of its character: the cornice, balcony, dormers, and widow's walk, unmistakably part of the revival, help to suggest a date. (Since a dolls' house is often a copy of an earlier house, the architecture alone would be inadequate evidence.)

The gracefully arched windows have well-defined keystones and, on the inside, lace curtains tied back with crimson ribbons, which appear to be original. Matching net may be found behind the red stained-glass lights above both the entrance and balcony doors. (The latter are a paneled pair; the lower single door contains a square frosted pane.)

Although the lemon-yellow house with its blue-gray trim has an open back and is, except for a division between the first and second floors, a shell, it is such an appealing shell that a lack of interior detail is readily forgiven.

CA 1880. HEIGHT: 26"
WIDTH (BASE): 17 3/4"

EASTERN SHORE COTTAGE

Another bit of regional architecture, this pleasing cottage, found on Maryland's Eastern Shore, is an approximation of many a small country residence of Victorian vintage to be seen in that picturesque region.

A careful carpenter—perhaps a father or a brother—made this simple cottage with its two rooms, one upstairs and one down, and with its open back. The walls are unfinished, but there is a piece of floral carpet on the lower floor and curtains at the numerous glass windows, suggesting that once upon a time it was furnished and inhabited.

VICTORIAN.
HEIGHT: 22"
WIDTH: 13"

REGIONAL ARCHITECTURE FROM YORK, PENNSYLVANIA

Although this small townhouse from York, Pennsylvania, lacks a shutter or two, and the front steps are a substitution, it represents its area architecture so fairly that it is shown without further apology. The absence of a couple of shutters is no more than what one might expect on any house of this vintage, especially when the shutters are workable, and therefore losable. These, on leather hinges, with shutter pins to keep them in place, are white-paneled on the first story, green-louvered on the second.

What the vintage may be is not precisely known, but the arrangement of sash bars on the windows and the type of detail in the workmanship suggest the mid-Victorian era. The elegant bracketed cornice is surmounted by a roof of a pattern almost identical to the one on the mammoth Harding sisters' house from neighboring Frederick, Maryland, page 17.

Except for lace curtains at the windows, there is no interior detail. There is evidence that a partition between the first and the second floors was once present, but it was missing when the house was acquired. As an example, however, of miniature regional (exterior) architecture, this small gray house with its pair of red brick chimneys and green and white shutters, warrants recognition.

SECOND HALF OF NINETEENTH CENTURY.
HEIGHT: (NOT INCLUDING CHIMNEYS): 22" WIDTH: 19 3/4"

A "TOUR DE FORCE" FROM BALTIMORE

When she was about twelve years old, a young Baltimorean named Gertrude Horsey Smith, who was born in 1872, made this irresistible house and its furnishings with paper. This vest pocket mansion can be described best, perhaps, as a tour de force.

Its three stories rise grandly to a height of eight inches plus a skylight. The third floor is composed of a mansard roof with "enormous" dormer windows. The latter have fancy frames—with lintels of elaboration similar to those of the numerous windows on the lower floors. There is everything to be expected of an eight-inch mansion—and more. There are two story bays on the left and a proper foundation with arched basement windows.

There are paper lace tie-backs at the windows and paper stair carpet on the stairs. The dining-room table is laid with a paper "cloth" which is fringed. There are pillows on the high-backed bed

in the master bedroom. There is even a two-branch gasolier suspended over the dining-room table. And there's a grand piano. And a sewing machine.

The fact that this fragile creation has survived intact for considerably more than a century is another tribute to the skill of its young maker. Happily, her house has provenance, so often lost with more substantial structures. We even know the name of the man the young artist later married (Charles Eager Moore) and the fact that she lived till 1952—eighty years.

CA. 1884. HEIGHT: 8 1/2"
WIDTH: 8"

EVEN A HANGING PAPER LAMP

A "COLONIAL REVIVAL" FROM MASSACHUSETTS

CA.1900. HEIGHT (NOT INCLUDING CHIMNEYS): 32"
WIDTH (NOT INCLUDING EAVES): 24"

The architectural firm of McKim, Mead and White, Edward Bok (the celebrated editor of *The Ladies' Home Journal*), and a New England kitchen displayed in 1876 at the Philadelphia Centennial, have all been given credit, in various measures, for the Colonial Revival. "The interest that was awakened," Marshall Davison writes, "sprang partly from nostalgia, partly from a quest for a new indigenous style of American architecture and partly from a form of ancestor worship."[1]

This dolls' house is a modest example of the genre, but it summarizes with clarity as well as simplicity the houses "beginning to spot the countryside as early as the 'eighties with columned houses with Palladian details in the windows and cornices."[2] This house has no columns except for the rounded pilasters which flank the doorway, but it has a wooden fanlight surmounted by a pediment and the conventional number and arrangement of windows on its façade. It is the style of the windows and the doors, however, which betray the late-nineteenth-century origin of the house. The dark varnished doorway with its vertical glazed panes is to be found on many a late-Victorian residence. And although there is one concession to a Colonial multi-paned window above the door, the others are the triple-paned style to be seen on many houses built in the 'nineties in New England (and especially in Massachusetts).

Some of the most elegant dolls' houses are whimsical about such practicalities as stairs and back doors, but this house has both; its back is almost identical to the front, except for the style of

the door which is wood-paneled rather than glazed, with a tiny projecting roof in lieu of the pediment.

Made with Yankee ingenuity, the façade is a sliding section which, like the back, may be slipped off entirely, revealing the inevitable "center-hall plan" of such houses. All interior woodwork, including window frames, the one fireplace, and the staircase, with its nicely turned newel posts, is dark varnished—another suggestion of era. The original curtains and draperies still hang at the windows, all of which have paper shades (half-way down for all eternity) with bead pulls. Green velvet portières hang between the rooms.

This relatively modest Colonial Revival is an appealing representative of "ancestor worship" in miniature.

1. *The American Heritage History of Notable American Houses,* New York, 1971.
2. *The Tastemakers,* by Russell Lynes, Harper's, 1949.

AN 1889 WASHINGTON D.C. HOUSE WITH PROVENANCE

A fifteen-room dolls' house with both architectural pretensions and provenance is usually looked upon with admiration and anticipation. The Washington, D.C. house illustrated has both, but it also includes one dolls' house flaw. Instead of opening from the front, or even the back, this one is built in sections, set one upon the other, and in order to furnish it, one must lift off the sections, floor by floor. To look into it, one must follow the same process, or obtain glimpses through the windows.

The house, however, does have the aforementioned "architectural pretensions," reflecting many mid-nineteenth century tall townhouses still standing in the District of Columbia. Though many of these are row houses, this one, with windows on the sides and a removable two-story veranda, is assuredly no row house, but with its tall turret crowning a steep dormer, it resembles those in townhouse rows still lining many a D.C. street.

After these words were written, a message was found beneath the bottom—XMAS 1889—and initials: "B.M." A most exciting discovery.

There are five rooms on each of three floors, and a sixteenth room—a "secret" windowless room—in the dormer section beneath the turret. (The turret lifts off, this dormer section lifts off, and then the third floor dormer with windows lifts off. Assorted dormers!)

The builder was skillful and thorough. A bay on one side of the house, interior staircases (one circular) and the detailed balustrading on the piazza (as it may well have been described at the time) are a testament to his work. Only his concept, shared by more than one dolls' house builder, is flawed.

As for the provenance, a yellowing sheet typed by me perhaps thirty years ago contains information provided by the D.C. antiques dealer from whom it was purchased. (Inasmuch as the average dealer is customarily silent about sources, this was a small triumph, though some of the information appears to be a bit disjointed.)

"The dolls' house was given to Zulime Whitney, born in 1872, by her grandmother (Mother?) Mrs. Hattie Luana Whitney. Mrs. Whitney and her three children lived at 1121 I St., N.W. (with the McCardles). (The twins, Myra and Wallace, were born in 1869.) She gave the house to her own granddaughter, Zulime Whitney Diehl, in 1928)."

HEIGHT: 40" WIDTH: 26 1/2"

A HUGE VICTORIAN WITH KITCHEN WING

Here is a miniature residence which defies the word "miniature." It is not only the most sizable structure in the collection, being a foot wider than even the imposing Mexican mansion[1], but it is the only example with a kitchen wing—and a butler's pantry.

An educated guess places its age before the turn of the century. There is a workable early doorbell with a patent date of Nov. 1888, though this might be a bit earlier than the house itself. It has balustrading identical to that in the "mystery" houses, although such a happenstance might be attributable to a source which supplied more than one builder. It features hardwood floors and though not as refined—in their parquetry—as those in the

"mystery" houses, these bear a clear relationship.

Actually, several related matters might suggest that this mammoth creation may be a prototype for the "mystery" houses. The house came to me with the incredible present of dolls from Mrs. Menoni[2] about thirty years ago. At the time, I did not ask for information. Mrs. Menoni is deceased and the Pennsylvania dealer from whom it undoubtedly came is also deceased, but it is clearly American.

Because the house is so large, it, like the Mexican mansion, comes apart in sections. The weighty, pitched, hinged roof with its double-windowed dormer, lifts off (with the aid of four strong arms) and the porch section beneath is also remov-

HEIGHT: 4' 2 1/2" WIDTH: 7' 2"

1. page 412
2. page 180

AMERICAN. CA. 1890. HEIGHT: 4' 2 1/2" WIDTH: 7' 2"

able. Needless to say, the kitchen wing and the butler's pantry are also readily detachable. Like the house façade, that of the kitchen swings open. This is a sunny kitchen, with its own glazed door on the front, and a window, and with windows on side and back. The butler's pantry, which connects the kitchen to the house, contains four well-designed shelves.

It must be said that the rooms in this otherwise remarkable house are a challenge to furnish.

There is no problem about the kitchen, or the grand staircase hall, one up and one down. Or about the two large rooms on the third floor, each with a circular window and with an arched wall between them. It is the small rooms which lead off the staircase halls which require thought. There are two on each side, one behind the other, containing windows but very little space. One at the rear, with

LAMP WITH
BRISTOL GLOBE

GILDED SOFT LEAD
CAGE ON STAND

CHAIRS ATTRIBUTED TO MÄRKLIN

GLIMPSE INTO GARDEN ROOM

ASPHALTUM WALL CLOCK

DETACHABLE KITCHEN WING

PORCH WITH EARLY HANDMADE WICKER FURNITURE

a door, would permit a bath. Another, a nursery perhaps. The appealing glass room on the second story is clearly meant to be a garden room, and has been dealt with accordingly. There is space for a small dining room adjoining the butler's pantry.

The imposing staircase is furnished with the same circular balustrading which caps the kitchen wing and which embellishes the side porch. All the windows are casement windows. The tall double doors to the front entrance are paneled. An early twentieth-century lighting system, with small round frosted bulbs, added at some point in the history of the house, has been refurbished.

The gossamer curtains on the third floor which are early, and the red-and-white checked curtains which may have been an addition, were the only furnishings which accompanied it. Those which have been added include a rare—probably unique—wicker suite with period upholstery on the side porch.

THE "QUAKER OATS" HOUSE

This relatively modest townhouse has—especially to a collector—a great deal in its favor. It has provenance; it was built for young Elma Zimmerman of New York City ca. 1895[1]—it contains its original furnishings—and—most intriguing of all—it was fashioned from a Quaker Oats crate. A picture of the base, on opposite page, is shown to prove it.

Elma's father ingeniously added a third floor to the top of the crate, which is hinged from the top. The façade he built for the two lower floors is hinged from the side. He hung a bell on a hook above the door (impractical, but interesting), and thoughtfully provided a metal mailbox next to the door.

Except for the transitional chandelier in the dining room, and the bathroom pieces, almost all of the furnishings are original to the house, including the out-sized piano lamp in the parlor.

The lamp rests on a marble-topped stand by Schneegass. The parlor, bedroom, and dining room are all supplied by the Waltershausen maker, which, given the New York City origin of the house, probably was obtained from F.A.O. Schwarz. There's a red-plush parlor set in the parlor, a piano with the dining-room pieces, and a sewing table (its original scissors and thread intact) in the bedroom. All of this furniture is of the popular "yellow cherry." (The catalogue description.)

The kitchen contains an under-sized iron stove ("DOT," probably by Hubley) and the dining-room table is covered, literally, with an over-sized pewter tea set. This is a true dolls' house—a toy house.

On the third floor, next to the bedroom, a set of bamboo furniture furnishes a sort of top floor "recreation" room—if one may employ a term unknown at the time. There is a tennis racket of early shape, perhaps hand-made, a golf bag with one club, and a pair of Indian clubs. The bamboo set is

CA. 1895. EXTERIOR HEIGHT: 31" WIDTH: 18"

1. This date was supplied by a family member from whom the house was purchased.

the very modest bamboo, but unusually complete, with two chaises, a hall rack with mirror and a corner stand—along with the usual table and chairs.[1]

A most realistic linoleum floor covering, faux-grained to resemble wood flooring, is to be found in parlor and dining room. Tile wall coverings of similar realism may be seen, each different, in kitchen and bath.

A portrait of Abraham Lincoln in an ornate gilt dolls' house frame, hangs over the piano.

BASE OF HOUSE

"MISS UNIVERSE"
ATOP PEDESTAL

NOTE WALLPAPER

1. Although this furniture occurred with variations, this appears to be the identical set advertised in *The Youth's Companion* in 1901 with the comment: "This set of toys is made by the Japanese, whose ingenuity in making toys is unequalled."

THE "GAY NINETIES" HOUSE

Sometimes one is suspicious of the perfection of certain dolls' houses. Were they made as toys or models? One can have no such doubts about the "Gay 'Nineties" House: its architecture is nothing which even the most tireless model-maker would wish to commemorate. Its façade begins bravely at the base with balustraded porches across the front, interrupted by a proper staircase. The pair of columns on either side support an upstairs balcony. So far so good. Then, alas, the graceless space between the bal-

cony door and the third-story windows requires, if nothing else, a leap in imagination. Or some sort of leap. It resembles an overly generous space above the lip of a homely man which he decides to camouflage with a moustache. And indeed there has been an attempt at an architectural moustache here: Country Tudor paneling has been applied below the windows as a sort of afterthought. There is a tall chimney at the rear of the pitched roof.

Swing open the hinged front and there is anoth-

UPSIDE–DOWN
CUPID CHANDELIER

CANDY BOX
BOOKCASE

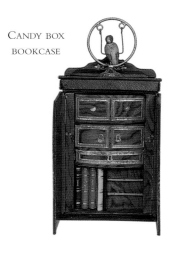

HEIGHT: 60" WIDTH: 41 1/2"

er small problem. It is true that a graceful column flanks the doorway on either side of the second-story hall, and an attractive window seat fits into a parlor bay. There is also a winding staircase from the second to the third floor, but there is no interior staircase whatever on the ground or third floors.

In a full-sized house, these matters could be seriously discouraging, but in a dolls' house such inconveniences are minimized. The "Gay 'Nineties" House, with its mica windows, net curtains and original wallpapers, thoroughly furnished in "Gay 'Nineties" style, is a favorite of dolls' house visitors.

Formerly known as "The Michigan House," (inasmuch as it came from Michigan!), this tall doll residence has been re-named. Its owner may be blamed. It was empty when it arrived, but inspired by uninhibited original wallpapers, it has been furnished in an uninhibited "Gay 'Nineties" style. It is perhaps a rather specific example of a house which is irresistible in miniature but would be resistible in full-size.

The crimson paper in the dining room is a case in point. A room 15 by 16 inches in this paper is warm and vivid; a room 15 by 16 feet would be impossible—and often was. Wallpaper in Victorian dining rooms, says Osbert Lancaster, was nearly always crimson, a color considered "stimulating to the appetite."

In the parlor, on the other hand, the green-patterned paper has an elegant sheen, a suitable back-ground for the "ormolu" furniture. A brass whatnot is crowned by a bisque bride-and-groom under a glass bell, and the parlor table has an album of views of Loch Lomond. (This bride and groom obviously took the Grand Tour rather than the more standard wedding trip to Niagara Falls.) A phonograph with morning-glory horn and a bird in a gilded cage (hanging in the bay window), provide music of divergent styles. The hall, which divides parlor and study, includes a wall phone, a rustic umbrella stand with mirror and shelves above, and a gilded metal standing card tray—a gilded boy with upraised arms does the standing—complete with cards.

The bedroom at upper right contains the standard massive marble-topped pieces, plus that most massive furnishing of all, the armoire. This one, with mirrored doors, is obviously a necessity in a closetless house such as this. The traditional grass mattings, a Victorian necessity for summer floors, may be found in the bedroom. Such Chinese matting was used all year by families that could not afford carpet in winter. The radiators, in a house in which central heating came early, are suitably bronze.

FATHER RELAXES IN HIS STUDY

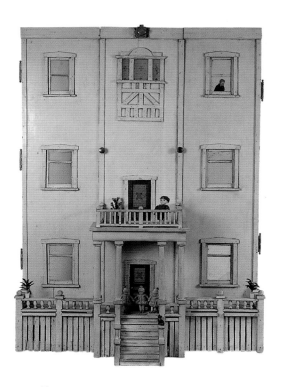

FAÇADE FOLDS BACK IN TWO SECTIONS

SEMI-DETACHED HOUSES FROM WASHINGTON, D.C.

Every city has its proper share of semi-detached houses, and Washington, D. C. is no exception. This pair came to its present owner with the information that its builder had emigrated from Germany to the District of Columbia and had built this disarming duplex at the turn of the century.

Certainly it is atypical of D. C. semi-detached houses, most of which, with small front porches marching monotonously across them, bear no relation to the red-white-and-green piece of ingenuity to be seen here. In this irresistibly colorful piece of gingerbread, arched windows, coigning, and miscellaneous rustication mingle in giddy profusion, clearly in tribute to the builder's Teutonic origin.

A theory was advanced by a perspicacious visitor that the pair of semi-detached houses might well be a pair of semi-detached shops. He based this theory on the presence of the narrow but deeply projecting windows at the side of each of the front doors, which lock with an ornamental key. This opinion may be reinforced by the room arrangement on the right-hand side which includes a small front vestibule with its own door into the rear room. (The "house" on the left contains a single chamber.) However, it is possible that this division was made in order to conceal the early transformer behind the inner wall, which once served to illuminate the plump, old-fashioned light bulbs.

There is a second entrance to this room on the side, where a hinged section of the wall, containing a sizeable arched window, may be opened, again perhaps, with relation to the lighting arrangements and their accessibility. The rest of the house opens from the front, also in segments. Like those on the ground floor, two sections on the second floor, each containing a deep room, also are hinged for access. The single room on the third

floor opens in the same manner, and on both floors a hinged section of the wire railing lowers to allow this.

A large supply of hinges was required by the builder. One of the many ingenious features of his remarkable piece of work relates to the left-hand section of the roof. When this is lifted off, and part of its hinged side lowered, a wooden swing, suspended from chains, moves into place when its wooden framework is raised.

Inasmuch as a black stovepipe runs from the ceiling of the ground floor to the chimney, it is evident that a stove with additional pipe once fitted into the opening (which is finished off with a circular metal rim). It is unfortunate that the stove and other (probable) furnishings were lost. Marvelous paper wall and floor coverings remain in all rooms, and most of the lace curtains, in various patterns, are at the assortment of windows.

CA. 1900.
HEIGHT (NOT INCLUDING CHIMNEY): 34"
WIDTH (AT BASE): 24"

These include several appealing pairs of pointed Gothic windows on the back, for this house is presentable at any angle. Only interior stairs were omitted, owing undoubtedly to the exigencies of space, for, seemingly, no other detail has been overlooked.

A Practical House with Panache

It is mortifying that I've mislaid the origin of this unusual house, which I'm certain is from the East Coast and which came to the collection many years ago.

Although it lacks a façade, there are well-

designed embellishments to suggest what the anonymous builder had in mind. The builder was clearly competent—and practical—and imaginative. There is no front door, but the strong-bracketed pilasters, repeated with a projecting balcony

American. ca. 1900. Height: 45" Width: 31"

on the second story and the small projecting roof above, suggest what we might have expected to see. Crowning the whole is a steeply pitched triangle—the roof—which encompasses the third story and the one large room it contains.

The hall with its modest winding staircase, bisects the kitchen and dining room. In lieu of an upstairs hall is the bath, with attractively "tiled" green-and-white walls and actual linoleum flooring. All the other rooms have been papered with antique wallpapers (from the well-known Wisconsin cache,[1] and antique fabric floor coverings from the Museum supply. All of a proper

turn-of-the-century vintage.

No furnishings came with this very practical house, practical for a child and practical for a collector, with its easy access and appealing design. (Individual segments of plexiglas have been provided for each of the rooms, to dissuade dust.)

The most unusual of the furnishings which have been added may be a velvet-upholstered parlor set.[2] There are pressed composition medallions with a pair of rabbits in each chairback. The sofa is a veritable zoo, with a dog and a deer nestled in the velvet, and a dove on the frame for good measure.

A CANDYBOX DESK

SOFA AND CHAIR WITH PRESSED CARD RABBITS AND DEER INLAY

PUPS AMONGST THE PLUMBING

1. See page 20.
2. Pictured above.

FIVE ROW HOUSES FROM EAST BALTIMORE

Urban renewal seemingly has claimed acres of Baltimore's brick row houses with their little white steps. More than a few remain, but still it was reassuring to come across this row of five, and to rescue them, sitting forlornly on a curb at a Pennsylvania flea market in 1971, at two o'clock in the afternoon.

Although this quintet was not made for use as dolls' houses, they might readily qualify. They came with the information that they had been part of a Christmas garden in a firehouse in East Baltimore.

Years ago many Baltimore firehouses had elaborate Christmas gardens, constructed by the firemen during the year, in their spare time, and displayed to the public at Christmas.

This substantial fragment, nearly five feet long, required some restoration. Though only a few partitions remained, it was evident from the construction that each of the five row houses contained two rooms, one up and one down, and that wallpaper lined the walls, a few shards of which lingered.

These carefully observed copies even have their

CA. 1900. HEIGHT: 18" WIDTH: 56"

street numbers—"10" through "18"—on the glass panes above the workable doors, and one wonders wistfully whether the street name was also specified. The brick paper, which was peeling, has been stabilized. The rundown row was apparently made many years ago to represent houses built in the 'eighties or 'nineties. With their hooded chimneys (covered in brick paper of a smaller scale), and their seamed and sloping roof-tops, they appeared to lack, beneath white shades still neatly drawn half-way at their windows, only an aspidistra or a fern behind the glass.

Curtains of old lace have been supplied, and a moderate number of furnishings have been placed within. A number of residents linger on or near their white steps. One of these is being photographed by a photographer operating a camera—an early and rare penny toy.

At Christmas the museum supplies a wreath[1] for each of the five doors—and, for the Fourth of July, a bunting.

Hooded chimney

Rare penny toy camera

1. Buntings on the doors are replaced at Christmas with wreathes.

GERTRUDE'S HOUSE FROM HALIFAX, MASSACHUSETTS

Aclassic example of the pitfalls to be avoided in the dating of dolls' houses is supplied by this self-assured specimen.

When it was offered (by mail) by a Massachusetts dealer, years ago, she mentioned a house number on the door. "Such cryptography," as I've written elsewhere, "is always alluring (one dreams of discovering the street name and locating the full-sized original), but in this case, the description was inferior to the actuality." When the house arrived, there was no address, but each of the pair of entrance doors bore an infinitesimal silver plate. One of these said "Gertrude" and one said "1904."

Given its true mansard roof and other mid-Victorian details, Gertrude's house might have been thought several decades earlier. Supplied the specific date, even the most casual amateur of architecture cannot fail. Presumably this was a copy of the house in which young Gertrude lived when the miniature replica was given to her, perhaps on her birthday, possibly at Christmas, but unquestionably in 1904.

The dealer from whom Gertrude's house was purchased said that it came from Massachusetts, and she had even supplied the name of the town: Halifax, on the south shore of Boston, not far from Plymouth.

Even without a shred of history, this would be a notable dolls' house. From its arched piazza, which runs the depth of the house, to the cupola, glazed with four different tints of stained glass, Gertrude's is a most realistic miniature residence.

Beneath the mansard roof, the façade, with its two-story bays, lifts off to disclose a staircase. This one ascends not only to the second floor, but, realistically, to the attic, and there is a proper balustrade for a doll of uncertain age, and joints, to cling to.

The floor plan is similarly real: back rooms open off front rooms. There are three each on the first and second floors in addition to the staircase halls. A bathroom with a built-in tub and square commode and, for privacy, "windowphanie" at the window (in an evocative and geometric pattern of yellow, black, and red) is located above the kitchen. Both of these rooms may be entered through the hall but can be seen only from the back which is open (and now protected by Plexiglas.) The two principal rear rooms are visible from the back and, through wide openings with proper moldings,

CA. 1904. HEIGHT: 35 1/2" WIDTH: 26"

SILVER PLAQUES ON DOORS

INTERIOR OF FRONT

Rare bathroom with built-in commode and tub

Interior of back

from the front. Probably there should be portières between these rooms.

Gertrude's house has original wallpapers and the almost inevitable net curtains. There is a red glazed window in the hall.

Handmade furniture came with the house, possibly made by the dolls' house builder, but, except for a parlor set upholstered partly in crimson and partly in blue velvet, and a hall tree with miniscule hooks, the best that can be said of it is that the maker was a clever carpenter, but not a dolls' house cabinetmaker.

A few of these pieces, too large for the rooms, and a bit clunky, may be seen through the attic windows. It was a delight to refurnish this charming house with pieces of the small scale which the delicately-scaled rooms suggest. As I've written elsewhere, dolls' house furniture makers in the

METAL COT, ONE OF PAIR, ORGINAL DRAPERY

FILIGREE METAL PIANO

nineteenth century did not work in terms of scale, but of size. Mid-nineteenth century toy catalogues show a bed or a desk in several sizes. One's eye, if a reasonably knowing eye, may decide. In a room it is, of course, sometimes possible to include discrepant sizes, if the items are placed judiciously—perhaps in different sections of the room. If one insists on defining scale in Gertrude's house, most of the pieces are possibly two-thirds of an inch to the foot.

In the kitchen, there is space for little more than a table, and the smallest of the series of iron kitchen ranges, but built-in floor-to-ceiling shelves permit a substantial display of crockery and other kitchenwares.

Bamboo furniture in a rare, small size is centered in the parlor. The bamboo is a reflection of the Thonet furniture which became popular in the second half of the nineteenth century. The bedroom has been furnished as a nursery with a pair of filigree metal cribs still hooded by a rare survival—their pink cotton, lace-edged canopies. Twin infants occupy the cribs.

Carpets of old paisley or old velvet have been laid in most of the rooms. In the bathroom—the ultimate Victorian dolls' house bathroom—the original green-and-coral "tile" floor in a diamond pattern sets off the built-in wooden tub and commode. A rare painted tin shower—with its curtain, as usual, missing, has been added.

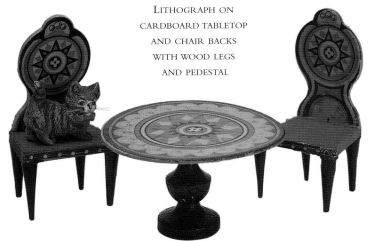

LITHOGRAPH ON
CARDBOARD TABLETOP
AND CHAIR BACKS
WITH WOOD LEGS
AND PEDESTAL

BENTWOOD CHAIR,
TYPICAL OF MANY
SETS, STYLES, SIZES

THE PIANO-HINGE HOUSE

In Chevy Chase, Maryland, many years ago, there was a modest establishment known as Grandma's Antique Shop. "Grandma" was a Mr. Williams. The contents of such shops were usually described as "a general line," and when Mr. Williams had something of interest, the price was reasonable.

There was a front porch on the rather ramshackle shop, and when I visited my 89-year-old

father in a nursing home several times a week, I'd pass Grandma's, turning my head in Mr. W's direction in the hope that one day there'd be a dolls' house on that porch.

One day, in 1959, there was, and I regret to say that I made a U-turn so precipitously that I was

AMERICAN. CA. 1910.
HEIGHT: 22" (PLUS CHIMNEYS)
WIDTH: 31 3/4"

lucky to avoid a wreck.

On closer inspection what met my eyes was the apparition pictured nearby. Many years later, when The National Trust for Historic Preservation made a series of Christmas ornaments of the Museum's houses, this one was included. For the ornament, I dubbed it, rather awkwardly, "a ca. 1910 Eclectic," though I now refer to it as "The Piano-Hinge House."

However, as I wrote in the blurb which accompanied the ornament, "it is as eclectic as a piece of architecture can be...very grand and Romanesque below and very modest and Main Street above."

An unassuming bungalow-style dormer, ca. 1910, looks down upon a two-tiered arcade with elegantly carved columns set between two bay windows on the first story, with matching fluted columns supporting pedimented arches on the second. The maker was clearly a carver by nature. All the first floor windows, front and sides, and the front door, are capped with carved arches. (The second-story windows have projecting lintels.) There is a dentilated molding beneath the eaves.

The façade swings open on its brass piano hinges. A third piano hinge offers access to the dormer. There are interior columns upstairs and down and one long elegant room with a mirrored wall. For a more plebian touch there are rods between the front and back rooms, to hold portières, draperies usually of velvet, which today might be considered "room dividers."

There is a built-in fireplace with an overmantel in the wide hall, and a staircase. An ingenious device, consisting of interior window frames with removable glass, provides easy access for a window-washer. The original net curtains, on removable rods, may serve as a reminder to turn-of-the-century dolls' house restorers that original net curtains are found in so many turn-of-the-century dolls' houses, and that net is a good bet for a blank window of the period.

Except for the curtains, the house, of course, came unfurnished. The scale of the rooms has lent itself to the smaller-sized Gottschalk and Schneegass pieces. The "elegant" room with mirrored wall has been supplied with the filigree metal[1] tables and chairs from the Paris company of Simon & Rivollet, also of the correct period for the house.

SIMON & RIVOLLET FILIGREE FURNITURE

MIGNONETTE WITH RARE GILDED SOFT-LEAD FIREPLACE

AMERICAN. CA. 1910. INTERIOR: HEIGHT: 22" (PLUS CHIMNEYS) WIDTH: 31 3/4"

---

1. David Pressland in his comprehensive book, *Penny Toys* (New Cavendish Books, London, 1991), identifies the substance as "lead alloy."

"THE EDISON HOUSE"

When this unassuming structure was acquired, it was accompanied by a tag which identified it as "The Patrick House, Haddonfield, N.J."

For a curious reason, it is known to its present owner as "The Edison House." It was acquired from a New Jersey dealer with what was obviously an early lighting system, defined by hand-blown pear-shaped bulbs with pointy glass ends and U-shaped filaments. When, with trepidation, the cord was plugged in, the sizeable bulbs lighted up. A friend dubbed it "The Edison House," in tribute, no doubt to Mr. Edison's contribution to incandescent lighting, and that name has remained. (It

AMERICAN. CA. 1910. HEIGHT: 35" BASE: 34" X 17" (PLUS STEPS)

THE EARLY HAND-BLOWN
BULBS STILL LIGHT

is not inappropriate that Thomas Edison's laboratory, now a museum, is, of course, in New Jersey where this house originated.)

In the hope that the rare bulbs, one in each of the six rooms and in the attic, would continue to burn, a dimmer was installed, and the bulbs have cooperatively continued to light (fingers crossed) for a number of years.

The house itself, with no façade below its steeply pitched roof and prominent dormer, is modest in decor but well built. There is a four-inch tall base, a feature which many dolls' house builders misguidedly omit, from which the well-designed front steps project, and there are seven glazed windows. In addition to those on the side walls, there are three on the back wall (another detail often omitted by dolls' house designers), a pleasing trade-off for the lack of a façade.

The original net curtains and green window shades lend atmosphere to the windows, and the original wallpapers, admittedly a bit wan (with stripes and floral patterns resolutely beige) remain on the walls. A rather ingenious device relates to the staircase which is placed against the back wall of the living room. This terminates in an upstairs hall with doorways to bedroom and nursery, and projecting walls which not only offer access to the rooms, but an extra dimension to the interior. A boy on his way upstairs may be glimpsed near the top through the bedroom doorway, and a mirrored console and a cat—whatever else—may be seen on the landing itself outside the nursery.

The house has been furnished modestly, in keeping with its character. There is Schneegass "yellow cherry" in smaller scale in the dining and bedroom. There is a "penny toy" sewing machine in the bedroom. (Unfortunately, since the publication of David Pressland's splendid book[1] penny toys have become a luxury.) A doll seated on the Mission-style sofa in the living room may gaze at an early framed portrait of the U.S. Capitol on the wall, and a framed portrait of the American flag on a table—obviously this is a patriotic family. A pewter dinner service by Gerlach is on the dining-room table. Other accessories by this prolific German company—an early electric fan, a grandfather clock and such necessities as oil lamps and radiators are to be found throughout.

GERMAN RADIATOR

EARLY ELECTRIC FAN

PENNY TOY SEWING
MACHINE BY MEIER

1. Ibid, page 80.

PENNSYLVANIA RAILROAD WORKER'S HOUSE

We, alas, don't know his name, but we do know that this carefully-crafted cottage and its furniture were built in the course of two years—1912 to 14—by a Pennsylvania Railroad worker in Pennsylvania. Although the date is specific, the style represents an almost indefinable era, one which is likely to inspire nostalgia in residents of a number of Eastern states or, at the very least, make them feel at home.

The front porch, the two-story bay, the careful clapboard and a pitched roof of some complexity (to accommodate the several dormers) are meticulously clad in shingles or clapboard. There are three patterns of shingles, presumably hand-cut by the careful builder. There are green window shades at each of the windows, neatly pulled down half way to reveal lace curtains. There are round shingles on the roof which match the white shingles on the bay. Shingles of a more complex pattern surround a small attic window (though there is no attic inside), one of two.

An interesting kitty-corner back door, see page 84, and a lift-off panel which covers the back of the house give access to the rooms.

The gifted maker of the house lavished as much attention on the interior as he did on the exterior. The eight rooms, four up and four down (approximately[1]), are bisected by a central staircase with banisters on both sides. The back rooms are implied: there are no walls, but a pair of columns at the base of the stairs are opposite matching columns on the side walls, which define the room spaces.

It is true that there is no privacy in the bathroom, but the handcrafted tub, basin and commode are so well made that a non-doll finds this unobjectionable. Oddly, the only built-in fixture in the kitchen is a basin identical to the one in the bath, complete with proper faucets.

All of the furniture is similarly successful, and perfectly evocative of its period. From the round table and mirror-topped sideboard in the dining room to high-backed beds in the two bedrooms, the furniture is very 1912 to 1914. One of the beds is brass in style but, oddly, is of copper. There are two dark-wood "dressers" and washstands, the latter with towel-rails above, to match the dark-wood bed.

There is an upright piano with bench, and a

1912-1914. HEIGHT: 24" WIDTH: 23"

MORRIS CHAIR AND PERIOD LAMP AND TABLE

---

1. The bathroom and kitchen are wall-less additions.

small assortment of very "period" chairs, including a Morris chair and high-backed rockers. Accessories, such as period lamps and vases have been added.

The rooms are unobtrusively wallpapered with pleasing borders. The word for this house is evocative—of an era and a style.

A copper bed

Pennsylvania railroad worker's house (interior)

Note back door

A "LITTLE HOUSE" FROM MAMARONECK

This neatly handcrafted New England "center chimney" is helpfully stamped, "Maker of Little Houses. W. P. Weiss. Mamaroneck, N.Y."

This is the only "little house" by Mr. Weiss which I have encountered, and suspecting that Mr. Weiss did not make many, and made those he crafted by hand, I venture to include it amongst handcrafted houses.

In any case, the house bears the classic simplicity of a Tynietoy house, but it appears to be earlier. The lower half is clad in the same well-made siding which has been painted green on the roof. The upper half is scored to represent a wider siding. It is plentifully supplied with glazed windows, two up and two down on the

back and two on each side. There are even two small fanlights under the gables. Three interior doors upstairs have knobs. Oddly enough the front door has none.

The façade sensibly slides off, revealing one large and one small room on the ground floor, separated by an arch. There is a staircase in the larger room which properly ascends to the second floor where it is concealed by a door, perhaps to give privacy to a possible bath in the front, with the other two doors opening to the bedrooms.

When these pages were nearly complete, I acquired the fence. It seemed to belong to this house and was duly installed.

EARLY 20TH CENTURY. HEIGHT: 20" (PLUS CHIMNEY) WIDTH: 21"

A Glittering House from Manayunk

This house and its garage glitter and glisten with a coating of bits of colored glass strewn upon its surface. From a Philadelphia community with an Indian name,[1] the Manayunk house was thought, when it was acquired, in the early 1980's, to be a copy of an existing house.

The thoughtful dealer who sold it attempted to learn the whereabouts of the original, only to be told that it had been torn down years before. There were a number of such houses in the Green Lane section of Manayunk, she said, with deep dentils beneath their roofs and similar porches. The houses were of granular stucco. The colored bits of glass, clearly meant to simulate this, give the house almost a folk art quality.

Even if there were no other evidence, the detached garage would serve to date the house to the 'twenties, or possibly as early as the 'teens. There is an elderly lighting system with small, round clear-glass bulbs, possibly added later.

The builder clearly gave a great deal of thought to his plan. The re-painted pitched roof lifts off, and the back, fastened by latches, opens in three hinged sections, each with a porcelain knob. The bay section, which swings open, contains nine of the nineteen glazed windows, some of them arched and some pedimented. Although there are windows on the third floor exterior, there is no actual third floor, but lace-edged net curtains are in place at all the windows. There is a total of six rooms—eight, if the staircase halls up and down are counted. There is a proper railing on the staircase.

The endearing potted plants in the upstairs windows are abloom with cloth flowers. The pair of chairs with matching table were stored in the garage.

It's the glitter which sets this house apart from any other and gives it its considerable sparkle.

EARLY 20TH CENTURY. HEIGHT: 27" WIDTH: 27"

1. An Algonquin term probably used by the Lenape Indians (Delaware), literally a direct reference to the Schuylkill River "where we go to drink."

A PIONEER HALF-INCH HOUSE FROM MAINE

It is unlikely that the term "half-inch" as applied to dolls' houses was in existence when this small house was built. The builder was ahead of his time. He had no access to scale roofing or siding or plumbing. He made his own. And this pioneer built, perhaps unconsciously, a "half-inch" house.

When it was found, in the mid-1990's, in a Maine antiques shop, there was no clue to the identity of the skillful builder, and no date. There are hints: the style of the windows on the façade is clearly Victorian, possibly copied from the builder's own home. The interior suggests a later origin. It is a mélange, withal a charming mélange, of styles: a Georgian fireplace with a dentillated molding in the living room, an elegant winding staircase of

similar vintage, Elizabethan latticed windows in the rear of the living-room and dining-room, a mirrored door in the bedroom. The front door behind the double-columned portico is a cottagey Dutch door.

This is one of two houses in the Museum's collection with gutters and downspouts,[1] and one of the few with workable shutters (on both front and back). The builder was a mechanic as well as a cabinetmaker. Courtesy of an ingenious metal mechanism, the roof lifts off on both the house proper and its kitchen wing. Another metal contrivance serves to hold both sections of the façade in place. A metal narrow switchboard at the rear of the house contains eight switches to light each small room indi-

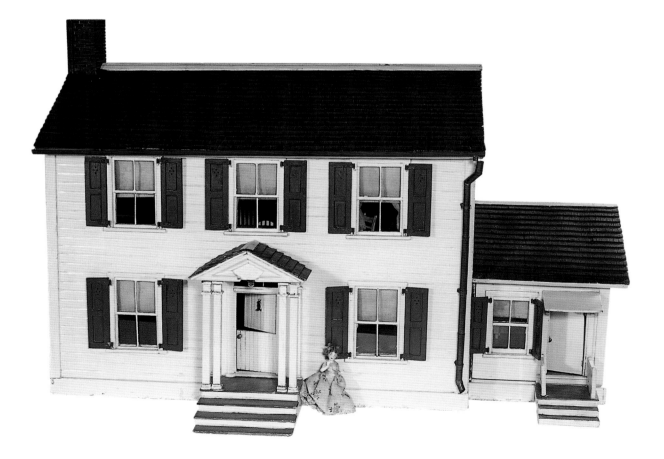

EARLY 20TH CENTURY. HEIGHT: 13" (PLUS CHIMNEY) WIDTH: 22"

1. See page 42.

vidually. There are brass chandeliers obviously hand-made in the two principal downstairs rooms, and simple ceiling lights in the other rooms as well as a light over the front door.

A few pieces of furniture which came with the house, and a few which are built-in, suggest a date as late as the 'twenties or even the 'thirties. The bathroom fixtures, especially, appear to have been added later. The bathtub has been built into a plat-form (with a built-in slot for soap), which is attached to the wall over a strip of wainscoting, clearly pre-existing. There is a built-in shower but the commode is missing. In the kitchen there is a built-in breakfast nook (a table between two tall benches) and a built-in stove. A matching wooden refrigerator with opening door and carved ice trays was not attached. Oddly, there is no sink. A few furnishings include a well-made rope bed and a varnished washstand—"antiques."

There are yellowing window shades at all win-dows. Sadly dilapidated net curtains remain at a few. One strip of faded shrubbery, apparently made from sponge dipped in green ink or paint, suggests that even landscaping was not neglected by the conscientious builder.

THE 1932 BUDD GRAY HOUSE FROM CONNECTICUT

Although it is the most modern house in the collection, this white clapboard "colonial," exquisitely built, and with its complete provenance, is one of the most satisfying in many ways.

The four bedroom house, with attached garage and (painted) lawn, is similar to many full-sized houses built in the 'twenties and early 'thirties on tree-lined streets in quiet suburban neighborhoods. It was meticulously constructed by Budd D. Gray of Greenwich, Connecticut for his three small granddaughters and given by one of them, many years later, to a museum in Boothbay Harbor, Maine.[1] His name, town, and the 1932 date are engraved on a brass plaque under the eaves. (Would that more dolls' houses—and houses—contained such information!)

Thoroughly filled with its original furnishings, the house, when it arrived, was accompanied by a vintage Kingsbury car with a New Hampshire license plate in the driveway.[2] When the overhead door of the garage is raised, a light comes on! This is one of many notable details by the painstaking Mr. Gray, who clearly spent many months of continuous labor on a small building of interest to many of today's innumerable dolls' house builders, both for the excellence of its design as well as for its craftsmanship. The fanlight over the front door and the sidelights were copied from the entrance to the early Greenwich house in which the Grays lived.

For the statistically inclined, there are twenty-four pairs of workable windows, 7,330 wooden shingles on the roof and thirteen doors hung on butt hinges and with spring fasteners. There is also a swinging door between the dining room and kitchen. There are window screens available for a house built in pre-air-conditioning days.

EARLY 20TH CENTURY

1. Acquired for The Washington Dolls' House & Toy Museum in 1980.
2. Molded into the rubber tires is the name of the town in which Kingsbury toys were made—Keene, N. H. (This car was snatched from its heavy Plexiglas case in 1998 and dramatically recovered a year later in 1999!)

EXTERIOR HEIGHT: 31"
BASE: 54" X 44"

The house, actually, has much in common with the Tynietoy mansion in the collection, which is a few years earlier, from the mid-'twenties, see page 145. Accordingly it has not seemed too much of a liberty to place shrubbery, a bench, and a sundial, all by Tynietoy, on the lawn.

The Tynietoy mansion opens from the front, and has more of a "toy" quality rather than the real-istic detail here. This is more of a model house, and if one were of proper size, one might comfortably move right in. In this house both the front and back lift off. There are locks on both, though the key is absent. There is complete realism, front and back, with a columned porch at the rear entrance, a full complement of windows, and to commemo-rate a relatively recent service since departed, even

VINTAGE KINGSBURY CAR

a few bottles of milk at the back door.

There are oak floors, quartered oak stair treads, mahogany newel posts and banister, hooks and hangers in the closets, and removable double curtain rods in all the rooms. On the latter hang curtains and draperies carefully made by Mrs. Gray who also supplied linens, blankets, and other needle-crafted furnishings.

There is Tynietoy furniture in the dining room, the bedrooms, and the nursery. The latter has nursery rhyme figures appealingly painted on the walls.

DETAIL OF ONE OF THE
REMOVEABLE SCREENS

DETAIL OF INTERIOR

REMOVEABLE REAR OF HOUSE

PART II

U.S. Houses, Commercially Made

An "Automatic Combination Doll Villa"

A Stirn & Lyon patent dolls' "villa," different from the New York firm's "Mansion" and "Combination House" (pages 98 & 100) is illustrated herewith.

Unlike the pressure-printed duo, the façade of this Colonial Revival-styled house and its unusual garden is lushly printed in lithographed paper-on-wood. The other two houses are intriguing in their own way, but pale by comparison. The only family resemblance relates to the low fence that surrounds the garden which is composed of similar pressure-printed wood.

This is a folding house with a rather curious concept. The interior is given short shrift. Between the colorful façade with its green shutters and pedimented dormer, and the plain back, which hook together, there is a wooden floor which may be lowered into place. When closed, the façade of the house fits between the garden and this rear section, like a sandwich.

CLOSED

CA.1875. HEIGHT: 18" WIDTH: 17 1/2"

The plain walls of the single room permitted by this device are, compared to the rest, bland. There's an accordion fold at their center and a few elaborate windows printed in black ink on their exterior, and that's it.

The garden, on the other hand, is lavish and the fact that the positioning of the figures and accessories was left to the discretion of the young owner has not helped. The fountain, the bushes, and the children are mounted on small wooden blocks with a wire brad at each side, and these figures can be folded down readily when the house is closed. The brads fit under metal staples which resemble wickets—and surely croquet would have been a more suitable game than badminton for this lawn! As the picture indicates, the fountain has been properly located, but the players are crowded by the strangely placed bushes, and the small girl emerging from the tasseled tent looks lonely. These figures are placed between the house façade and the garden, and when the toy is closed, they are ingeniously protected by the low wooden fence.

Under the lid, there is information about other Stirn & Lyon toys. Referring to themselves as a "Manufacturer of Patent Combination Toys," they list a "doll house mansion, bridge, grocery store" on one side, and "menagerie, stable, circus, game of Rinaldo" on the other. Unfortunately, when the house was manufactured, the patent had only been applied for, and no date is provided. Given the Colonial Revival aspect, ca. 1885 appears to be reasonably logical.

This is a strange and fascinating piece.

A Doll "Mansion" By Stirn & Lyon

One can picture a father on Christmas Eve of 1882 struggling to assemble this "Combination Doll Mansion," just as fathers of recent years struggled with the notoriously strange instructions for Japanese toys. Or perhaps it lay unassembled, wrapped in its wooden box under the tree, and on Christmas morning father and child coped with it together.

It is to be hoped that the young recipient wasn't expected to set up the house herself. If she was, she may have suffered from a frustration syndrome the rest of her life. Mansard roof, dormers, balcony and all, this toy house came "knocked-down," in a sizeable wooden box (24" by 10"), and with its thin wooden siding and tongue-and-groove (and dowel-and-peg) construction, putting it together (one speaks from experience)[1] is an exercise in patience and dexterity. The relatively flimsy result may not have been worthwhile for a family of dolls in 1882, but it is an intriguing piece of miniature architecture for a collector more than a century later.

Unfortunately, because the box becomes the ground floor of the house, it has had hard usage, and bits are missing of the handsomely lithographed label, an idealized rendering of the mansion, a stable, and an elegantly turned out Victorian lady, but most of it is intact, including what every collector most longs to know: "Combination Doll Mansion, Stirn & Lyon, NY." And though the date was lacking, this information is intact on the smaller "Combination Doll House," and on the "Combination Grocery Store" (page 326). The first says, "Patented 1881 by Stirn & Lyon, N.Y." The date on the lid of the store is even more specific: "Patented April 11, 1882." How many years these were made is unknown to me, but with all of the pieces there are to lose, and the fragility of many of them, the fact that even a few have survived suggests that they were manufactured for several years at least.

The mansion, the smaller house, and the grocery store all have a family resemblance, both in their patented construction and in their appearance. The framework is composed of corner and interior beams which peg into the foundation and connect the top with the lid. The second floors of the two houses rest on ledges glued to the inside walls. The windows, pressure-printed on the light wood to resemble shutters on the mansion, and four-light sash on the small house, were cut out and then partially re-fastened with adhesive tape so that they may be opened in pairs, in the manner of a casement. (One was opened by a two-month-old kitten who went inside and made himself at home.)

In appearance, both houses and the store are heightened by a lovely reddish stain which is applied to parts of each structure: the four pilasters across the front of the mansion, the dormers, cornice, balcony, and chimneys, are all of this hue. This provides an effective contrast to the similarly pleasing deep cream shade to which the unpainted wood, printed to imitate bricks on the mansion, and possibly brownstone on the smaller house, has turned with age.

---

1. The mansion, it must be confessed, was set up and glued into position before it was acquired, by a prior owner. Our experience was with the smaller "Combination Doll House" shown here, and with the "Combination Grocery Store" (page 326).

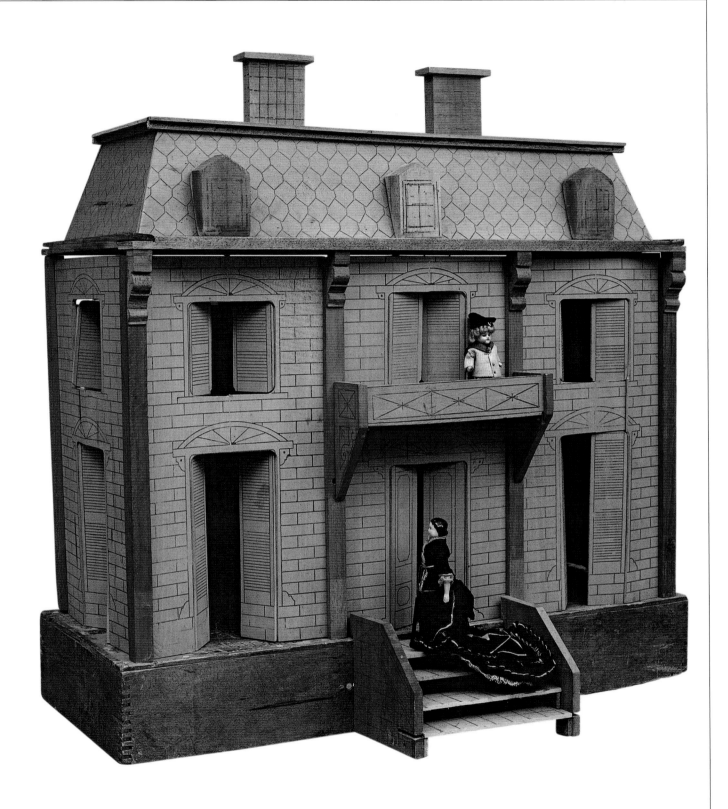

PATENTED 1881. HEIGHT: 24" (NOT INCLUDING 3" CHIMNEYS) WIDTH: 26"

A "COMBINATION DOLL HOUSE" BY STIRN & LYON

Of similar construction to the Stirn & Lyon mansion, the "Combination Doll House" replaces with a cornice the mansion's mansard roof with its dormers and chimneys. The cornice, which attaches to the top of this house and shields the flat roof, is not unlike the false fronts often seen on late-nineteenth century buildings in full-size. (Mercifully beyond the reach of restorers and "modernizers," these upper sections usually survive intact, often with a date to let us know when each was built.)

There is also a relationship to England's box-back dolls' houses such as those by Silber & Fleming (page 181) and, later, Lines Bros. (page 203). Such houses have been aptly described as houses with "Queen Anne fronts and Mary Anne backs." These are definitely "Mary Anne" but appealing on their own terms.

LID BECOMES BASE

PATENTED 1881.
HEIGHT: 22" WIDTH: 18"

THE "MYSTERY" MANSION

In 1974, I wrote at length[1] of a fascinating series of houses which had begun to surface, mostly on the Eastern Seaboard. They were sturdy dolls' houses, all big, but varying in size and number of rooms. Most had such common characteristics as parquet floors in colorful patterns as well as exterior rustication—chamfered wood strips applied as coigning and wherever else it seemed to strike the builder's fancy. There were paneled doors both inside and out.

Because of the considerable detail, a theory was bandied about that these houses must have been made in prisons (where only prisoners would have had sufficient time on their hands!) This theory seemed highly imaginative.

In 1971, F.A.O. Schwarz reproduced its 1897

AMERICAN. CA 1895. HEIGHT: 46" BASE: 55" X 24"

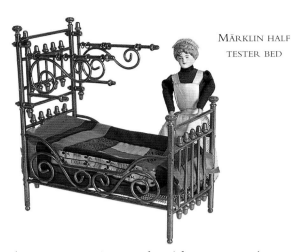

MÄRKLIN HALF
TESTER BED

RARE MÄRKLIN
UPHOLSTERED
METAL CHAIR

Christmas Review and, with some excitement, I discovered an illustration of one of the smaller models. Unfortunately, Schwarz hadn't and still hasn't, a clue as to where these houses were made, but the late Ashby Giles, of Schwarz's antique toy department (alas, no longer in existence) reminded me that because Schwarz had a branch in Boston, these houses might well have been made in Massachusetts.

In any case, in *Dolls' Houses in America*, I dubbed them "mystery houses," a phrase which appears to have "caught on." More than a generation later, the origin of the houses remains a mystery.[1]

Although the builder of the Museum's example is unknown, it has otherwise its complete provenance. It was given, at about the turn of the century, to Annie Pinkney Watt of New York City, born in 1889. Inasmuch as the Watt family resided at 605 Fifth Avenue, it requires little imagination to suppose that it was purchased at Schwarz, then on West 23rd Street.

This splendid specimen (the owner of one of these referred to hers as "a great ark of a house"), is almost five feet in width, with a wing, dormer rooms, and staircase halls. (There is one model which is even more mammoth.) Although this mystery house lacks rustication and inlaid floors, the basic structure is the same, along with such

1. This house is not to be confused with the South Jersey House, featured in *The Doll House Mystery*, (page 37)

LAMP WITH
ORIGINAL FABRIC
SHADE COVER
OVER OPALINE

details as a latticed basement foundation and stairs leading to the small wooden lawn. All of these houses are, sensibly, front opening.

The house was purchased from Annie Pinkney Watt's great-niece, the late Mrs. Anne Pinkney Watt Wiechmann, a Washington area resident at the time of the purchase.

The imposing house contains ten rooms, including an attic room on the left side and one on the front along with the staircase halls. Upstairs, the lady of the house has turned her back on the viewer, possibly to speak to someone below, as she stands before the well-turned balustrade of the winding staircase. A rare, work table is nearby.

An "ormolu" hallstand with built-in looking-glass above brightens the downstairs hall, fitting as though made for the space, a thing gratifying to interior designers of full-sized houses as well as dolls' houses.

Although it was apparent that some of the furniture had been lost or mislaid, much, happily, was still with the house including some rare and fascinating pieces. Among these is the parlor set, in maroon, of the rare Märklin upholstered-on-metal genre: tufted, tasseled and be-fringed, a pair of Märklin brass half-tester beds with wire springs,[1] and a pair of banquet lamps with opaline shades. With the latter, rarer still, are the original fabric shades—very period—which fitted over the opaline shades (assuming one can bear to cover opaline shades!).

The curtains and draperies are original to the house. Because the wallpaper had been damaged by dampness, these were replaced with antique papers from a precious supply.

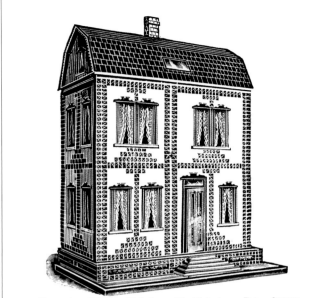

Above size, 45 inches high, base, 24 x 35 inches.   Price, $33.00
Dolls' Houses, in many styles and sizes, $2.00, $3.00, $5.00, $6.50, $12.00, $13.50, $20.00, $26.00, $33.00, $50.00, $80.00
Dolls' Rooms $1.75, $2.50, $3.50, $4.75, $6.00

FROM SCHWARZ 1897 CATALOGUE

1. A pair of these, lacking the half testers, were pictured in Schwarz's 1913 catalogue, obviously a popular item over a long period of years. At an antique show years ago, I told a dealer who displayed one (without the half tester) as "a salesman's sample," that it was advertised in F.A.O. Schwarz's 1913 Christmas review for $1.25. He was not pleased.

TWO HOUSES: TWO UNKNOWN MAKERS

Other than their lithographed paper-on-wood construction, these two houses share only their American origin and the fact that we do not know who made them.

The first, and foremost of these, fascinates me with its lithographed chimneys casting lithographed shadows, and its suggestion of early Arts and Crafts architecture. (The foolish little turret, perching like a parasol, above the front door, seems the only false note.) There is a two-inch strip of horticulture on the base.

The back is open to reveal one very tall room inside—the ultimate Victorian parlor. The lithography within, as vivid as the lithography without, is dominated by an impressive tile fireplace with an equally impressive roaring fire. A thoroughly

upholstered "easy" chair, typical of the 1880's, may be the 1890's artist's idea, quite rightly, of comfort. A floor lamp with a huge yellow, fringed shade, undoubtedly of silk, matches yellow draperies on each side wall. Through each window, one may see the identical tree in the distance. There is a small fringed hearth rug, not abutting the hearth, but in the middle of the room, over a bordered carpet.

There has been a theory among collectors, which seems reasonable, that this might be an early Bliss.

★ ★ ★

The lithography on the second house shown herewith is totally different in character. In a

LATE NINETEENTH CENTURY. HEIGHT: 15 3/4" WIDTH: 10 3/4"

British publication,[1] Evelyn Ackerman, author of the excellent Gottschalk book, head-lined this house as "A Rare Whitney-Reed," and cited a catalogue illustration included in *Dolls' Houses in America*, as proof that this was one of the vanished houses of Whitney-Reed. That was published in 1974, and, as several examples in the present volume indicate (pages 127-129) the houses hadn't vanished at all, and their somber lithography and sober rooftops bear little resemblance to the rather giddy design of the color specimen shown here.

Mrs. Ackerman detects "a striking resemblance,"

though she does not supply details. She was judging, however, from small black-and-white catalogue illustrations, and hadn't the advantage of seeing the three shown in color. The lithography—doors and windows among other details—are entirely different in character, and there is no stone coigning as seen on the mysterious structure, with its highly imaginative roof-line, shown here. Even the wood columns fail in their several turnings, to correspond.

One day a catalogue with this curious toy house may appear, suggesting a maker heretofore undiscovered.

CA. 1884 -1903. HEIGHT: 12 1/4" WIDTH: 9 3/4"

1. *International Dolls' House News*, Sept. 5, 1997.

"Dolly's Playhouse" By McLoughlin

In May 1905, *Playthings* printed an obituary of John McLoughlin, the celebrated New York manufacturer of games, blocks, books, and various paper toys. According to the article, McLoughlin, in 1855, had taken his brother Edmund into partnership, establishing the McLoughlin firm.

The McClintocks have observed that John McLoughlin, "being an engraver by trade, was interested in good printing, with emphasis on color, which appealed so strongly to children."[1] They might have added that such printing "with emphasis on color" also appeals strongly to latter-day collectors. Four of his dolls' houses, illustrated in these pages, are prime examples of his work.

CA. 1884–1903.
HEIGHT: 18" WIDTH: 12"

1. *Toys in America,* Public Affairs Press, 1961.

When Montgomery Ward, in 1903, advertised "Dolly's Playhouse," they really failed to do it justice. With a dimly printed illustration not much more than an inch tall (McLoughlin should have helped with Ward's catalogues), they described under "folding doll houses," a specimen "two stories high, made of strawboard and wood, lined outside and in with paper printed to represent carpets, wall paper, brick walls, and windows."

"This is a very fine residence for any family of small dolls," they asserted, and they might well have added, "even a royal family." Although the rooms are only two, they are so palatial that even a princess, of the proper size, might feel quite at home.

The drawing-room (it is too sumptuous to be called a parlor), with its elegantly paneled walls hung with paintings in gold-leaf frames, and its ornately carved white marble mantel with "ormolu" clock and "garniture," surmounted by a ceiling-high "looking-glass," is the Victorian drawing-room incarnate. If, as Frances Lichten has written[1], "lavish outlay on window draperies was a particular stamp of worldly success," the head of this dolls' house must have been extremely successful. (After all, he paid 75 cents for his house in 1903.) Lace curtains, which are clearly Brussels lace, are accompanied by gold-leaf cornices from which hang tasseled lambrequins of mauve (of course). But the decoration that gives the room much of its opulence is the green carpet which is centered with a multi-colored floral medallion of astonishing elaboration, and surrounded by a floral harmonizing border. And horticulture is overhead as well as underfoot: the fact that the ceiling is of the identical pattern, with somewhat more subdued coloring, may well have been overpowering to all but the sturdiest dolls.

The second floor, with striped wallpaper and a blue, gold, and white figured Brussels carpet, is

LID

almost prim by comparison, but it is suitably fashionable nevertheless.

In its construction the house is ingenious. The principal section consists of hinged walls and floors which swing into position and are then firmly slotted by the lithographed paper-on-wood cornice which fits over a wooden strip at each side of the front. The shingled roof, which then is placed over the pediment formed at front and back, miraculously stays in place. The chimney fits snugly into an opening in the roof.

It is clear that this house was sold during the course of a number of years. The late Marian Howard, whose careful research in the fields of paper dolls and their houses is well known, related that in a 1875-76 catalogue in her possession, this very house, made of wood at that time, was illustrated. It is also illustrated and advertised on the back cover of a McLoughlin Bros. ABC book, published in 1884.

1. *Decorative Arts of Victoria's Era,* Scribners, 1950.

THE SMALL WORLD OF R. BLISS

Current collectors of Bliss architecture may find it amusing (or possibly disconcerting) to learn that this collector acquired her first Bliss piece, the "Seaside Cottage," in a West Virginia antiques shop, in 1948, with a few pieces of furniture, for eight dollars and fifty cents. It was the first Bliss house on what became in her own collection a few years later, "Bliss Street," shown on pages 110-111.

In the intervening years, "R. Bliss"[1] has become a household—a dolls' household—name.

The R. Bliss Manufacturing company of Pawtucket, Rhode Island, was established in 1832 with the manufacture "of wooden screws and clamps" for the use of piano and cabinet makers,[2] and did not become involved with the making of toys till more than half a century later. Then they

"BLISS STREET" CA. 1895 AND ONWARD. "SEASIDE COTTAGE" HEIGHT: 24" WIDTH: 18"

1. Some years later identified as Rufus Bliss, by the late Blair Whitton in his paperback, *Bliss Toys and Dollhouses,* Dover, 1979.
2. Ibid.

made amends. The examples on the following pages may serve to highlight the sequence of houses, stables, firehouses, armories, churches, and other buildings which constitute their small and appealing lithographed paper-on-wood world.

With the exception of Schoenhut, whose dolls' houses came later, and possibly of Converse, perhaps no maker of American dolls' houses is better known, and though the houses are also sturdy, realistic, and charming, and warrant their fame for these reasons alone, the name of Bliss is best known for a very simple reason: it was lithographed, along with the bricks, doorways, window frames, and gingerbread ornamentation onto the papers applied to the buildings themselves. Frequently the name is on the front door, sometimes on a pediment, occasionally elsewhere. On some houses it is missing entirely. In any case, in a field where so much material has been destroyed,

and relatively little information is available, dolls' house collectors have long been grateful to the firm in Pawtucket.

Numerous toy manufacturers, both in the United States and abroad, made houses and related toys of lithographed paper-on-wood, but it seems unlikely that any outsold those made by Bliss. Judging by the quantity that have survived, it is clear that many were built, in an enormous variety of sizes and styles.

In 1907, Bliss took a full page in *Playthings* to advertise the line of dolls' houses which had been launched "about twelve years" before, and which the firm declared had been "an emphatic success from the very start."

"Not many years ago," they asserted, "every doll house sold in this country was imported. These goods were unsatisfactory in every way, but nothing else was to be had." Then Bliss introduced "A

"Bliss Street"
Length of street: 11 1/2'

ISSMAYER TOURING CAR

ANNIE POSING WITH "SEASIDE COTTAGE"

AN ELEGANT SUBURBAN HOME.

FOR GOOD LITTLE PEOPLE.

No. 575.

The children are perfectly delighted with this beautiful house ; and well they may be, as neither time nor money have been spared in its design, construction, and finish. The front on hinges, the spacious verandas, cosy rooms, clear mica window-panes, handsome lace curtains, and artistic decorations make this house an ornament suitable for any home. Outside measurement, 11¾ 18¾ 27 inches. Packed, set up, in strawboard box.

A MODERN CITY RESIDENCE.

A DOLL MANSION UNEQUALED.

No. 576.

Of all the attempts made in the designing and construction of doll-houses, this house is the result of the most successful. A perfect beauty, admired by both old and young. Many are the little girls who will become the happy possessors of one of these elegant homes for their dollies. Packed, set up, in good substantial box.

large line...including Stables, Stores, Cabins, and so forth, as well as houses. All were made in American designs to suit the tastes of American children...of well-seasoned lumber...(which) not being subject to climatic changes...eliminated the greatest objection to these goods."

"An Elegant Suburban Home," the $4 size shown, may be seen on Bliss Street (the end house on the right, page 111), and surprisingly, it contains only two rooms, one up and one down. The third story is sham, forming what might be described these days as a "cathedral ceiling" to the second floor. On the other hand, another Bliss Street residence (extreme left, page 110), not shown in the catalogue and possibly later than 1901, is very little larger in base dimensions and height, but this one contains four rooms and a rare Bliss staircase. The staircase has a

simple metal rail downstairs and a metal balustrade upstairs which matches the railings on the exterior.

The 1901 catalogue alludes to "the splendid interior decorations" of the houses, the lace curtains, and "clear mica windows." Although a reference is made to hinged fronts and doors, the four-room house with the staircase may be opened on each side, and the three-room "Seaside Residence" (to the left of the small stable on Bliss Street) on one side, to give access to the kitchen on the left. The front may be swung open as well. The houses are to be found both with lithographed foundations and painted wooden ones.

The 1901 catalogue also pointed out that Bliss houses were "designed and modeled by a practical architect"—assuredly another secret of their success.

An Unmarked Bliss House

When this house with its lithographed interior was acquired in 1971, I'd never seen another. It was obvious that four posts were missing across the front porch (now replaced) but the lithographed interior, to be seen through the open back, was in pristine condition. With one of those curious coincidences of timing so often encountered, a week or two later, during a visit to the Strong collection in Rochester, I saw two similar houses. Shortly thereafter, Mrs. Betty Chart of California sent me a picture of another.

HEIGHT: 24" (INCLUDING CHIMNEY)
WIDTH: 19"

Mrs. Chart felt that her house had many characteristics of a Bliss, and wondered if any Bliss houses were unmarked. Before my Rochester visit, I could not have answered her question, but one of the dolls' houses there, unmarked on the outside, had the familiar marked Bliss doors connecting the four rooms, two up and two down, inside.

One of these houses was exactly like Mrs. Chart's, with two mica curtained windows downstairs at each side of a lithographed door and another one upstairs between two lithographed windows with drawn shades. The porches had the metal rails (possibly a later addition to the Bliss line), rather than the wooden railings upstairs and down, and the turned wooden posts on the front porch.

However, as we learn, variations in Bliss houses are infinite. The other Strong house, similar to mine, with wooden railings and posts, was conventionally made, with the customary papered interior. The house illustrated here comes apart for packing, and as the illustration suggests, the walls

are elaborately lithographed. All exterior detail on the house is also lithographed, with no mica windows or operable doors on the front to interrupt the interior decoration.

The latter is of the distinctive blues, reds, and gilt, highly glossed, that one associates with much of the Bliss furniture. Exuberant floral patterns paper the walls, surmounted by an alphabet border—cupids gambol upon the letters that surround the three walls from "A" to "Y." Dolls and/or children traverse the walls of the upstairs border.

Children, as they well might, dominate the decor—in pictures on the wall, and even as mantel ornaments. A pair flank an enormous clock on the mantelpiece, and two more surmount the clock itself. There is a fire, roaring summer and winter in the fireplace, and elaborate crimson draperies are at the windows—through which views may be observed. Four elaborately draped windows are upstairs, but the rest of the bedroom furnishing is left to the imagination of the young owner.

BLISS BEDROOM, ORIGINAL BOX (TALLEST CHAIR: 5 3/4")

"BLISS PLACE" (AROUND THE CORNER)

With the enormous productivity of the R. Bliss Company, any dolls' house collection worth its salt has more Bliss houses than even a reasonably long street can accommodate. We turn the corner here, so to speak, and offer a few others— on "Bliss Place."

The most imposing of these has one small idiosyncrasy: The small door on the second floor contains the much-sought Bliss name. The larger entrance door below does not. The porch posts are of wood, the lace-curtained windows on the façade are of mica. All else, including the dormer window, is lithographed. The two rooms within are papered with neatly scaled prints.

★ ★ ★

The two small, seemingly twin Bliss houses have a few minor external differences. The one which retains its chimney has a modest wood projection over the front door and the ground floor window is of mica rather than of lithography. There is a major difference in the interiors: the house with the chimney contains two rooms properly wall-papered, the other, an amusing and confusing surprise. As its portrait indicates, two

small girls are asleep in their brass bed upstairs. The remainder of their bed and the toys beneath it continue to the lower floor.

By happenstance, many years ago, I acquired a

HEIGHT: 20" (NOT INCLUDING CHIMNEY) WIDTH: 18"

A FEW MORE HOUSES FROM RHODE ISLAND; LATE NINETEENTH CENTURY. HEIGHT: 9 1/4" WIDTH: 7"

box of large-scaled Bliss bedroom furniture, with the lid. On the lid are the same two sleeping children, and four more—in two additional beds. Moreover Santa himself is outside, next to the chimney and on the right-hand side of this sizeable lid (11" by 16"). Somehow all of this (and more) is logically arranged. The Bliss company, in a moment of whimsy—or economy—decided that a slice of this charming scene, in lieu of wallpaper, would serve the purpose.

Incidentally, it is of interest to note that inside the cradle which was part of the bedroom set, is embossed, just visibly within the cardboard side, "June 26, 1888," pre-dating all Bliss catalogues known to me.

These houses are 9 1/4" tall with a base 7" by 4". The metal bicycle built-for-two, to be seen in front of the house with chimney, is assuredly

rare, and so is the miniscule basket hung on the handle-bars.

★ ★ ★

The remaining house is the well-known and aptly named (by collectors) "The Key-Hole House." The windows on the façade are all of mica, and the design is imaginative, to say the least. The wallpaper is large and floral, clearly made for a full-sized residence.

HEIGHT: 9 1/4" WIDTH: 7"

"KEYHOLE HOUSE" BY BLISS. PAT. 1895. HEIGHT: 15" WIDTH: 11"

LID: 11" x 16"

"HOME OF MOTHER GOOSE"

The 1896 Bliss catalogue asserts: "This series [there are three sizes] of the Home of Mother Goose will be found a desirable companion to our 'House that Jack Built.'" Very desirable indeed—with or without Jack's house. This delightful toy is rare, undoubtedly owing to its fragility as well as its complexity.

The catalogue describes it as "An old-styled Mother Goose house...represented with two piazzas, one on either end, two dormer windows, birdhouse, and dovecote." The wood base, with wood posts for birdhouse, dovecote, and chimney pots, is surmounted by the structure "lithographed in fine shades," in the words of the proud maker. The open interior is lushly lithographed inside and out and the closed "end" is equally picturesque.

With the meticulous Bliss attention to detail, the latticed windows on the back of the house are clearly imitated on the tiny birdhouse, while those on the front resemble the four-paned windows on the front of the house! (It is, of course, rare, if not impossible to discover a birdhouse or a dovecote on a dolls' house of any persuasion.)

One Bliss inconsistency: Mother Goose, looking like the motherly lady with spectacles we know her to be, is printed on the latticed-windowed back, where she may be seen watering roses. Bliss, for once failing us, includes among the cut-out fibre board figures representing the nursery verses, a young girl labeled "MOTHER GOOSE." There are, therefore, two Mother "Geese" and three fiber board cut-out geese.

The three geese and the young Mother Goose bring the total of fiber board cut-out figures to eighteen, all on wood stands. The latter include such major players as "Little Bo Peep," "Little Boy Blue," "Mistress Mary" (looking very contrary indeed) and "Tom, Tom, the Piper's Son" with the goods on him—the stolen pig under his arm.

BY BLISS. PAT. 1895.
HEIGHT: 15" BASE: 14" X 5 3/4"

"The House That Jack Built"

When this lavishly lithographed structure was first encountered, in almost mint condition, at a Maryland antique show, it looked vaguely English, and it seemed—as indeed it still does—more stable than house.

It didn't take long to discover that it wasn't made in Britain. Stamped beneath the gabled roof is precise documentation: "Pat. March 12, 1895. Manufactured in U.S.A." And then, in 1986, when the ATCA[1] reprinted the 1896 Bliss catalogue, there it was, "The House that Jack Built," along with two other more inexpensive versions.

(Earlier, it had been located in the 1898 catalogue of a Chicago importer and jobber, W.A. Cissna & Co., where it was identified, inexplicably, as "Modern Jack's House." It had been clear even before the Bliss catalogue surfaced, that, though unmarked, these fanciful "houses" were made by Bliss.)

What is mysterious is why this curious building is referred to as a house. The decor is similarly enigmatic. Although inside there is a sizeable room, reached through the open back, with blue-and-white printed walls and red-and-white printed floor, the exterior as the illustration suggests, is strictly barn-like in aspect. Both on this model and the next size, there are similarly lithographed façades (the detail condensed on the smaller structure) with a milkmaid milking a cow while a farmer stands by, scythe in hand. The gentleman in the top hat at the left-hand entrance resembles a country squire. A small rotund figure lithographed in the upstairs window (repeated on the back) is totally unidentifiable, and there seems very little to relate to "the farmer sowing the corn, that kept the cock that crowed in the morn, etc., etc., in the house that Jack built."

With the sixteen cut-out figures which accompanied the house, however, there's a strong kinship; of the nine which remain here, a few are labeled: "THIS IS THE DOG" and "THIS IS THE RAT." The rat, by the way, is the size of the dog. A second dog in his dog house good-naturedly watches two birds drink out of his bowl. "THE MAIDEN" is also present, along with assorted, un-labeled sheep and other animals.

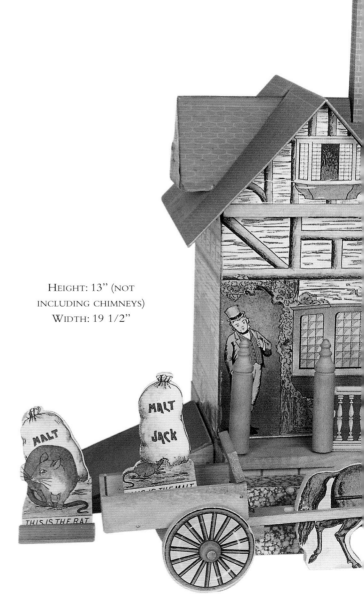

Height: 13" (not including chimneys)
Width: 19 1/2"

1. The Antique Toy Collectors of America, to whom I'm indebted for much original catalogue material.

In the catalogue, the smaller house is shown with only two gables, rather than the three in our example, and one chimney rather than two. The smallest version is recommended as "a companion toy with (their) two larger ones" and it looks like a house. A huge finial, in lieu of a chimney, sprouts surrealistically between the twin gables.

Actually, as the catalogue description suggests, there are variations between the large example shown and the catalogue version, and the design may have been altered in a later year. The chimneys and lithography under the eaves diverge. Most strikingly, the catalogue version lacks the two-inch base visible on our example, and it also lacks the balustrade with wooden posts. The base accommodates the steps and the pair of ramps to be seen in the photograph.

The catalogue alluded to a dray and a tip-cart with horses, to be seen herewith, and pointed out that the house "comes knocked down in box with full directions for setting up. Retails for $1.00."

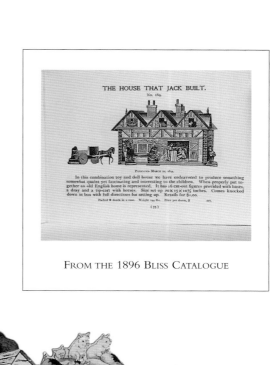

FROM THE 1896 BLISS CATALOGUE

THIS IS THE FARMER

THIS IS THE DOG

AN ADIRONDACK COTTAGE

In the late 1960's, in a New York State antique shop, this collector saw the apparition pictured here. The lithographed paper-on-wood log house seemed almost surrealistic with its lithographed paper-on-wood Indian head (which in metal might have served creditably as the radiator cap on a 1926 Pontiac!), coasting eternally in profile down the second-story dormer. With the deer head on the uppermost gable (repeated on the rear), the effect was of a dolls' house seen in a dream.

The purchase of this house was resisted at the time, and one never expected to see its like again, but it was remembered when the small log version (page 121) was acquired. Then, some months later, the files of a 1904 issue of *Playthings* yielded up the apparition, lithographed logs, deer head, Indian head, and all! The National Novelty Corporation, a toy trust founded in 1903, and one which would certainly require antitrust counsel today, displayed, in a double-

page spread of miscellaneous toys, and in all its rustic glory, the dolls' house from the New York State antique shop with (as the illustration below indicates) the label: "Adirondack Cottage. Novel Doll House."

Although it appeared from this place name that the cottage had not wandered from its native state, the identity of the manufacturer, owing to the seemingly circumspect nature of The National Novelty Corporation, is difficult to establish positively, but the evidence points to Bliss. The thirty-seven manufacturers who were part of the group in 1904 were referred to as "branches," and these included R. Bliss of Pawtucket, Rhode Island, and Whitney-Reed of Leominster, Massachusetts, both of them makers of lithographed paper-on-wood dolls' houses, among other toys. An extensive list of the toys manufactured by Whitney-Reed in their 1902-3 catalogue specifies such miniature buildings as an "Observatory," an "Armory," and even a

HEIGHT: 17 1/2"
WIDTH: 17 1/2"

ADIRONDACK COTTAGE. NOVEL DOLL HOUSE

FROM *PLAYTHINGS*, 1904

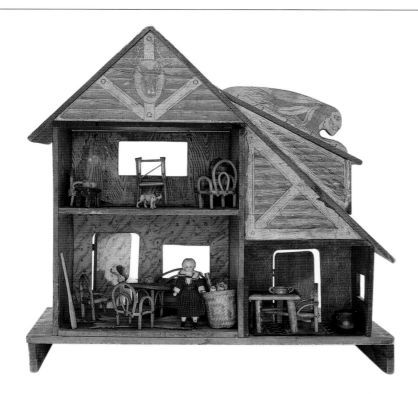

By Bliss. 1904.
Height: 17 1/2" (to peak of roof)
Width: 12" (base)

"Camp Dewey," but all dolls' houses are listed as such without further description. If an Adirondack cottage was among them, it was neither illustrated nor described. A Bliss 1901 catalogue throws no light on the subject, but since the cottage was not advertised by The National Novelty Corporation till 1904, it may not have been in 1901 even a gleam in its maker's eye.[1]

Of the remaining manufacturers in the group, there is no clue to relate one of them to the Adirondack cottage, but it is peculiarly satisfying to have found the illustration and the Adirondack identity of the log house even if the identity of the maker is presently relatable only to The National Novelty Corporation, a group defunct by 1907.

By some miracle, the Adirondack cottage in the New York State antique shop in the late 1960's was still there in the summer of 1972—and its purchase was not resisted this time around. It contains three rooms plus a small attic room formed by the dormer; access to the latter is gained by the Indian head which serves as a sort of handle to the section.

With the meticulous detail one associates with Bliss, even this tiny room is papered, as are the other three, with papers on walls and floors suitable for a cottage in the Adirondacks—"knotty pine" or some other rustic finish in perfect scale. Both front doors, like the dormer-with-Indian, are hinged and workable. The back of the house is open, and lithographed segments identical to ones on the front (i.e., one on the pediment above the two-story section and one beneath the dormer section of the roof) are duplicated on the back, along with the Indian and his dormer.

The "popsicle-stick" embellishment above the dormer has been replaced along with the chimney.

To judge by the small two-room house, which has glazed windows, glass was also originally in the windows of the larger model, which is otherwise in remarkable condition. The smaller house, also in excellent condition, has two rooms and an open back, and is a more modest Adirondack cottage. It is 17 1/2" tall by 9" wide not including eaves, and 7" deep not including balcony.

---

1. In a 1907 advertisement, Bliss referred to the line of "stables, stores, cabins and so forth" they'd introduced.

A FOLDING BUNGALOW BY MCLOUGHLIN

The box which contains it is about an inch in depth, but the exquisite McLoughlin lithography is in full bloom—almost literally—both inside and out, when this "folding bungalow" is unfolded. And it may be assembled in a twinkling.

The hinged roof is one of the two sections in which the house—of heavy card—is constructed. This ingeniously slips over the twin dormers which hold it in place, and it, in turn, keeps the hinged façade in place. When the façade is lowered, it becomes a garden, complete with pond, shrubs, and flower beds. A multitude of tall, arched, latticed windows on the first story (sixteen, in actuality), give a Renaissance Revival flavor to the façade which is also well-provided with vines.

Inside, there are two rooms, courtesy of a folding center panel which divides the interior into two rooms when in place. The latter is even more lushly, if illogically, lithographed than the exterior (i.e., where windows are on one side of the exterior, a fireplace is on the inside). Among the amenities are stained glass, oak paneling, and plate rails bearing sufficient pitchers, plates, and jugs to supply a well-stocked antiques shop. More importantly, information about carpets and draperies, and anything else one may wish to know about decor of the period is plentifully provided.

CA. 1905.
HEIGHT: 7" WIDTH: 17"

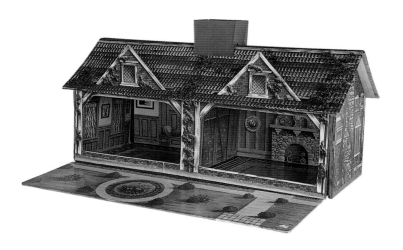

McLoughlin's Folding House

In 1894, a Baltimore woman, Eleanor McCulloch Smith, was successful in marketing her patent for a folding house. McLoughlin Bros. of New York were successful in selling it.

In 1896 the price was right: McLoughlin's catalogue lists a folding dolls' house of which the retail price was six cents! The larger model was fifteen. For this sum, the buyer received "a series of partitions radiating from a common hinging point" magnificently presented in the lush lithography for which McLoughlin is celebrated. No detail has been overlooked: a parlor, bedroom, dining room, and kitchen are lithographed with every late Victorian appurtenance or decoration known to wall or floor. Oriental rugs, floral wall-papers, stained glass, velvet portières, mantels crowded with bric-a-brac, and even a feather duster are printed upon the premises in the most exuberant late Victorian manner.

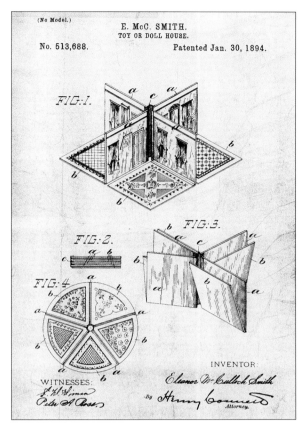

ORIGINAL PATENT

TWO OF THE FOUR ROOMS. CA. 1894. HEIGHT: 12" WIDTH: 24" (OPEN)

All of this folds into a book-like format, thirteen inches square and an inch thick.[1] Adding furniture seems almost irrelevant but the temptation has not been resisted.

The furnishings of the rooms shown are not elaborate. Almost any of the right size and vintage and of reasonable quality look "at home." More is gilding the lily.

It is clear that these toy houses were very popular. Many have survived. Mrs. Smith should go down in dolls' house history along with McLoughlin.

Box lid

1. The six-cent version is thinner. These were also issued as four individual rooms.

"DUNHAM'S COCOANUT DOLL HOUSE"

The above heading (with coconut misspelled) is incised in red and black on the top of the wooden house. Typical four-light windows with arched tops and fancy lintels are incised on the "brick" sides.[1] "And that is all there is to indicate that one is in the presence of a dolls' house unless the engagingly lithographed papers applied to the walls and floors remain in the four rooms."

In 1974, when I included that sentence in *Dolls' Houses in America*,[2] I knew of only three examples. Only "shreds" lingered in one, the colors were faded in another, and a crack down the back, which appears to be common to most, was "severe" in the third. "But," I added, "they still beguile."

These houses were, of course, essentially crates with four levels. It is not known whether or not the crates arrived with the lithographed walls in place. Presumably, the boxes of coconut would have chipped the delicate papers. A theory recently published[3] that the papers arrived "in place" because "all known examples follow the same configuration of rooms" may be challenged: a kitchen would inevitably be on the ground floor, with the dining room above and the bedroom at the top, leaving the remaining floor for the parlor.

If this theory is correct, there is still no information about how the houses were assigned once they were emptied: a present to the children of a favored customer? A raffle? A premium?

In any case, in the intervening years, other examples of the Dunham's house have turned up now and then, but what eluded me till a few years ago was the rare paper furniture made for the house. When, at long last, a set was acquired, there was, on my part, great rejoicing.

CA. 1890'S. HEIGHT: 29" WIDTH: 11"

1. On one of the houses, the detail is of lithographed paper-on-wood. "Trade Mark Registered" is printed under the side of this one.
2. Charles Scribner's & Sons. New York.
3. *Antique and Collectible Dollhouses,* by Patty Cooper and Dian Zillner. Schiffer Publications. 1998.

The kitchen table offered information about the manner in which the furniture was dispensed: on the underside is printed: "If you want another piece of furniture like this, send us the Cake Trade Mark from a half pound package of Dunham's coconut...and ask for piece of furniture No. 4." The New York City address of the "Premium Department" was given.

On the top of the table, to no one's surprise, is a coconut cake. Indeed, few latter-day admen can approach the ability of Dunham's to promote their products. Even the backs of the easy chairs have large circular Dunham's logos the size of (and possibly in lieu of) pillows. An identical logo dead center on the kitchen range might serve, for one of the room's occupants, as an archery target.

There is, of course, a considerable amount of furniture lithographed on the walls themselves. Dolls in this house were clearly meant to subsist on the maker's product; there are three boxes of Dunham's coconut on the bottom shelf of the kitchen cupboard, the only provisions to be seen in the kitchen.

Bright and cheery, the dining room is dominated by a huge aquarium on a substantial four-legged base and a mammoth moose head mounted on the wall. Four plants bloom exuberantly beneath the windows. There is nothing as dramatic in the parlor, with the exception of a most imposing fern. "Love Song" is the title of the sheet music which rests on the upright piano. The inevitable aspidistra sprouts from a black and crimson porcelain jardinière on a pedestal.

However these lush backgrounds were acquired, the resulting ambience is peculiarly satisfying to those of us who are antiquarian dolls' house collectors; it offers vivid guidelines to the furnishing of other old dolls' houses whose interiors may be more spacious but are less specific (or permanent) then Dunham's about the manner in which they, and the full-size houses they imitate, were furnished.

DINING TABLE

ADVERTISING MINIATURE
(NOT PART OF SET)

CHAIR HEIGHT: 4 1/2"

THE HOUSES OF WHITNEY-REED

It is well known that sometimes one speaks too soon. In 1974, in *Dolls' Houses in America,* I made a point of referring to the "Vanished Dolls' Houses of Whitney-Reed." Since then, I've acquired three. One of these is "The New Practical Doll House." A catalogue illustration of this house, fortuitously discovered at the time, was shown in lieu of the "vanished" original, and it is shown again here. It is taken from the firm's 1902-03 catalogue (page 129).

I did have the grace to state that it might be "something of a presumption to refer to Whitney-Reed's dolls houses as vanished." In any case, I journeyed to Leominster, Massachusetts and visit-

TURN OF THE CENTURY. HEIGHT: 20" WIDTH: 15 1/2" (AT BASE)

HEIGHT: 14 3/4"
WIDTH OF BASE: 9"
VARIATION OF CATALOGUE
ILLUSTRATION NO. 81 (SEE NEXT PAGE)

THE NEW PRACTICAL DOLL HOUSE
HEIGHT: 14" WIDTH 24 1/2"
SEE CATALOGUE ILLUSTRATION, TOP, NEXT PAGE

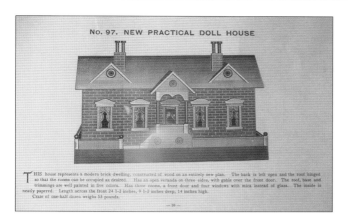

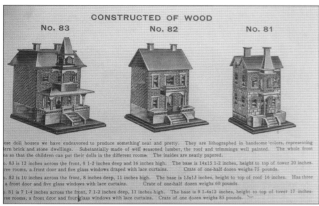

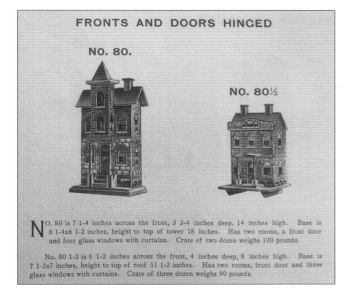

UPPER: FROM 1902-03 WHITNEY-REED CATALOGUE
LOWER: FROM 1897-8 CATALOGUE

ed Mr. William H. Green, who had been head of the Whitney-Reed Chair Co. in 1957, when what remained of the company was sold. He was aware of "no existing specimens," but he kindly permitted me to reproduce illustrations of dolls' houses in the earlier 1897-98 catalogue.

In the five-year interval, the company had developed "a new line," of which one was "The New Practical Doll House." These, "constructed of wood on an entirely new plan" represented "a modern brick dwelling." However, just in case the "New Practical" house, with an open back, a hinged roof, and windows of mica instead of glass proved to be too practical, part of the 1897-98 line were still available.

In that year, houses in eight sizes had been described, though the two largest were not illustrated, and all were Bliss-like structures "lithographed in handsome colors," with hinged fronts, glass windows, and curtains. In 1897-98, the heading on three of these was "up-to-date in Style and Finish." In 1902-03, this was amended to read "Fronts and Doors Hinged," and the two largest models, as well as the smallest, were no longer listed. The houses in both lines were "neatly papered inside."

In any case, the museum's trio of houses includes two illustrated in the 1897-98 catalogue. The larger of the two appears to be almost identical to #83 in the catalogue illustration. This is 20" tall and, like the smaller example, has glass windows. The white wooden railing on the front porch may be the only variation. (There is none in the catalogue version.)

TWO UNIDENTIFIED AMERICAN HOUSES

In their well-researched book,[1] Dian Zillner and Patty Cooper show "A Series of Lithographed Houses by an Unknown Maker." They also offer the unattractive appellation of "gutter houses," suggested by a collector of lithographed toys when he noticed on these houses a strip of over-scaled molding where gutters would normally be found on a full-sized building.

The smaller of the two shown herewith lacks such a molding, but the lithographed front doors and the window interiors are identical to those on "the smallest" of these houses in the Zillner-Cooper book. The gutterless house shown here is even smaller. Their "smallest" house is identical in measurements and lithography to our larger example, and is clearly the same house, though the vivid reds to be seen on our specimen appear to have faded out on theirs.

Over the years, more than one factory made dolls' houses, and I respectfully suggest that one-day, with luck, a catalogue may be found which shows these presently anonymous houses to be from a small factory of short duration. Or these might be earlier and more modest versions of Bliss houses before the company quite "got the hang" of what they later did so well.

CA. 1890. LARGER HOUSE: HEIGHT: 10 3/4" (PLUS CHIMNEY) BASE: 7 1/2" X 5 3/8"
SMALLER HOUSE: HEIGHT: 8 3/4" BASE: 3 1/2" X 6 1/2"

1. *Antique & Collectible Doll Houses*, Schiffer, 1998.

A "Ta-Ka-Part" Doll House

The cutesy name printed under the base of this folding lithographed house fails to tell us what we most wish to know: who made it and where. However, there is a great deal of other printed information beneath its sturdy wood base about the maker's three products. In addition to "Doll Houses," there are "Doll Furniture" and "Trunks," and a paragraph about each. We are also informed that these toys are "NEAT AND DURABLE," and that this is "A TOY THAT IS A TOY INDEED." There were "Patents Pending." Whether these patents eventually were granted is not clear.

In addition to the base, there is a matching chimney and cornice, all of red-stained wood. Matching wood brackets support the removable roof. There are neatly printed wallpapers within. The lithographed door does not open, but the yellow clapboard below, the red-and-yellow brick above, the green shutters and white curtains are an appealing combination. Even the crimson, which outlines the windows, reminds us that full-sized houses at the turn of the century and before were often many-hued.

Inasmuch as I have never seen or heard of another TA-KA-PART house in more than half a century of dealing with this subject, it is likely that not many were made.

TURN OF THE CENTURY. HEIGHT: 12 1/2" (PLUS CHIMNEY) BASE: 10 7/8" x 5 3/4"

A "Dandy Toy House" By Grimm & Leeds

"Your collapsible toy house is a winner." No less a merchandising authority than John Wanamaker is quoted in an advertisement by the Grimm & Leeds Company of Camden, New Jersey, in a 1905 issue of *Playthings,* the toy trade journal.

Probably there were assembling instructions inside the missing box lid of the example pictured, but the butter-fingered owner managed to construct this cardboard gem in two or three hours of triumphal engineering. Talent only was required; no glue. The structure is an ingenious arrangement of folding cardboard with only the porch and roof sections reinforced by blocks. Junctions are formed by heavy cardboard pockets in walls into which floor and roof sections are inserted. There are four rooms, two up and two down, a beguiling sprigged wallpaper, and lace-edged dark blue window shades behind mica windows. Only one floor strip

was sheared off in assembling—a tribute to the strength of the aging cardboard.

On the bottom of the box, the foundation of the house, was the name "Leeds Toy House," the manufacturers name and town, and the patent date of September 22, 1903. It is clear that the company lost no time putting these into production.

As the 1905 advertisement reveals, the firm made this large, four-room model as well as a two-room version. There were four models: "One Dandy Toy House" in two sizes and "One Colonial Toy House" in two sizes. In the same 1905 advertisement in which J. Wanamaker is quoted, a photograph of a substantial sheaf of orders dominates a tiny cut of a two-room specimen and we read: "Sales one store 500 houses." With such a success, it is not surprising that more than this one example of a toy so fragile has survived.

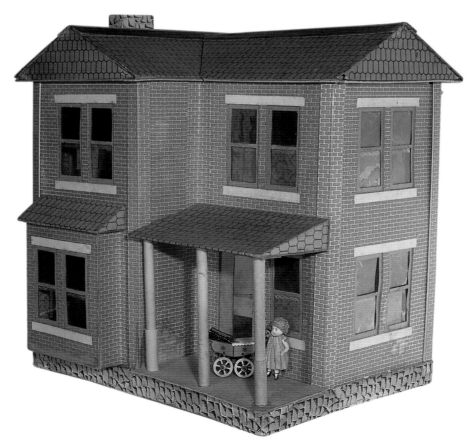

CA. 1903. HEIGHT: 20 1/2" (INCLUDING CHIMNEY) WIDTH: 19" DEPTH: 12 1/2"

CONVERSE, CASS, ET AL.

A maker of wooden boxes, who accidentally discovered the toy business when he made his small daughter a tea table from a collar box, turned Winchendon, Massachusetts into "The Nuremberg of America." His name was Morton E. Converse, and his company, no longer in existence, was, at one time referred to as "the largest toy-manufacturing firm in the world."

Among many other toys, he made dolls' houses and furniture, and he is represented here by several of his modest houses.[1] The tallest, probably the earliest of these, is the twenty-inch (plus chimney) specimen in which an embossed cat may be seen peering out of an attic window, and two embossed, identical, rather glum matrons are gazing, one to a side, out of windows on the first floor (page 135).

With the exception of five glazed windows on the façade, all of the other details are embossed directly on wood. The windows, shingles, and additional architectural elements which such makers as Bliss and Gottschalk lithographed on paper and then applied to the wood, are simplified by this process. The colors are more limited, being

CONVERSE BUNGALOW WITH BING ROADSTER
HEIGHT: 9 3/4" (PLUS CHIMNEY) WIDTH: 11"

1. See also Roosevelt Stock Farm, etc., page 364.

mostly red, blue, brown, and sometimes, green. Details are also fewer, but unlike the lithographed paper-on-wood houses, there are no delicate bits of paper falling off to madden collectors several generations later.

The façade swings open to reveal two rooms, one up and one down. There is a sham attic above. The Converse name is on the embossed rug, which appears to be a Navajo. This house was discovered many years ago during a visit to Martha's Vineyard.

The rug in the large bungalow also is embossed with the Converse name. This model, very green and red, may have had Santa Claus in mind. It has an applied gray "stone" chimney and appears to be later than the two-story house. Actually it is very similar to the specimen pictured in a 1913

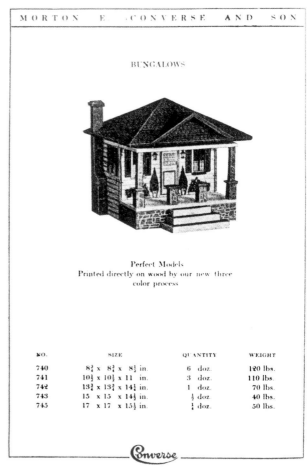

MORTON E. CONVERSE AND SON

BUNGALOWS

Perfect Models
Printed directly on wood by our new three
color process

NO.	SIZE	QUANTITY	WEIGHT
740	8¾ x 8¾ x 8½ in.	6 doz.	120 lbs.
741	10½ x 10½ x 11 in.	3 doz.	110 lbs.
742	13¾ x 13¾ x 14½ in.	1 doz.	70 lbs.
743	15 x 15 x 14½ in.	½ doz.	40 lbs.
745	17 x 17 x 15½ in.	¼ doz.	50 lbs.

Converse

1913 CONVERSE CATALOGE

MASON & PARKER BUNGALOW. CA. 1913.
HEIGHT: 12" WIDTH (AT ROOF): 14 1/2"

Converse catalogue. This came in five sizes. Ours is 12" tall, plus chimney, and 14 1/2" wide, at roof.

In describing the Converse house in *Dolls' Houses in America,* many long years ago, I referred to the smaller ones in the collection as either by Converse or Cass of Athol, Massachusetts. Athol, I

pointed out, is a mere fifteen miles from Winchendon, and Cass houses were printed in similar colors and a similar manner. It is known that there was a certain amount of "parts-swapping" between the neighboring firms, and in the later catalogues identical toys were, in a few cases,

THE "RATHER GLUM" MATRON

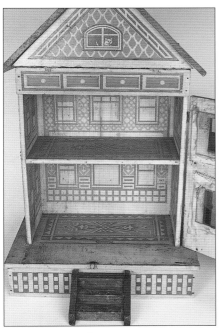

INTERIOR

HEIGHT: 20" (PLUS CHIMNEY) WIDTH: 12"

SMALLER MASON & PARKER BUNGALOW.
HEIGHT: 11 1/2" (PLUS CHIMNEY) WIDTH: 13"

at least, marketed by both.

Assuredly, this is true, but suddenly, in the spring of 2001, there was an addition to the literature! In England, Nick and Esther Forder in their excellent publication, *International Dolls' House News,* came up with another American maker and also from Winchendon. They reproduced two houses from the 1915 catalogue of the Mason & Parker Mfg. Co. These bear a strong family resemblance to several houses shown herewith—ones I had believed to be Converse or Cass. The three feature columns in the identical stained wood with similar turnings, and both have interior printed features—windows, "wallpapers"—interior decorations—exactly like the example shown in color in *International Dolls' House News.* The bungalow alone has square columns and is clearly a close relation to the other house illustrated in the 1915 Mason & Parker catalogue.

Inez and Marshall McClintock referred to an

early partner named "Mason" Morton Converse "found" in Winchendon.[1] There is more but we shall leave the tangled Converse, Cass, Mason & Parker web to be sorted out by future dolls' house historians.

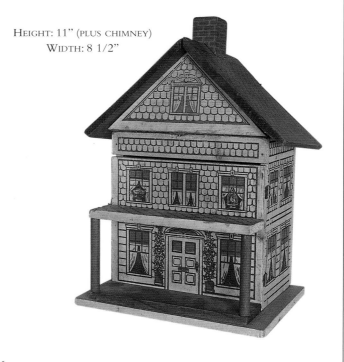

HEIGHT: 11" (PLUS CHIMNEY)
WIDTH: 8 1/2"

1. *Toys In America.*

A McLoughlin House With a Garden

FOLDING DOLL HOUSES
$1.00 each

On its most imposing lithographed lid (18" by 20"), "New Folding Doll House" is scrolled in equally imposing letters. The façade is repeated on the lid, and over the pedimented double doors, "McLoughlin Brothers New York" is printed. Nothing is said about the garden which is charmingly lithographed on the inside of the façade. When this is lowered into place, there are four beds with palms and shrubs surrounding a circular pool encircled with similar greenery.

This house is wider than "Dolly's Playhouse;" the latter is taller and the interior grander. These rooms are more cottagey, though similarly vivid. There is great emphasis on windows—and win-

CA. 1911[1]
HEIGHT: 16"
(PLUS CHIMNEY)
WIDTH: 17"
DEPTH: 10 1/2"

1. This is shown in a Christmas catalogue of "Toys and Games" issued by Woodward & Lothrop, a Washington department store in 1911. The box is illustrated above right.

dow seats. A fireplace on each of the two floors, and the interior style, clearly reflect the Arts and Crafts movement which had shoved Victorian opulence aside in many households at the beginning of the twentieth century. The effect, however, is far from subdued. Carpets in bold patterns highlighted by crimson and Christmas greens festoon the floors.

The fireplace on the ground floor is surmounted with lithographed wooden niches containing numerous examples of—no doubt—arts and crafts pottery. There are numerous pillows on the window seats and numerous pictures on the walls. All sides of the house are lithographed inside and out with a vast assortment of windows.

The windows are multitudinous, and it is typical of the generous McLoughlin company and/or the era (when fewer corners were cut), that the two sides, which probably a maker today would have been content to duplicate, are separately printed— one side with side doors and windows—the other with bays. And all of this courtesy McLoughlin's marvelous mechanisms, which enable the owner to fold the house, roof, and detachable chimneys into the wooden-sided, one-inch deep box!

LID OF HOUSE

HEIGHT: 16" WIDTH: 17"
DEPTH: WITH
GARDEN EXTENDED: 23"

SCHOENHUT BUNGALOWS AND OTHER HOUSES

A Schoenhut catalogue for 1917 describes "a whole new line of dolls' houses" and the trio herewith illustrate the "stone"[1] bungalows and two-story structures in several of the sizes available.

The well-known Philadelphia firm, famous for its toy pianos, dolls and circuses, had been founded in 1872 by Albert Schoenhut—who had come from Germany after the Civil War.[2] The 1917 catalogue promised that these dolls' houses would be "less expensive than the fine imported doll houses, but at the same time much stronger, more durable, and beautiful."

ABOVE AND BELOW: LARGER BUNGALOW.
HEIGHT: 20 1/2" (PLUS CHIMNEY) WIDTH: 24"

1. "Floor and frame is of wood, sides of pulp construction in imitation stone." This description may be found in a Montgomery Ward catalogue of the period.
2. Dian Zillner and Patty Cooper in their very informative book, *Antique & Collectible Dollhouses* (Schiffer Pub. Co.), have discovered a possible connection between Schoenhut and Gottschalk.

Judging by the excellent condition of the three examples pictured, this promise of durability has been kept. The houses also include a charming interior feature mentioned in the catalogue: lithographed doorways on the walls "showing a perspective view of another room... producing the illusion of a house full of fine rooms." In the larger models, there is a glimpse of a bath with footed tub and a butler's pantry with brightly patterned oiled paper on the glass doors. There's also a lithographed fire in a lithographed fireplace and lithographed portières.

In the large bungalow the sides swing open to reveal two rooms apiece, and the roof may be tilted, and held in place, rather like the lid of an old phonograph, to disclose the top of the interior staircase and two attic rooms. The staircase, with attractively turned balusters, is of wood, as it is in the large two-story houses. In the two-story houses shown here, the staircase is printed.

The smallest Schoenhut contains only one room on each floor, but all of the houses feature net curtains on their glass-paned doors, and lace-trimmed net curtains are at the windows. In the larger houses the lithographed wallpapers are exuberant—very striped—very floral and thoroughly bordered.

SMALLER SCHOENHUT. CA. 1917.
HEIGHT: 13 3/4" (PLUS CHIMNEY)
WIDTH: 10 1/4"

LARGER, TWO-STORY SCHOENHUT.
CA. 1917.
HEIGHT: 24 1/2" (PLUS CHIMNEY)
WIDTH: 19"

An Appealing Mystery From Philadelphia

This appealing house is something of a mystery—one I long to solve. The Pennsylvania dealer who sold it to me believed it to be from Philadelphia and it has a number of features which support this belief. See pages 142-43.

With its meticulous detail, a combination of metal and wood, it appears to be commercially made, a Colonial Revival house of the 1920's, or possibly of the 'teens. The elaborately pierced metal fanlight above the front door, with its matching sidelights, is echoed by the wide fanlights, front and side, on the wing. The latter, especially, have a Philadelphia look. They relate to the imposing pair of dormers on the third story, with their arched twelve-light windows of a pure Palladian style. The wing, with its pierced balustrading above, contains the "sun room," often seen in houses of the period.

The house sits upon a foundation, an important element often overlooked by dolls' house builders. This one is scored and (clearly) hand-painted to resemble stone—a detail which questions the commercial origin. There are many "custom" details such as metal shutter pins to fasten the workable wooden shutters. French doors in the dining room and a mirrored door in the bathroom are dark-stained, another suggestion of the period. There is white "tile" wainscoting in the bathroom which retains its tub, basin, and commode.

The walls which separate the hall and dining room are flanked by squared columns on deep bases. In the dining room itself, there is a window seat under the Gothic-style bay window. There are glazed French doors leading to the kitchen with its latticed windows. There are also latticed windows

CA. 1920. HEIGHT: 17" (PLUS CHIMNEYS) WIDTH: 32"

at the back of the living room. A pair of arched casement windows is on the side wall. (The designer was clearly infatuated with windows.) On the third floor, there are small fanlights on either side.

In the living room a "brick" fireplace with a well-designed Adam-type surround, leads properly to the red "brick" chimney, the back of which climbs the interior wall on the sunroom side. There is a red "tile" hearth and the only remaining piece of furniture—a mantel clock—is in perfect scale on the mantel.

Tootsietoy furniture of the 'twenties fits perfectly into these rooms, which are entered from the back. A Kilgore washing machine logically fits into a small back room on the lower floor. The three-inch-tall bisque inhabitants are rare in this size and are deserving of their house which is also rare, if not unique.

AN APPEALING MYSTERY FROM PHILADELPHIA

THE "UBILDIT PLAYHOUSE #3"

Possibly because paper Christmas wreaths were affixed to the glass windows, and the lithographed brick paper on the exterior is very red indeed, I've always thought of this substantial bungalow as a "Christmas house."

Its name tells its story. It was a house to be assembled by a loving parent, or an older sibling, possibly the latter inasmuch as a brochure which fortuitously has been preserved with the house asserts that UBILDIT is "The Name for Educational Playthings."

Happily, it came accompanied by, not only the brochure, but by comprehensive documentation of the type collectors long for and are seldom supplied. The detailed assembly instructions even include as a first step, an admonition to "keep hands clean when setting up, otherwise the outside finish will be finger marked." (This instruction may not be essential for posterity, but I find it interesting.)

Not even the assorted small envelopes in which the "70 bolts and nuts each and 60 washers" and hinges, etc., etc. resided have been discarded. (The nut and bolt construction, incidentally, though visible, is not intrusive.)

The F.P.M. Corp'n, The sole licensee for The Santa Claus Toy Manufacturing Co. Line[1] of Rochester, N.Y., applied for patents which may or may not have been granted. In any case, this is "Playhouse #3," and I've never seen another of any model, suggesting that it was not particularly successful and was made for only a short period. This is surprising inasmuch as the house is sturdy and attractive with its latticed windows and trellises of metal and its columned portico, dormer, and chimneys of wood. (There are also wooden window boxes and perhaps the "4 sprays flowers" and "4 sprays green fern" listed in the brochure were removed when the paper Christmas wreaths were added by the young owner. Flowers, however, still cling to the lattice.)

All of this is affixed to heavy fiberboard, or something similarly strong.

The back half of the roof opens on hinges, and below there are two sizeable hinged openings at the back of the house to give access to the two rooms. The walls are printed with attractive wallpapers.

Because this is such an appealing house, one longs to know how many models there were and what the other models were like.

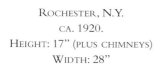

ROCHESTER, N.Y.
CA. 1920.
HEIGHT: 17" (PLUS CHIMNEYS)
WIDTH: 28"

1. Another Yuletide aspect.

THE TYNIETOY MANSION

Established in 1920 by two Providence, Rhode Island ladies, Mrs. Marion I. Perkins and Miss Amy Vernon II, "Tynietoy" has become almost a cult with a goodly following of dedicated collectors. There is even a club for those of us who are charmed by their toy-like interpretation of period architecture and furniture.

Most coveted of the houses is "the mansion," the largest and grandest of the line. In 1991, the Museum was fortunate to acquire one of these with many of its furnishings. The thirteen-room, three-story mansion replaced a rather dowdy eight-room cupboard house which contained a great deal of Tynietoy furniture, some of which was added to the mansion. The façade, which lifts off, reflects the Colonial Revival architecture of the 'twenties[1] to be seen in many a suburban lane

in the eastern United States. (This is closely related to the Greenwich, Connecticut house to be seen on page 90.) There are rooms rather than a garage behind the garage segment. The great 58" width required that when shown in the Museum, the façade necessarily was hung above the house.

A handsome colonial mansion, unfurnished, with garden, cost $170 in those halcyon days. Without garden, it was $145; furnished, with garden, $247. (A fraction of its value now.) Furnishings were modestly priced. Although production continued as late as the early 'fifties, the pieces, as noted above, are being assiduously collected today.

Inasmuch as the series of houses and furnishings Mrs. Perkins and Miss Vernon commissioned were largely handcrafted, the inclusion of Tynietoy under the category of commercially-made exam-

MID-1920'S. EXTERIOR HEIGHT: 32 1/2" (PLUS CHIMNEYS) WIDTH: 58"

1. This is not to be confused with the earlier Colonial Revival of the late nineteenth century.

ples may appear to be untoward. The production was relatively small, but the fact that Tynietoy was sold commercially over a period of several decades has guided this choice.

If wing chairs with painted wooden upholstery are an acquired taste, many amongst us have acquired it. These painted Tynietoy sofas and chairs supplement chests of drawers and tables—and even knife urns—of stained wood. One of the features of the mansion they occupy is the hand-painted mural on the music-room walls. There is pleasing

TOONERVILLE TROLLEY

RARE ASTOR PIANO STOOL

LADY IN "BEACH PAJAMAS,"
HAIRDRYER ON CHAIR

painted over mantel "paneling" and classical wood pedimentation over the doors. (The latter are shaped and applied.)

Other interior amenities include a Palladian window on the rear wall in the staircase hall, a butler's pantry, and glazed multi-paned doors on either side of the living-room fireplace, which lead out to the garden.

The bisque-headed residents of the mansion, representing an affluent family of the mid-'twenties, include such personages as a gentleman listening through earphones to a super heterodyne radio, a "flapper" wearing "beach pajamas,"[1] and a young fellow playing with a miniscule (and rare) "Toonerville Trolley."

The house is quite thoroughly furnished, largely with Tynietoy furniture, and with a number of German accessories of the period. (The hair dryer in the bathroom exactly resembles one used by the author in the 'twenties and early 'thirties and still to be found in her attic.)

In addition to the superheterodyne, another example of early radio is represented—the "loudspeaker," with its flamboyant horn, and the triangular aerial, both of which plug into the radio. When turned, a very small crank on the loudspeaker makes "static," a 1920's constant of 1920's listening.

An early model vacuum cleaner with a rubber hose (nearly always missing) is another useful accessory.

PAINTED MURAL
IN ROOM
DESIGNATED AS
MUSIC ROOM

1. If "beach pajamas" seems an esoteric term, a pair of full-sized ones were made by the author in a seventh-grade sewing class at John Eaton School in Washington, D.C. in 1931. (See page 147.)

TWO CARDBOARD COLONIALS

Like the Colonial Revival Houses of the 1920's which they imitate, these two cardboard "colonials" seem, at first glance, so similar to one another that it takes a moment to realize that two companies—not one—are responsible for their manufacture.

The somewhat smaller house, below right, made by the Wayne Paper Co. of Ft. Wayne Indiana, I had always thought of as a Tootsietoy house. With a bit of dolls' house snobbery (and a keener interest in earlier houses), I'd placed it, years ago in the attic, though I'd brought it downstairs in recent years. I'm grateful to Dian Zillner,[1] who has done pioneer work in researching these more recent—no longer very recent—houses, for the information that "It appears to be the same house advertised in the Tootsietoy catalogue as a Dowst product."

The house with the wing, below left, has been identified in the Zillner-Cooper book as "The Playhouse Doll House No. 200," manufactured by the Sutherland Paper Company of Kalamazoo, Michigan. It is more decorative than the Tootsietoy house, with such additions as printed shrubbery and window boxes. There are curtains of actual lace in the cardboard windows, clearly original. The front lifts off, where the Wayne House hinged façade divides in the middle, making access convenient but awkward. However, there are such printed details inside as pictures on the walls, a tile floor in the kitchen, and wainscoting. There is also a sturdy flight of cardboard stairs. The printed shrubbery is perfunctory, but the front door is considerably more detailed than the simple door on the Sutherland house. There are double doors with a fanlight and sidelights.

These houses are a modest contribution to the record of early twentieth-century architecture.

SUTHERLAND HOUSE.
HEIGHT: 16 1/2" (PLUS CHIMNEY)
WIDTH: 18" (PLUS 6" WING)

CA. 1925-1930. WAYNE PAPER CO. HOUSE
ADVERTISED AS "TOOTSIETOY" BY DOWST.
HEIGHT: 16" (PLUS CHIMNEY) WIDTH: 18"

1. *Antique & Collectible Doll Houses,* Schiffer, 1998.

A SPANISH "MANSION" BY TOOTSIETOY

Although the Dowst Manufacturing Company of Chicago chose an unnerving name for their line of metal vehicles and dolls' house furniture, nothing could stop Tootsietoy. They were a great success when they were launched in the early 1920's and they are, as the current phrase is, highly "collectable" today.

The furniture became so popular that the next step was obvious—houses to contain it. Dowst brought out various models, beginning in 1925 with "a fine brick Colonial home."[1] In 1930, they introduced a Spanish mansion. The latter undoubtedly was related to the Spanish Colonial revival in California and also, somewhat later, to the rise of Hollywood, where the revival flourished. What went on in Hollywood was noticed throughout the country: Patios appeared in Pennsylvania; stucco haciendas turned up in South Dakota. Northern gales swept iron grille-work balconies intended originally for Southern breezes.

1930. HEIGHT: 19" WIDTH: 26"

1. See page 149.

The Tootsietoy mansion "designed by one of America's greatest architects who specializes in the Spanish type of architecture," was made of "heavy book-board and colored in oil colors (washable) in nine colors…" The maker considered its product "the finest house five dollars can buy."

In 1930, the Spanish mansion was obtainable both furnished and unfurnished. The catalogue showed the five rooms of furniture, "all packed in an attractive shipping carton." (The bathroom and kitchen fittings were fastened to lithographed cardboard linoleum; the other three sets of room furnishings were attached to lithographed Orientals.) The furniture was by no means the same as the line which Tootsietoy had launched

seven years earlier. Dowst kept in step with the times and the painted metal manner was there, but the styles were updated; the old-fashioned round dining-room table was gone, the 1930 beds were provided with tin removable spreads, and even the kitchen chairs were re-tooled—a vaguely Windsorish style replacing the 1923 (also vaguely) Queen Anneish one.

Tootsietoy was at its realistic best in kitchens and baths. In 1928, the firm advertised bathrooms "in the new orchid and green finishes," and kitchens in "two new colors, red and green, just like the colorful kitchens so in vogue." As described in toy catalogues of the 'twenties and early 'thirties, as I've noted elsewhere, the line offers enough information about the period to supply a standard essay upon its furnishings and decorating.

The "over-stuffed" living-room suite to be seen within the opened left-hand wing, probably meant to represent cut velour, is vivid in bright orange and bright green. The grand piano shown below is fitted with a workable top, music rack, and keyboard cover.

TOOTSIETOY GRAND PIANO

REAR OF HOUSE

Part III

English Houses,

Both Stately and Modest

A Georgian Baby House

This quite beautiful Georgian house came to me with the extraordinary gift of dolls from Nancy Petrikin Menoni. It was unaccompanied by provenance. There were no furnishings, with the exquisite exception of the gossamer curtains which have been rehung, and with the early commercially made fireplaces attached to the back walls.

The façade lifts off in an unusual manner, with elaborate wooden finials which peg in at either side of the pedimented roof. The portico protects a handsomely paneled door, flanked by a pair of fluted columns. The house has a sandstone finish and, with its elegant proportions, it is clearly the work of an assured cabinetmaker.

Height: 3'10" (plus chimneys) Width: 40 1/2"

RARE PEG WOOD DOLL WITH
PORCELAIN HEAD AND LIMBS

CLOTH DOMESTIC WITH "HASTENER"

For years it languished unfurnished, owing to the difficulty of providing suitable furniture for so early a house. Recently there came to me what I trust was an inspiration: many years ago the late Laura Treskow, my helpful London source for several years, sent the Regency Town House, shown on page 169, and a Georgian Town House, with a quantity of unsorted furniture, most of it early nineteenth century, and presumably from both.

The latter Georgian house has simple but elegant proportions and may be seen on page 159.

The "inspiration," has been to plunder the altered Georgian, which is now in the process of restoration, and to furnish its larger and more splendid contemporary, shown herewith, including much of the furniture which crossed the ocean with the Georgian Town House and the Regency Town House.

When the façade is lifted off, there is a charming surprise: the interior is provided with a facing which enhances each of the six rooms, a decorative scallop at the top of each. There are no staircases or interior doors, but early wallpapers and floor coverings which appear to be original, lead the eye into the rooms. Especially appealing is a sandstone-textured paper, scored in blocks, in the kitchen and the downstairs halls. There is a kitchen

A RARE PAIR OF AIR-TWIST WINES
WITH EARLY ROCK AND GRANER TABLE

floor in harmonizing beiges and browns. Only the downstairs hall floor covering needed to be replaced, with the ever-useful paisley. The other rooms have early wool carpets in varying patterns.

There is a window in each room, in addition to those on the façade. Even the two halls, upstairs and down, are lighted by a sizable arched window at the rear of each, infusing them with light.

In the kitchen, the attached fireplace is faced with iron. In the other principal rooms, the three tin fireplaces with their built-in brass grates and fenders (the one in the bedroom quite petite) are also affixed to the walls.

The "plundered" furnishings include an exquisite set of wheelback windsor chairs with saddle seats, obviously hand-crafted along with the Tudor-style table. These might have been made at any time during the long history of the house but were undoubtedly antique before I acquired them forty years or so ago. The same gifted hand may have carved the highly detailed posts with its gilded and pineapple-carved segments on the lovely canopied bed upstairs. The bed, however, is more

readily datable by its pretty chintz fabric which, coincidentally, appeared on another bed in another Georgian house which came to light shortly before these words were written.[1]

It is possible to write an entire chapter on the furnishings to be seen here, such as the bottle-jack and screen ("hastener") in the kitchen, shown on previous page. (When this tin contrivance was set in front of the fire, and wound, it turned the roast. The ham still hangs from the hook. The screen protected the cook from the intense heat when she reached in to baste the meat.)

The red tin candle holder with extinguisher still clinging from its bit of chain may be, like the chairs and tables, more Regency than Georgian—as is the peg wooden "char lady" relaxing in the kitchen and the housekeeper with her fierce (embroidered) expression presiding in the drawing room.

The rarest of all the dolls is to be seen in the bedchamber. On our first trip to London, in 1948, she was the only dolls' house piece of consequence I discovered in more than a month of searching.[2] Antique dealers did not bother with such toys in those days. (Perhaps I didn't speak up sufficiently: one dealer thought I was inquiring about antique dog houses!) With her porcelain head and limbs, she is seated in her tub, ill advisedly, though, in her red porcelain slippers.

Many years ago, from Laura Treskow, my fortuitous source in London, I acquired an extraordinary collection of what she believed to be eighteenth century glass (some pieces may have been a bit later). These included the two "air-twist" wine goblets on the dining-room table. Other pieces from this collection are displayed on the tilt-top table, itself unusual, in the foreground.

---

1. *International Dolls' House News,* Vol X by the knowledgeable collector-dealer, Anne Timpson.
2. In the mornings, in the library at Bethnal Green, I pursued research on *A History of Dolls' Houses.* In the afternoon, I "searched."

A GEORGIAN TOWN HOUSE

When this elegant townhouse came to me from Britain, in the late 'fifties, it was accompanied by the Regency Town House, shown on page 169, with a mélange of furnishings, presumably from both.

To say that the interior had been "restored" would be an understatement: interior walls and a staircase were obvious additions, but nothing had disturbed the lovely proportions of the façade with its twelve-paned, slightly arched sashed windows and its simple, glazed fanlight over the door, the lovely café au lait painted and scored "stone" surface, or the black painted and scored hipped roof above it.

Unfortunately, the door was unmistakably a poor replacement. Strips at the base of the house indicate that the traditional stand is missing. Within, the three stories had been subjected to various "improvements." The third floor had been divided into three rooms, courtesy of a papered cardboard wall, which was immediately removed. A staircase opening in the floor was covered.

The two lower floors were not as readily alterable: the interior walls, though of wood, were obviously not original. An inoffensive beige and tan striped paper was to be found on the walls of all three floors. The walls in one room had been stripped and were bare. The furnishings have been plundered and many of them placed in the

Georgian house, below.

In the existence of a house two centuries old, full-sized or miniature, more than one renovation is likely. The most noticeable addition, which provided a possible clue to the date of at least one set of alterations, was a winding "Chinese Chippendale" staircase, rising from the ground floor. This was backed with a paper strip from a British publication, "The Bystander," dated 1912. The Chippendale balustrade is well made of wood, perhaps by the same hand which added a built-in dark wood dresser with a matching wall

WHEEL-BACK
WINDSOR

HEIGHT: 41" WIDTH: 23 3/4"

cupboard in the kitchen and corner shelving in the other ground floor room. There was also a tin fireplace in the kitchen which appeared to be hand-done, but none of this is of the quality of the house itself. These features have been removed and preserved.

Of the furnishings which accompanied the two houses when they crossed the ocean, those which, to a reasonably educated eye, appeared to be the earliest, were placed in this house at the time. These included a wonderful set of hand-crafted wheel-back windsors, shown on previous page, and a set of painted country chairs of a style which would be referred to in the United States as "arrowback." It is possible that both sets of chairs were by the same hand which fashioned the Chippendale balustrade, but these were far more finely made than the interior shelving.

Mysteries, alas, will forever remain, but my theory is that originally, this house contained one room on each of the three floors. The house is in the process of one more restoration to correspond to this theory. A paneled door carefully copied from a house of similar date, has replaced the "poor replacement."

In *A Book of Dolls and Dolls' Houses*,[1] published in 1967, I asserted that this house "might be as early as 1760," relating this date to a "two-story house of the Adam period at the Manchester Art Gallery (England) with almost identical twelve-light windows" and "a similar hipped roof with twin chimneys." On the other hand, the ca. 1720 house at Stranger's Hall, Castle Museum, Norwich, with far more and far finer detail, has a similar arrangement of windows, with one room on each of its three floors, and I shall not presume to compare it.

A Postscript: after this house was photographed, rather starkly, I decided that the wonderful carriage and its motley company, shown below, should appear in front of it. Why I can't recall where this incredible piece was acquired, perhaps forty years ago, I don't know. It had clearly been in a glass case, and undoubtedly came from England, and therefore may very well have been removed for shipping. The most exquisite embroidery on Bristol board—the carriage itself of the most perfect satin stitch with tufted seating within—appears to be conveying a member of the British Royal family. It is possibly the Queen, Victoria herself, who is emerging from the carriage (though she alone wears no headdress or crown, which may have slipped off in the long-ago packaging). The Georgian house was clearly built several generations before her reign, but was, of course, still standing when she and her entourage emerged in front of it. On the front of the carriage is embroidered what appears to be a visual pun: "Draw me not without cause and return me not without honor—," a homily associated with Excalibur, King Arthur's sword. Here, of course, a carriage is being drawn, not a sword. And, anachronistically, why is a Victorian carriage and family involved? It is an enticing mystery. Perhaps someone will read these words and solve it.

EMBROIDERED BRISTOLBOARD
CARRIAGE

1. Charles F. Tuttle. Tokyo

ENGLISH BABY HOUSE

An acquaintance saw this handsome house, more than thirty years ago, in the window of an elegant Manhattan antique shop and was kind enough to send the address. It was the Christmas season and for display the house was slathered with imitation snow. (Traces of the latter were still being removed years later.)

This is truly a "baby house" in the best sense. Vivien Greene has written that rather than in the nursery, the baby house stood on the landing, and

CA. 1840. EXTERIOR: 61" (INCLUDING STAND) WIDTH: 44"

BOOKCASE WITH AUTHORS

PLATE RACK

she has suggested that the term is applicable large-ly to 18th century treasures designed by architects.

Actually, I have seen the term used for humbler American dolls' houses as late as the mid nine-teenth century. This one is typically British. Perhaps the most traditional feature of the English dolls' house is the stand on which it rests, usually, as in the case of this attractive specimen, an inte-gral part of the architecture. Here the supports are carved to resemble stone. Matching realism may be seen in the coigning, applied in individual blocks, which, along with the lintels above the windows, are painted a lovely taffy shade. Door panels and shutters are imitation-grained. The pair of chim-

neys are properly capped with chimney pots, two apiece, to accommodate the four fireplaces within, and ornamental verge boards—almost baroque—emphasize the pitch of the roof. Vestiges remain of where there may have been a brass or wood plaque above the door with a house or family name, pos-sibly removed by the original family or the dealer, and lost, alas, forever.

Inasmuch as it came with most of its early fur-nishings intact (a number of late Victorian addi-tions have been replaced) and in excellent condi-tion, this house may be dubbed "a treasure."

The early marbled bookend papers which, dis-creet investigation reveals, originally covered the

SPUN-GLASS WINES

DRESSING TABLE MIRRORS

KESTNER CONCERTINA DINING TABLE

walls, are happily undisturbed in the halls. In recent years, an outer layer in the kitchen has been carefully removed to reveal the original.

A proper staircase with landing and balustrade dominates the center halls. Although two rows of tacks were all that remained of the stair carpet, antique paisley is a pleasing substitute.

Well-made metal grates are built into the wooden chimneypieces and these are filled, in proper scale, with genuine coal. It is curious that, in a residence with so much careful detail as this one, no provision is made for going from one room to another. A doll who happens to be in the hall may go up or down, but not from one room to the next.

Several early dolls survived this indignity, including a nice peg-wooden cook with her original coral-sprigged cotton gown and commodious white apron. Three blond bisque sisters with their mid-nineteenth-century flat hairdos and flat shoes have been supplemented by a bisque nanny with her equally mid-nineteenth-century sausage curls, her striped tan uniform, and her white cap.

A number of pieces in the early rosewood—Biedermeier style—came with the house. In the bedroom, there's a small sleigh bed. A toilet mirror with drawer below rests on a three-drawer chest with the bone supports usually to be seen on these earlier pieces. There's also a black-and-gilt metal bed

with astragal-twist posts capped with gilt ball finials. Exuberant pink silk bows were placed on head and footboard by some long-ago young owner. (And who are we to remove these?) Another unusual metal piece is a washstand with a well-preserved faux marble top, possibly Rock & Graner.

Because there was no proper dining-room set in this very proper house, a parlor set of the well-known French genre (with floral paper-scrap trim and with coral silk seats on the chairs) was moved into an upstairs room, and a rare Waltershausen "concertina" dining table with suitable chairs was substituted. An early set of spun glass wine goblets, in which the wine is suggested by port-colored glass, embellishes the table.

The most remarkable piece with the house—and I've never seen another—is the bookcase. Tales are told of full-sized libraries whose uncaring, un-reading owners install books by the yard with not a single printed word within their handsome bindings. The Biedermeier bookcase in this house features books by the inch—of probable mid-nineteenth century origin, to judge by the authors represented. In the bookcase itself, decorated in fanciful gilt motifs and surmounted by an owl in relief, such giants as Voltaire and Goethe keep company with such relatively forgotten authors as Voss and Uhland. [1]

1. A scholar might write a learned treatise on the contents of this bookcase!

A "VICTORIAN GOTHIC"

As British a dolls' house as one would expect to see, this small early Victorian Gothic is a modified (to say the least) castle, a thing of turrets, buttresses, battlements and, irrelevantly, of chimney pots. It is built to fit into its own stand which, like those of many English dolls' houses, blends with the house and completes it. One must examine this stand carefully to see where it ends and the house begins.

When the door handle, on a spring latch which fastens the façade, is turned, the two windowed sections spring open on either side of a fixed front door panel. With their four-paned mullions, the arched Gothic windows on the ground floor (and the two with simpler lintels above), betray their Victorian origin.

The 1840 date is an educated guess. This irresistible small structure is assuredly no later.

The rare Gothic exterior is, to adopt a current phrase, what this house is "about." Within there are four small, unadorned rooms, but each contains a chimneypiece with a built-in metal grate. These correspond to the chimney (with logic often ignored by dolls' house makers). These are somewhat hidden by the fixed front, but may be seen from the side windows.

The small rooms require reasonably diminutive furnishings. A rare white metal set in a Gothic pattern, consisting of six chairs and a table, has been placed in the dining room. The rectangular top is glazed with a blue, shimmering surface. (The latter is accomplished, presumably, by placing a crinkled, tinsel-like paper beneath the glass.)

A bed of early style, with a domed canopy, presides over the bedroom. Pieces of early Biedermeier of the smallest scale, including a secretaire with bone supports and a dentelated molding of great delicacy, are placed in the three principal rooms.

Although chairs with silk seats do not appear to be suitable for a kitchen, they have been introduced into this one owing to their presence in a set of simple two-toned wooden pieces, unvarnished and inlaid, which are of a genre obviously made over a period of many decades and very suitable for a kitchen. This furniture is to be seen in a mid-nineteenth-century German catalogue, from the Erzgebirge region. Its inlay—the only ornamentation, is appealing. A "copper," to be found at the time in every proper British kitchen, and in perfect scale for this one, occupies a corner.

VICTORIAN GOTHIC
SOFT-LEAD FURNITURE

THE "COPPER"

ENGLAND. CA. 1840. EXTERIOR: (INCLUDING INTEGRAL STAND, PARTIALLY SHOWN) HEIGHT: 41" WIDTH: 23"

THE MARSHALL COLLECTION

One fortuitous day in 1979, there was a phone call from England from a friend and former museum staff member, Mary Hamilton Moe. She was visiting friends in Cheltenham where her husband was stationed during World War II.

An antiques dealer in Cheltenham had for sale in his "back room" the early nineteenth century contents of a dolls' house accompanied by a most intriguing provenance: in a worn notebook labeled "The Georgian Dolls' House," Algernon Edward West (1865-1944) was quoted in reference to "the old dolls' house made from a cupboard by Gt. Grandfather Marshall for his girls about 1800." A further note: "This Marshall was the father of the Rev. John William Henry Marshall (1803-1841), rector of Ovingdean, Sussex, England who had himself been the rector."[1]

When she phoned from Cheltenham, Mrs. Moe noted that the house was of little interest. It was actually a rather cramped cupboard, but if I wished to go ahead with the purchase, she'd arrange to bring the contents to me when she returned. She sent pictures and a list of the "contents" which featured eleven early, exquisitely dressed peg-wooden dolls and their remarkable possessions.

After thinking about this major acquisition for several days, my kind husband agreed to purchase the collection, which became one of the earliest and most dazzling (to its new owner) of the exhibits in the Museum. I arranged to leave the cupboard in the custody of a dear friend in Birmingham till I could cross the ocean and see it for myself. [2]

EARLY KITCHEN UNIT.
HEIGHT: 6 1/2" WIDTH: 11"

TUCK COMB LADY WITH HER FIRE SCREEN
AND EARLY METAL FURNISHINGS

1. These notes were made by Kenneth Cyril Arnold Barrie Savory, half nephew of Evelyn Lovett Hawker whose uncle was Algernon Edward West. They were made in July, 1977 at Casa Resolis, Luz De Tavira, Algarre, Portugal where Mrs. Hawker lived at the time of her death (1976). I regret never having spoken to Mr. Savory, who must be given great credit for arranging to keep the collection together. (An English auction house wanted the collection, but would have "split it up.")
2. My friend was quite right about "the cramped cupboard." When I saw it, some months later, I was glad that meanwhile I'd acquired a sizeable glazed case to display its myriad treasures. In the small cupboard, relatively few would have been visible, and I gave it to my English hostess.

THE FAMILY. TALLEST DOLL: 4"

As their group portrait suggests, the eleven members of the doll household are exquisitely dressed, their period garments in perfect condition.

With them came a framed portrait (a "miniature" in its original sense), of the Reverend Marshall and his "book" dated 1810. One could write a book of one's own about this collection. For the Museum display, nothing has been added or subtracted—not even the box of fifteen early "Frozen Charlottes" which appear to be irrelevant and are later than most of the pieces.

From the flame-stitch and needlepoint carpets to the rare, self-contained kitchen unit, it is difficult to limit one's admiration—and mention—to a relative few of the treasures. Especially notable are

the metal coronation chairs, the souvenir watch with the date of birth of the Prince of Wales in 1841, and several tiny hand-made albums. The latter may well have been made by the Reverend Marshall's "girls" for whom the house was begun. On the backs of two wood-backed engravings are the names of Louisa Maria Marshall and Emily Mary Marshall, assuredly, the "girls."

One of the albums contains Lilliputian watercolors; there is one of a girl and her doll which is a treasure in itself. Louisa Maria and Emily Mary may also be responsible for the dolls' costumes and their additional garments—exquisitely made bonnets, dresses and "pockets." The furniture includes early metal pieces by Evans and Cartwright—the rare Regency clock and rectangular table in faux mahogany and, rarer still, a circular table painted green with a floral pattern.

For a bibliophile, but very much a part of the collection, is the aforementioned crimson leather book with the Reverend Marshall's name in gold on the cover. It is "Baxter's Pocket Book or Gentlemen's Country Remembrancer...for the Pocket or Desk for the year 1810." This is illustrated with a hand-colored map of the county and is, for a volume nearly two centuries old, in near mint condition.

In the small notebook in which the careful Mr. Savory recorded the family history, he lists the furnishings of the house. There is also, tucked in the back, a real estate ad with a photograph of "A Gracious Georgian Rectory in the old village of Ovingdean...on the Edge of the Downs Near Brighton." This was clearly the charming rectory in which The Reverend Marshall and the Marshall collection resided, so many decades ago.

A FEW OF THE GARMENTS

THE REV. MARSHALL HIMSELF

COMMEMORATIVE ITEM. READS:
"VIVA REGINA BORN ON
9TH OF NOVEMBER, 1841"

TINY WATERCOLORS IN A
CHARMING ALBUM.
HEIGHT: 1 1/2"

EVANS & CARTWRIGHT WASHSTAND

SOFT-LEAD CORONATION CHAIRS AND CLOCK

AN ENGLISH REGENCY TOWN HOUSE

When this house was sent from England in the 1960's, it was described as Regency. I questioned this at the time, suggesting that "Early Victorian" appeared to be a more accurate designation.[1]

However, I admitted that the exterior appeared to be "a modest interpretation" of certain Regency features, with the roof, balustraded parapet, matching balustraded windows, and classical window cornices. In any case, I labeled it "Early Victorian," probably influenced by the fact that the interior is suffused with Victorian decor. Osbert

Lancaster[2] had referred to "the last flicker of the great classic tradition of English architecture" which he called ""Kensington Italianate."

"This," I thought, "might link the house with the 'forties and 'fifties when houses very similar to this one were built in multiplicity in Kensington, Paddington, and Belgravia." One clue to an earlier date may be the Venetian blinds painted on the glass inside the pedimented windows. Fashionable in the eighteenth century, their vogue began to wear off around 1840, at which time, according to Frances Lichten,[3] "Green, their usual color, was going out of fashion." Inasmuch as the blinds of

EARLY NINETEENTH CENTURY.
EXTERIOR HEIGHT: 42" WIDTH: 25"

1. *Victorian Dolls' Houses*
2. *Here of all Places.* Houghton-Mifflin, 1958
3. *Decorative Arts of Victoria's Era.* Scribner's, New York, 1950

this house are green, I rationalized that perhaps they were painted on the windows by one not quick to follow style.

The house itself, of course, may have been a copy of an earlier house—one in which the maker lived. It is clearly not built by an expert craftsman, though certainly the builder was conscientious. It is not in the tradition of the craftsmanship to be seen, for instance, in the English Baby House, shown on page 161, where the coigning, for a small example, is applied in individual segments. Here it is painted, though the builder has gone to some pains with other details such as the pedimented windows and balustrades.

Nevertheless this is a fascinating house, with unexpected touches. The colorful, glazed transom over the front door is one of these: a knight's sil-very helmet, topped with a golden coronet, nestles in a lush backdrop of scrolls and related curlicues. (This appears to be of stained glass but is probably *windowphanie* or the English equivalent thereof.)

Whatever the date of the town house, it was clearly—and marvelously—redecorated at midcentury. There are velvet lambrequins on the mantels (two of which are corner ones) and all of the decor appears to be of similar vintage. There are charming, perfectly scaled wallpapers, assuredly made for dolls' house rooms, in tiny prints with floral ceiling borders. Unfortunately someone painted over the papers in the upper and lower right-hand rooms before the house crossed the ocean. The three remaining papered rooms (the kitchen is painted) were mercifully left untouched, somewhat faded but thoroughly evocative.

KITCHEN WITH "THE MODEL BAKERY"

SUNBURST FABRIC PANELS
ON FIRESHADE AND CABINET

EVANS & CARTWRIGHT CHAIRS

Most evocative of all—in one of the rooms where a picture was removed, a silhouette remains of the shape which hung there, exactly as it might in a full-sized room after a few generations.

Remarkably, many of the pictures and mirrors were left intact. Sixteen looking glasses remain—in seven different styles—including, in the drawing room, the oval pair which boast pricket candle-holders. One—and I've never seen another—has a pair of cloak hangers at its base. These mirrors are supplemented by a motley variety of prints in metal frames, and the fact that they are in the splendid clutter of their original positions, with infinitesimal nails attesting to the position of others, is especially appealing.

This house and the Georgian Town House, shown on page 159, came together from England many years ago, along with a fascinating array of furnishings. Unfortunately, these were sent unsorted and it was not possible to know which belonged to which house. However, most of these are no later than mid-century and one must be grateful (in this era of separation of houses and their contents) that these came at all. There are Evans & Cartwright pieces—tables, chairs, and a sofa—two of the metal chair-seats painted in rare patterns. A most unusual wood chest and matching fire screen contain fabric "sunburst" insets.

In the kitchen, an exceedingly rare tin unit with "The Model Bakery" embossed in the space between its operable oven doors, is fitted into a corner with wood shelves built-in above. The shelves hold a set of hot dish covers and other fitments. (In the days of large houses with long distances to the dining room, such covers were essential to keep the food "piping" hot till it reached the table.)

The oddest feature of this house may also relate to the latter: what appeared to be a dumb-waiter—or an elevator—was built into the alcoves which may be seen on each of the floors. This metal unit was attached to a pulley on the balustraded roof and was removed when essential lighting was installed. This, of course, was retained, and could be reinstalled easily by any occupants of the dolls' house who felt the need of this astonishing feature. It is rather crudely made of tin and is, frankly, a puzzle.

A very rare pair of dolls—a bearded gentleman in his smoking jacket and an elderly lady in her frilled cap—crossed the ocean with the houses. See below.

EARLY BEARDED GENTLEMAN AND ELDERLY LADY

TOWGOOD HOUSE

A worn and faded page covered with antique script heightens the charm of this small, slender, mid-nineteenth century town house from England. The rare page is an inventory of the original contents—undated and unsigned, but with a clue, invisible till held to the light, a watermark: "Towgood's Extra Super." Edward Towgood & Sons, Ltd., still manufacturing paper, offers us forty-four years, from 1836-1880, during which such paper was in use. The style of the house and the penmanship of the inventory place the page and the house in the earlier years of this range.

MID-NINETEENTH CENTURY. HEIGHT: 28 1/2" WIDTH (INCLUDING BASE) 25"

"Inventory of the Lilliput House" is the heading, and the modest contents of three rooms, kitchen, drawing room, and bedroom (one on each of the three floors), are carefully set down. It is interesting to see what were considered the essentials in a well-run baby house at mid-century. We note "bellows" and "toasting fork" in the kitchen, and "jug and basin" and "towel rail" in the bedroom, but nothing can be more arresting than the list of occupants themselves, departed at some unspecified date but of unmistakable family to judge from their highly specific names. When the inventory was drawn up, most of them were assembled in the drawing room, a cozy company consisting of "Mr. Woodhead, Miss F. Woodhead Mrs. Firbody, Harry Firbody, and Lucy Woodhead & Doll." "Betty the Cook and Mary the Housemaid," their family tree (fir?) unspecified, were properly below-stairs, while "Mrs. Woodhead

& Baby" were in the bedroom. The owner of the small house will never see an unidentified jointed wooden in the future without wondering if she or he did not, perchance, once reside in this neat-fronted, red brick house with its lace-edged blinds and metal door knocker. Meanwhile, another Woodhead family has taken up residence.

Four pieces of furniture and the kitchen fireplace came along with the Towgood House and its inventory at the time of its purchase. The tin kitchen grate with its fender obviously is original, having been built into the chimneypiece.

It is difficult to date the others. They are of the soft-lead filigree which a factory in Bavaria has been turning out since 1799, and up to the present. Some of the pieces are still being made from original molds, a fact which makes dating difficult. But these survivors are unmistakably Victorian. The small cupboard with door below and shelf

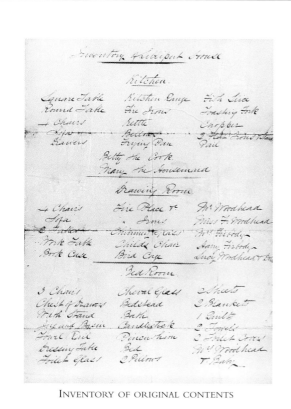

INVENTORY OF ORIGINAL CONTENTS

WASHSTAND (BABETTE SCHWEITZER), ONE OF ORIGINAL PIECES

CHAMBER SET ON ORGINAL METAL STAND

above has a feature which we have never seen else-where—an attached lead lamp base with glass chimney and Bristol shade. The washstand with its basin opening features not only a built-in mirror but also a molded-in red-painted lead candle in a candleholder at either side. On the chest, the mirror swivels, and the three drawers work; on the dresser, the door above is missing, but the doors below are in working order. All of these pieces are of the usual silvery lead, with the gilt wash often found on earlier pieces for embellishment.

One of the charms of this house is its diminutive size. It lends itself to furnishings of perhaps three-fourth-inch scale (3/4" to 1') and since dolls' house furniture of the early-Victorian period seems often to come in one-inch scale or larger, it was something of a challenge to complete the furnishing of such a house. Among the rosewood pieces with gilt stenciling are a square piano (all of 5" long), a dresser with shelves above and doors below, a marble-topped dressing table, a meridi-enne—the Mme. Recamier type of sofa with open end, complete in purple silk with roll cushion, and a half-tester bed, its vestiges of gossamer violet curtains clinging to their lace edgings.

PEG-WOODEN LADY WITH
HER RECAMIER SOFA

ORIGINAL TO HOUSE:
LAMP INTEGRAL

HALF-TESTER
BED WITH PEG-WOODEN
OWNER

MADAME ST. QUINTIN'S HOUSE

In the 1965 edition of *A History of Dolls' Houses*, I wrote: "One of the most thoroughly furnished of all possible dolls' houses, and one of the most attractive, is an English mid-nineteenth century one in the possession of Eunice Althouse of Oxford, Pennsylvania."

The house, of fifteen rooms, plus stair halls and attic, was purchased by the late Mrs. Althouse, a collector and dealer, in 1962, and it was to her great credit that she was willing to sell it completely furnished only, and had stood by this resolve for several years.

Though I could not afford the house, I drove to Oxford just for the pleasure of seeing it. The surprising manner in which I came into possession of the house, a number of years later, is another story.

Mrs. Althouse told me that the house came from an estate near Burford, England where it was built by the estate carpenter. The latter didn't go to too much trouble. A rather primitive boxlike structure

HALF OF FAÇADE.

ENGLISH. CA. 1856–58. HEIGHT: 5' 1 3/4" WIDTH: 5'

with a removable façade, the house is not in the stately baby house tradition usually associated with estate carpenters. As I wrote at the time: "the house is not the thing, but then its builder was beset with putting in all those walls, and with the flights of stairs for three of the four floors (plus attic), he probably had little time for flights of fancy."

It was the decorator—a nanny, a mother, a sister?—who indulged in the latter, and gave the house much of its character and charm.

Simple glazed windows with painted lintels on the removable façade and sides are supplemented in several rooms with paper windows decoupaged with paper views. Much of this scenery is of a horticultural nature, as lush as the pages of the Victorian seed catalogues whence, undoubtedly, these "views" originated.

There is also imaginative decoupage in other rooms. Ancient maps adorn the walls of one. A huge pair of Ming vases are glued to each side of the fireplace in another. The effect is colorful, ingenious, and delightful.

MADAME ST. QUINTIN

As is usually the case, more than one generation must have played with the house, and some of the furnishings are later, but a few, possibly dating from an earlier dolls' house owned by the family, are eighteenth century. In the dining room there is a marked Wedgwood oval tureen ca. 1790. The square pianoforte in the music room is also about 1780-90 and two hand-painted "ancestor's portraits" over the sofa in the drawing room are ca. 1800.

Only one doll, Madame St. Quintin herself, came with the house. An early peg-wooden with a rare painted Ferroniere (ornamental head band worn across the forehead), she is believed to date no later than 1840.

Because the house has always been known as Madame St. Quintin's house, it is of interest to note that Jane Austen attended for two years a school in Reading operated by two ladies, one of them a Madame St. Quintin. Although the house and doll are several generations later than this

coincidence, the presence of two Madame St. Quintins in that part of England at any time seems unlikely, and one assumes there is a family connection between the young owner of the dolls' house and the school.

There is a fireplace in each room, and a tea set in each bedroom, both drawing rooms, the music room and in the small sitting room above the kitchen. It looks like a house for a family who entertain a great deal (and who drink a lot of tea). But why is Madame alone and where are all the servants? Undoubtedly there is an explanation. The new owner took the liberty of adding a few furnishings including several early Rock & Graner pieces to the bedroom and a few dolls.

On a personal note, the house came to the museum in 1988 under the most astonishing circumstances. In the 'sixties before there was a museum, I received a phone call at home from a woman in California who asked my least favorite question:

BED CHAMBER SHOWING WINDOWS WITH DECOUPAGED SEED CATALOGUE PAGES

MADAME IN HER DRAWING ROOM

BEDCHAMBER WITH ADDITION OF RARE TESTER BED

did I know where she could find a dolls' house for sale? I did. I had recently seen Madame St. Quintin's house in Eunice Althouse's antique shop in Oxford. Being unable to afford it, I gave the information to my caller, Mrs. Nancy Tewkesbury (later—Menoni) and evidently I made a friend. Mrs. Tewkesbury, I later learned, bought the house and, over the course of perhaps a dozen years, a few other houses and a number of large dolls from Mrs. Althouse.

During the course of her collecting, Mrs. Tewkesbury phoned me now and then and we exchanged Christmas cards.

I shall never forget one phone call. Evidently tiring of her collection, Mrs. Tewkesbury phoned me and said: "is your driveway wide? I'm going to send you my collection." At the time I had no museum and I assured my caller that I could not possibly accept her generous offer. I remember saying: "You don't even know me, Mrs. Menoni!" and hearing her reply, "Oh yes I do!" In any case, there was a 45-minute phone conversation in which I continued to refuse. I also remember saying, finally, "My husband would never let me

accept it." She was finally persuaded and hung up.

Years later, a few years after I opened the Museum, she phoned and again offered her collection. Inasmuch I could then share it with the Museum's visitors, at long last I "graciously" accepted.

After Madame St. Quintin's house and the dolls were comfortably settled in the Museum and I related this story, one visitor said, "cast your bread upon the waters!" Of course I'd had no thought of "casting bread" but this incredible present added greatly to the Museum (especially the numerous dolls which were lacking in the collection), and I shall be eternally grateful to the late Nancy Petrikin Menoni.

CHEVAL MIRROR
WITH SHOP LABEL

"ORMOLU" MUSIC
STAND WITH MUSIC
HARP OF TORTOISE-
SHELL, PEARL INLAY,
AND BONE

MUSIC ROOM WITH TERRESTRIAL BACKGROUND

An Elegant Silber & Fleming "Box-Back"

This splendid Silber & Fleming "box-back" is somewhat larger than a quite similar house sold at Christie's South Kensington in May of 1999. Christie's described a house with "five bays and two stories...opening to reveal four rooms with staircase and landing, original Evans & Cartwright grates, opening interior doors...marbleized fire surrounds."

All of this also may be said of our version. One of the differences may be seen in the small photograph from Christie's catalogue: the Christie's house has balustrading across the front, under the upper windows, but it is somewhat smaller. Our house is 8 1/2" wider (and 3" taller). Perhaps this is why the entrance door is larger and more

imposing with space for a brass key-hole (key missing), along with a lion-headed knocker and a knob. There are well-designed pilasters on either side, and a graceful top light, the white-painted detail on the glass clearly original. Both top-light and pilasters are considerably more modest at the entrance of the Christie's house, and so is the white-painted woodwork including the door itself. One of the exquisite features of the larger house is the faux-grain finish on the door—and indeed throughout the interior.

Houses of this genre were known to have been sold at Cremer's Toy Shop in London early in the nineteenth century.

The lovely faux-grain finish on the front door

ENGLISH. CA. 1856-58. HEIGHT: 34" WIDTH: 49 1/2"

SILBER & FLEMING INTERIOR

is continued on the interior doors, and on the skirtings, all of them in remarkably mint condition. (In the Christie's house the woodwork is painted white or cream.)

The Evans & Cartwright fireplaces, nestled inside their elegantly faux-marbled surrounds, are positively majestic. Inasmuch as furniture which came with the house includes Evans & Cartwright pieces, there is an appealing consistency to the ambience in the rooms in which they are placed. Among these is the elaborate Regency clock which, with its exuberant plumes, adds panache to any setting, to say the least. Oddly enough, a tall-case clock I've never seen elsewhere was readily identifiable as Evans & Cartwright as well—its metal-rimmed face is identical, and on both the clocks the hands point to nearly five forty-five. The grandfather clock, its paint showing its age, was found in a shabby American house, of no pretensions whatever, which I bought years ago in order to rescue the clock. It is on the staircase landing.

But not all that came with the house, which arrived only partially furnished, is Evans & Cartwright. A French boudoir—its draped day bed crowned by a gilt-metal cornice—dominates the left upper chamber. (Another fine English house came furnished with a French suite, one for the dining room. Families who could afford such splendid dolls' houses very likely made visits to the continent with similar miniature results.) A lovely miniature on ivory,[1] of a lady who appears to bear a striking resemblance to Marie Antoinette, has been placed on the wall in this room. In its splendid filigree frame, it was acquired decades ago. (I regret that I can't remember where.)

The kitchen had pleasingly-patterned wallpaper, clearly old, but I suspected that under it must be the "poison-bottle blue" usually found in

TWO EVANS & CARTWRIGHT CLOCKS

ORIGINAL EVANS & CARTWRIGHT FIREPLACE INSERT

---

1. A true miniature. For years I fought the use of the word "miniature" as a term for dolls' house furnishings, rather than for small paintings. Having sold miniature pieces in our Museum Shop for nearly three decades, I finally bowed to the inevitable and use the term, occasionally—with care. But it is of interest here to acknowledge the presence of a true "miniature" in this small room.

kitchens (to discourage the beetles). It seemed a pity, as we did, to remove it: on one wall, very charmingly, were pencilled the heights of the dolls, with their names, just as actual children have sometimes been measured. (The blue was indeed beneath.) The kitchen dresser was missing. The American purchaser of the Christie's house kindly sent measurements and pictures of hers, which was then reproduced by Jim Reus.

Other early pieces which accompanied the house include a fine mahogany chest of drawers with bone knobs, and such accessories as a red and gilt painted Regency toast rack and a proper copper tea kettle on a brass footman. Two rare Evans & Cartwright chairs, hand-painted, with a striped seat on one and a floral medallion on the other, may be found in the nursery, so designated by the presence of two wire-work cradles which came with the house. The history of the tiny baby house, placed

on the Evans & Cartwright table, is unknown, but it appears to be "early" (a useful, catch-all word, withal vague, which seems suitable here).

After these words were written, the proud owner decided to place in the lower right-hand room one of the great treasures of her collection. This may be best described as "The Abell's Drawing-Room Suite."

A Maryland antiques dealer brought this exquisite set to the Museum in the late 'seventies. It was and still is in mint condition and the price was reasonable. In those days antiques were more affordable than now, needless to say.

The set not only was contained in its original paper-covered wooden box, but there was provenance: within the box ancient shards of *The Baltimore Weekly Sun* included the masthead dated "Saturday morning, January 18, 1868," along with the information that this remarkable piece had

HAND-PAINTED FIRESHADES,
BONE HANDLES

THE BALTIMORE WEEKLY SUN

ABELL FURNITURE SHOWING ORIGINAL BOX AND PART OF
THE BALTIMORE WEEKLY SUN FOUND IN BOX

come from *The Sun*'s publishers, the Abell family.[1]

With its red mahogany finish, its lovely upholstery of birds and flowers—and its most striking feature—"ormolu" mounts and other metallic elements, it was an exciting acquisition. The presence of the original box, also in remarkable condition along with its intriguing provenance, printed and oral, were, to coin a phrase, the icing on the cake. It is, of course, similar to the lovely set in the South Jersey house (page 34) and to the one in the Graddon family parlor (page 248) but it is larger in scale and grander. The chairs (page 185) are of a more elaborate construction, though the bird-and-flower upholstery is also to be seen on the South Jersey set. (The Graddon pieces are upholstered in a solid blue fabric.)

During a visit to Washington many years ago, my wonderful friend and fellow researcher Vivien Greene saw the pieces in the South Jersey house and related that she had seen them in an early catalogue in what was then East Germany. (Catalogue covers, with the firm's name, were frequently removed, making precise identification difficult.) Because its style is French, I had assumed it had been made in France, and this was striking information. In more recent years, this rare suite not only has been identified as having been made in Germany, but, more specifically, in Waltershausen, by Schneegass or Kestner.

Among the accessories with which it has been embellished, most worthy may be the exceedingly rare air-twist wines on the table.[2] The late Laura Treskow, a London dealer who, many years ago, provided a number of wonderful objects, wrote me about "a collection of eighteenth-century glass" she had discovered, and these were amongst the delicate assortment which crossed the ocean. Other pieces are shown on page 158. Because its owner hopes to be around long enough to include this glorious suite in a book about dolls' house furnishings, it nearly failed to be present in this one. Although it has been lent once or twice for special exhibits, I've never been able to bring myself to display it in the Museum or at home for fear its perfection would be diminished.

(The two chairs—the smaller one from the South Jersey set—measure 5 7/8" and 3 5/8", shown on page 35.)

A TRUE *MINIATURE* IN THE
ORIGINAL SENSE

EVANS & CARTWRIGHT
MARKED CHAIR

EVANS & CARTWRIGHT METAL SETTEE

1. There is a curious coincidence, a personal one, associated with this set. For a number of years, members of the Abell family lived a few houses from mine. A considerable number of generations removed from 1868, they were surprised to learn about the furniture.
2. These have been moved.

TWO MODEST "BOX-BACKS" BY SILBER & FLEMING

When I first wrote about the Silber & Fleming box-back houses in 1965,[1] and included an illustration from the company's 1879 catalogue, I referred to the "assortment of relatively modest dolls' houses made over a period of years in many sizes, and with innumerable variations, most probably by a craftsman working at home assisted by members of his family."

In *The Cricket on the Hearth*, Dickens described such a home operation: "Caleb and his daughter...at work...Caleb painting and glazing the four-pair front of a desirable family mansion." A 1960 article in *Country Life* referred to a report by the Jury of the Great Exhibition of 1851 which mentioned "the large number of well-designed and constructed dolls' houses made by English chamber masters," as such home artisans were called. Their productions were sold through jobbers and toy shops, and undoubtedly, over the years, similar houses were built by a succession of such craftsmen.

Certainly the "Palladian Villa," shown on page 196-197, and the considerably larger Silber & Fleming House, shown on page 181, are worthy of Chamber Master origin. The two shown herewith are considerably more modest, but unquestionably related. Both have balconies of pierced tin, painted green. The two-story example has a feature I have seen only on this one specimen—scalloped green awnings of heavy card, supported by wooden brackets. These are in lieu of the usual grandiose lintels (truly grandiose—painted in a sort of bright mustard hue and taller than one of the window panes each surmounts). The three-story specimen pictured appears to have a façade identical to "Miss Gray's house," ca. 1864, which, like the Palladian Villa, was illustrated in the ubiquitous *International Dolls' House News,*[2] and which was in the possession of Mrs. Moira Garland of Surrey, whose aunt's

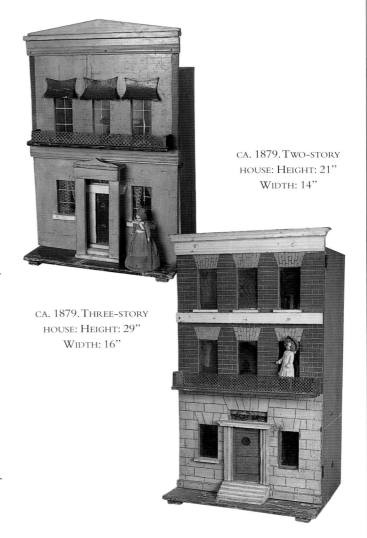

CA. 1879. TWO-STORY
HOUSE: HEIGHT: 21"
WIDTH: 14"

CA. 1879. THREE-STORY
HOUSE: HEIGHT: 29"
WIDTH: 16"

plaything it originally was. Mrs. Garland and I corresponded, but until I saw her house for myself, it was difficult to believe the gable on hers hadn't been an addition. There was another major variation: although other dimensions were the same, the depth of my version is 9 1/2"; the depth of hers is 17 inches. In the 1879 catalogue, there was a gabled roof model costing forty pounds, possibly a predecessor of Miss Gray's. Both of the houses pictured have more than one layer remaining of early wallpapers and their original wooden fireplace surrounds, several with tin fire grates intact.

1. *Dolls' Houses in America.*
2. Now in The Toy and Miniature Museum of Kansas City.

AN ENGLISH TOWN HOUSE

This English town house is so similar in style to British "box-back" houses, (shown on previous page), that one must make a point of noticing its modestly gabled roof and the fact that it looks perfectly at home nestled between two box-backs.

As we know, many dolls' houses of this period, sold through jobbers and shops, were made by craftsmen working at home, assisted by family members. There are many variations within the box-back genre. Here, in the related structure, the painted brick is larger than is usually found, and this covers the entire façade, whereas in the box-backs, the lower half is usually of painted stone. Another unusual feature is the glazed bay into which the entrance door is set.

One of the most charming features of this modest town-house[1] is to be found inside. The two upper stories are papered with over-scaled but delicate views of Kate Greenaway-styled figures in rural settings. There are gentlemen in knee-britches and boots and ladies in flowing frocks with bonnets of ribboned streamers. Those garments from the early part of the century, which the artist favored, offer a fairy-tale quality, enhanced by such sentimental fantasies as sunflowers with faces.

CA. 1880. HEIGHT: 29" (PLUS CHIMNEY) WIDTH: 15"

KATE GREENAWAY-STYLE WALLPAPER

1. However modest, this house, all twenty-nine inches of it, was brought to me from London by a friend who, with her husband, carried it on a plane, one of the most touching presents I've ever received.

A THREE-STORY ENGLISH CUPBOARD HOUSE

There is something about a three-story house with two well-proportioned rooms on each floor which beckons the eye. At a glance, one has a sense of a complete household, perhaps, and if the house is thoroughly furnished, the effect can be quite dazzling.

This English cupboard house is thoroughly furnished, and though its original floor coverings may be a bit too dazzling[1]—with floral printed patterns almost in conflict with the furnishings—the interior of this mid-Victorian English house may not beckon the eye, but certainly challenges it. Actually, one floor covering, a forthright mocha-shaded pattern in the kitchen, with harmonizing patterned paper on the wall, presented no problem. All of the early wallpapers are intact—and tasteful.

Also present are the original fireplaces, each a different and attractive commercial model. These fireplaces are flanked in each room by a pair of faux wood doors. Most are plain but the parlor pair bears

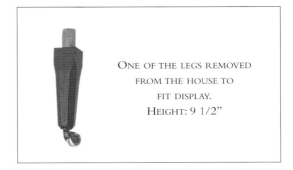

ONE OF THE LEGS REMOVED
FROM THE HOUSE TO
FIT DISPLAY.
HEIGHT: 9 1/2"

BISQUE NEEDLE WOMAN
PRESIDING OVER RARE
KESTNER WORKTABLE

KESTNER DESK WITH BRASS GALLERY TOP, SPECTACLES WITH
ORIGINAL GILT CASE AND RARE SWIVEL CHAIR

1. Several of these are so "busy" that for a few years, I covered them with segments of old velvet, but ultimately decided that original was better and removed them.

an unusual printed pattern and a gilt paper surround.

The house itself, although of quality construction (perhaps by an estate carpenter), has few architectural pretensions. Under the pitched roof, the façade swings open in two sections, well supplied with windows, but there is no door. Originally, the house was mounted on short wooden legs with brass castors, in lieu of the customary British dolls' house stand. Although it was necessary to unscrew and remove these for convenience of display, they have been, needless to say, preserved.

Except for the fireplaces and a lone chandelier, no furniture came with the house. The ubiquitous and appealing stenciled rosewood furniture from Germany, including a number of rare and early pieces, fill the three stories.

Of special interest is the parlor set. There are gilded patterns not only on the "ebony" frames, but also on the glistening crimson upholstery. The latter has the look of leather but is probably oilcloth, or a related fabric. An unusual extension table which accompanied the sofa and chairs (and the inevitable footstool) bears on its surface an appealing gilded design, which appears complete whether its two leaves are in or out.

Also rare are the embroidery frame with adjustable metal mechanism and original "embroidery," and a games table with gilt and dark checkerboard top. In its drawer are the original, slightly over-sized, pressed cardboard checkers of green and black. The metal shower bath in one of the bedrooms lacks its curtain but is also a rarity. A pair of infinitesimal spectacles in their original oval gilt two-piece case may be the most ephemeral of all the pieces—they might so easily have slipped out of sight. (Inadvertent pun.)

MID-NINETEENTH CENTURY. HEIGHT: 44" WIDTH: 40"

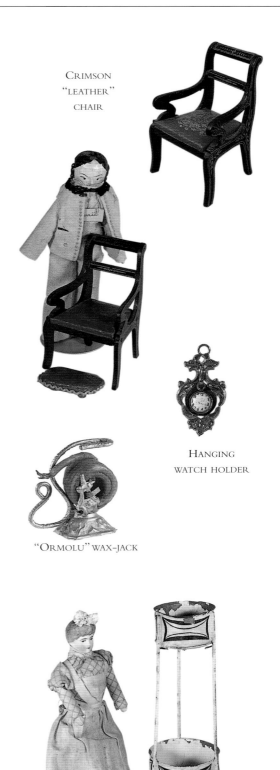

CRIMSON
"LEATHER"
CHAIR

HANGING
WATCH HOLDER

"ORMOLU" WAX-JACK

AN EARLY SHOWER WITH BISQUE CHAMBERMAID

"DOROTHY HALL"

The provenance of this sizeable house is incomplete, but it is, to say the least, beguiling. Even romantic. Years ago, its owner phoned from a Virginia suburb and offered to give it to the Museum. (In over half a century of collecting, I've had only one other such offer.)

With a staff member, I went to see it. It did not look like much. There were only parts of the original roof and the owner informed us that her great-aunt had removed the third floor and thrown it away![1]

However, it still contained the original staircase—extending to and beyond the missing third floor; and, on the façade were painted, in skillful script, a name, "Dorothy Hall," and a date, "1894."

Most intriguing of all, the generous giver related that the house was built by a Cunard carpenter for a Cunard captain's daughter. The Cunard captain, she told us, had sailed his ship aground and had come to the United States! (Assuming that Cunard would not be delighted to confirm this story, I have never, perhaps misguidedly, inquired.)

So much for its history. At the time I naively assumed that the captain's daughter was named Dorothy Hall. Later, realizing that in England, houses frequently have names ending in "Hall," I revised this ill-considered theory. Unfortunately, over the years, I lost track of the kind giver and the opportunity at least to learn the family name. (Because the house was so unprepossessing when it was acquired, I did not take it with proper seriousness at the time.)

Small screw holes in each of the ground floor rooms indicated that the third floor was not the only part of the house which had been discarded. The stand, which no proper British baby house would be without, was also missing. (One pictures nice little plump turned legs.) In lieu of this, a simple stand has

1. Further, if it was not accepted, she planned to throw the house itself away.

MÄRKLIN CHAIRS

RARE WALTERSHAUSEN VICTORIAN
GOTHIC FURNITURE

ENGLISH. 1894. HEIGHT: 53" WIDTH: 48"

EXTERIOR

been supplied to support the tall house.

We must be grateful, however, that what was removed from this imposing late Victorian town house was restorable and that the remainder was left intact. The restoration was splendidly accomplished by Jim Reus, a Maryland collector and dealer whose favorite pursuit is the restoration of antique dolls' houses. Both triangular sides of the pitched roof and half of the roof itself had survived and, when the third floor was replaced, the stairs looked entirely at home. The house, courtesy of Mr. Reus, shows no sign of the indignities to which it had been subjected.

Well-designed fireplace mantels in each of the six principal rooms contain their original metal grates. The one in the kitchen, typically English, has its brass tap. The rather eccentric oak cornices which crown the numerous casement windows and the sturdy oak staircase were also undisturbed.

Even the original paint scheme, with bands of contrasting color to suggest wainscot remain intact, along with painted "tile" floors in kitchen and hall.

In lieu of other coverings, old velvet was provided for two of the rooms, and antique paisley, with its warm reds and golds, for the others. Paisley also defines the sturdy staircase and its landings. The landings, especially the front segments, are virtually small rooms which contain sufficient depth for a few furnishings. Carefully selected panels of antique lace curtain the numerous casement windows.

The premises have been thoroughly furnished with pieces of the period, including a parlor set, early for the house, (heirloom to the doll family in residence, no doubt) with blue silk upholstery. This type of furniture, known variously as Waltershausen, where it was probably made, or

"Ormolu" wall pocket
with music

Asphaltum tray with cakes

Boule,[1] has been borrowed from its rare, original box. It is now known that much of this furniture, made by Schneegass of Waltershausen (Thuringia) was also made by Kestner, heretofore thought of primarily as a doll maker.

On the table is an asphaltum tray of cakes, delectable to the eye, and, on the desk, an early tin box of matches. The latter is labeled "Jo Kerr & Co's Safety Matches. Made in England." On the back: "I supply the matches. You the cigar." Possibly a bit late for the house, but irresistible to include.

A Märklin gasolier hangs in each of the principal rooms with later, turn-of-the-century electric chandeliers in the bedrooms. Two painted metal Märklin chairs, one a rocker, may be seen in the kitchen.

Many treasures have been bestowed upon this once derelict house, but one was added just as these pages were completed—an "ormolu" wall pocket. In nearly six decades of collecting, I have never seen another in miniature, though I have two in full size. (As I've written elsewhere, if I have an item in full size, I tend to want it in miniature—and vice versa!) The "Musik" has been added, but these pockets were also useful catch-alls for the daily paper or a magazine.

Victorian gothic set with original box

1. Described in early catalogues as "imitation ebony." This set is printed with the delicate white tracery which imitates the elaborate inlay of Boule, a French cabinetmaker.

A Palladian Villa[1] from Silber & Fleming

When this appealing structure with its imposing Palladian windows came into my possession in about 1965, we proudly posed our small daughter Amanda in front of its appropriately crimson façade for our Christmas card. One of these cards was sent to Miss Felicity Locke, the founder and editor of *International Dolls' House News,* then a small, informal bit of newsprint.

Miss Locke asked and received permission to reproduce the card in her modest publication. Not long after it was printed, I received a letter from England from Lady Samuelson in Sussex expressing her surprise: she sent pictures of a nearly identical house. Neither she nor I had ever expected to see another. An exchange of letters followed and later I was privileged to see her house and the rest of her collection. During the years, other versions have surfaced. A more elaborate example is taller (though barely wider) with a columned portico and a roof with three dormers.

These are upscale versions of a series of Silber & Fleming "box-back" houses. This name stems from a curious concept—a sort of false front covering a box-like interior and rising several inches above it (a bit of architectural dishonesty sometimes found on full-sized buildings as well). The hinged façade, opening in one section or two, appears in varying styles and sizes, often with a balcony balustrade of pierced and painted tin, or of wood, dividing the "stone" lower story from an upper one painted to represent brick. Elaborate lintels and other details are usually painted on, though three-dimensional elements—sills, stairs, and keystones are also to be found in varying com-

1. Webster's describes a villa as "a country residence." Inasmuch as most of the small, narrow box-back houses are clearly town houses, we take the liberty of referring to this as a "villa." On the other hand, the 1879 catalogue refers to "plain villas" in five styles, beginning at four pounds six shillings and going up to twenty-two pounds each, the latter a tidy sum in 1879.

HEIGHT: 30" WIDTH: 38 1/2"

HEIGHT: 30 1/2" WIDTH: 38 1/2"

binations, along with the balconies. There are even awnings on one model. "Silber & Fleming, London, Manufacturers, Importers, Warehouse-men and Agents" show, in their 1876-77, 1879-80 and 1889 catalogues, houses unmistakably of this ilk.

Although there are minor variations, the major features in Lady Samuelson's house and my own are identical—the nicely turned balusters on the balconies, keystones over the windows and the entrance, and, of course, the splendid Palladian windows.[1] It is of interest to see in a commercial-ly-made house of the late—possibly earlier—nine-teenth century a reappearance of an eighteenth century classic revival style.

One of the satisfying aspects of Palladian dolls' house windows, apart from their charm, is the vis-ibility they afford into their interiors. There are splendid views of the rooms, and one's cats are unable to intrude. [2]

The interiors of the house shown are a case in point. The ground floor windows, with their stan-dard twelve panes, are not as accommodating, but the upper floor (or first floor, as it is designated in Britain) reveals many treasures. The staircase, with its stylishly turned newel posts, the lovely (undoubtedly) original wallpapers, the paneled interior doors and the handsome chimneypieces, with their built-in brass grates and marbled wood

1. The panes, into which, with white paint, the windows in these houses are invariably divided, were obliterated in Lady Samuelson's, but it is miraculous when they survive, as they do, on my own version. Window washing is likely to remove them along with the grime. Achieving clean windows without effacing the panes is a tedious process.
2. The compatibility of cats and dolls' houses, and their owners, has often been noted.

THE METAMORPHIC BED

KESTNER SOFA DATED 1868

surrounds, are examples.

The Palladian house in Sussex[1] is probably later than the one in Chevy Chase. In Lady Samuelson's house, there is a small closet at the back of the downstairs hall which contains a "W.C." wedged in, she said, by the small hands of a granddaughter, where, in the "twin," there is only a sham door. There is no projecting chimney-breast in the kitchen in Sussex, as there is on the one in Chevy Chase. The fireplace itself differs. The kitchen in Chevy Chase contains the original built-in range with hot water tap, the usual "copper,"[2] and wooden sink, and there is also a shelf, and even a roller towel.

Except for such features as these, the house was empty when it came to me, as, sadly, is usually the case, and I have attempted to furnish it with pieces of the correct vintage, and from British sources.

One of the occupants, curiously, a Scotsman with his bisque legs painted in Argyle socks, and found in Connecticut in recent years, is clearly related to two Scotsmen with bisque legs, shown below, painted in Argyle socks, found elsewhere (I do not recall where) years ago, who may be seen in the drawing room.

Furnishings include a rare metamorphic bed (a similar piece in the U.S. would be referred to as a "Murphy bed") which appears to be a cupboard when closed and was made, probably, by Schneegass or Kestner in the dark printed "Boule."

TWO SCOTSMEN WITH BISQUE LEGS

---

1. The house may or may not remain in Sussex. I have not corresponded with Lady Samuelson in recent years.
2. In the "copper," a piece often misunderstood, the laundry was placed, and stirred with a paddle from above.

A BIG SILBER & FLEMING "BOX-BACK"

A friend discovered this sizeable and unusual Silber & Fleming "box-back" years ago in Cohasset, Massachusetts, but when it crossed the ocean is anybody's guess. I'm uncertain about what the builder had in mind—a double shop front with shopkeeper's residence above, or a residence with projecting and prominent bay windows on the ground floor? (Possibly it was to capture one of Britain's ubiquitous and inviting sea views—at Brighton, say, or Bournemouth.)

Rising to a height of five feet, including the stand, the house also has unusual depth: the deep

HEIGHT: 42 1/2" (PLUS 19" STAND) WIDTH: 32"

KESTNER
PIANOFORTE

EARLY SEWING
MACHINE

ÉTAGÈRE WITH VIENNA
BRONZE ANIMALS

WELL-DRESSED
TESTER BED

stand if not original is assuredly early, with a garden space, painted dark green, beneath each bay, and a convenient extension in front of these for the young owner (or, more likely, in recent years, a "mature" collector) to hold furnishings during the arranging process.

The six rooms have properly tall Victorian ceilings, though in such an imposing residence, the lack of a staircase is surprising. The tin fireplace remains in the kitchen and in the other five rooms. There is a chimneypiece which appears to be original, with arched opening, surround, grate, and attached curved fender, all of black. I've taken the liberty of dramatizing the simple mantel shelves in each room with lambrequins fashioned of an early braid which came from a generous friend in England.

When found, the rooms were painted a stark white. Another liberty was taken: antique wallpapers, from a rare supply no longer available, were provided.

Furnishings are fairly small-scaled—one's eye decides—but these are appropriate in an antique house. For collectors who insist upon the latter-day obsession with scale, these vary between "inch" and "three-quarter-inch." Among them are an asphaltum dressing table, in the upper right-hand bedroom and a thoroughly turned mahogany Victorian, étagère (or what-not) adorned with the most miniscule of Vienna bronze animals, in the parlor. There is also a sewing machine, of an early and rare style, with the head placed vertically before the operator rather than, as later, horizontally.

It was decided (by me) to ignore the shop possibility, whatever the big bays suggested, on the ground floor, in favor of a thoroughly furnished house.

"A REALLY SPLENDID MANSION" BY LINES BROS.

In their 1909-10 catalogue, England's Lines Bros. referred to this relatively modest house as "A really splendid mansion, elaborately fitted up inside and out." Though this may appear to be something of an over-statement, this is indeed a charming house, justifiably popular, to judge by the fairly numerous examples which have been found.

Evaline Sole, a previous editor of *International Dolls' House News*, wrote me, in a scholarly 1981 letter: "The Lines Bros. had to register some of their designs in 1909 to protect them from being copied—presumably by foreign competitors who would have the advantage of cheaper labor, materials or taxation." Actually, therefore, this design may be earlier than 1909.

CA. 1909. HEIGHT: 32" WIDTH: 33"

The façade leaves no spindle unturned or bracket uncut. The pair of two-story bays which flank the front door below and the casement windows above, lead to a pair of matching turrets crowned like coronets with spindled balconies—these in turn flanked by a pair of chimneys. Each chimney contains two chimney pots,[1] presumably to accommodate eight fireplaces (in a four-room house with staircase halls!) Perhaps we may pretend that the other four fireplaces are in the attic which, by the way, is sealed charmingly with glazed windows within elaborately lithographed tin frames. (This feature appears to be lacking in the 1909–10 catalogue illustration where bracketed wood windows match the others.) These contain the same green-lithographed paper Venetian blinds which are to be seen at most of the windows. (A few have been replaced and a few are missing.) All windows are arched and bracketed, except for the casement pair with its spindled balcony. The catalogue refers to the casement as a "French window."

The façade swings open on hinges—two-thirds to the left. The interior bays formed by the four

1. These were evidently lost. When the house was acquired, it was otherwise in excellent condition. These have been replaced.

SOFT-LEAD GOTHIC SHELVES
WITH MOLDED "OBJECTS"

exterior bay windows permit a few pieces of furniture in each, offering an interior appeal which complements the irresistible exterior. All floors, including the kitchen, have their original paper parquet, and the walls their original attractive papers.

The catalogue alludes to "staircase, doors to rooms and curtains." The staircase has a modest balustrade—no turned spindles as on the exterior—and has been supplied by me with paisley stair carpet. The fireplaces—chimneypieces, as they'd be referred to in their native land—are also modest, but contain metal grates. The one in the kitchen is wider.

The house has been furnished with a mixture of turn-of-the-century pieces, some earlier, such as an unusual asphaltum dressing table in one of the two bedrooms and a matching grandfather clock on the landing. "Yellow cherry" by Schneegass in the other has been supplemented by a French half-tester bed, nicely dressed with its original fittings.

Accessories include a large family of bisque pugs, a mother and five pups. (This was a German series of which I've seen at least six breeds represented.)

ASPHALTUM DRESSING TABLE

AN ENGLISH "HOBBIES" HOUSE

A few years ago, in a Maine antiques mall, I looked across a wide staircase and saw a vision on the other side. I was glad I'd taken the trouble to climb to the third floor. What I saw was the beguiling dolls' house shown herewith.

The style was unmistakably English, but I didn't realize till Faith Eaton's *Ultimate Dolls' House Book*[1] appeared with a similar but not identical model that this was not a commercially made house. As she related, it was built from plans published in a monthly magazine—*Hobbies* of Dereham, England, ca. 1926.

Then, going through files of *International Dolls' House News*, other versions began to sur-

1. *The Ultimate Dolls' House Book*, Faith Eaton. Dorling Kindersley, 1994

CA. 1926.
EXTERIOR HEIGHT: 22 3/4"
WIDTH: 24"

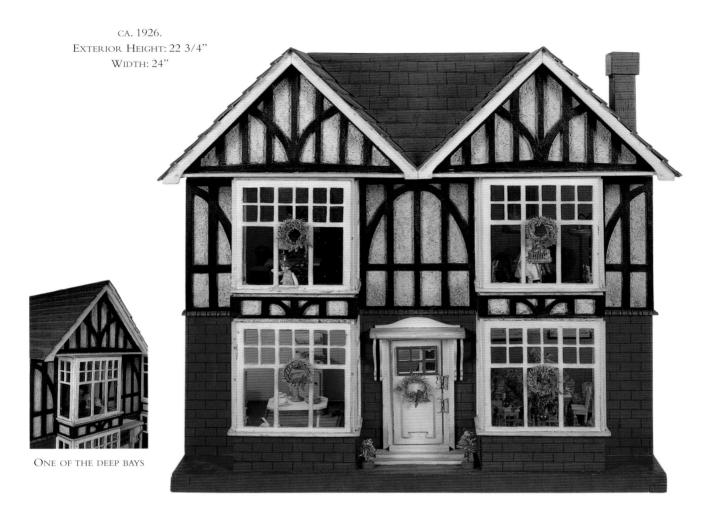

ONE OF THE DEEP BAYS

face: one is in the possession of Nick Forder, Editor of I.D.H.N.[1] where it was illustrated in a 1998 issue. He had acquired it ten years before from its original owner, to whom it had been given in 1935. This lacks interior stairs but has the addition of an attractive garage wing. This house has the original furniture, also made from *Hobbies* plans. Another, on display at Angel's Attic, in Santa Monica, diverges in various ways from the original plan, but has the unusual addition of a conservatory in lieu of the Forder's garage.

There are modest variations between Faith Eaton's house and my own. The measurements and details are almost identical. There are two chimneys rather than one on Faith Eaton's roof. The door and other wood trim are dark varnished rather than in the cream paint to be seen here. The finish on the half-timbering appears to be similar.

The four glazed bay windows, two inches in depth, give the house a great deal of its character and charm. I cannot resist mentioning the bottom of the house, not usually viewable. This specifically indicates that the base was fashioned from a crate which once contained "Pure India Tea."

All of these houses open from the back. The four rooms, bisected by staircase halls, up and down, are to be found in most of the examples which have surfaced (omitted entirely from one). A small partition has been added to the upstairs

1. *I.D.H.N.* offered the history of the company in a 1992 issue, relating that *The Hobbies Weekly* commenced publication in 1895 and, by 1935, the firm was advertising "27 Designs for House and Furniture."

TREE WITH ORIGINAL
METAL ORNAMENTS
INCLUDING A PISTOL!

RARE CELLULOID FURNITURE, MAKER UNKNOWN

hall in the Eaton house, allowing for a miniscule bath, and for a broom closet under the stairs. In our own version, there is instead hall space for a few pieces of furniture both upstairs and down.

The walls are painted, in contrast to the wall-papers in the Eaton house. The latter has period lighting. When found, our house had none. Here, "radio lights" have been supplied.[1]

An effort has been made to furnish the house with English pieces of the proper period. A Triang chair and fire screen bearing the familiar orange-brown-white cotton print may be seen in the living room. A liberty has been taken with respect to fourteen pieces of rare, "mystery" celluloid furniture which seem of the right vintage, though possibly too early for this house but which seem comfortable here. Their vintage may pre-date the house—I suspect them of an early "twentyish" origin—possibly even a late "teenish." An English collector who is a member of a plastics society in Britain, and who saw them while this compilation

was in progress, had never encountered them previously. Among them, all in a restrained arts and crafts mode, include a desk and chair, a piano with bench, a work table with lift-top, a hall stand with mirror above, a book-case, and a table and chairs. All are in the ivory celluloid I associate with a dresser set of the 'twenties I remember from my childhood. Black keys on the piano and a black face with white numerals on the tall case clock are the only "color."

A few German accessories, lamps, and an early radio with separate aerial and loudspeaker mingle with a few French chairs by Simon and Rivollet and the mysterious Arts and Crafts celluloid.

1. As recorded elsewhere, a number of years ago this writer, having become bored with Christmas lights found in many early twentieth century dolls' houses, and knowing nothing about electricity, stumbled upon the lights which were used to illuminate radio dials. These are unobtrusive, long lasting and give off little heat.

PART IV

EUROPEAN HOUSES: MANSIONS,

VILLAS, AND COTTAGES

THE "QUEEN ANNE" MANSION

This Edwardian mansion, in the "Queen Anne" style, surrounded by porches, surmounted by turrets and spires, and possessing a formidable assortment of windows of every shape and size, is a substantial piece of gingerbread of the genre to be found in full-size, at the turn of the century, in many an upscale American suburb.

Of lithographed paper-on-wood, it was commercially made in Germany for the American market by Christian Hacker, a Nuremberg firm

MÄRKLIN
FIREPLACE

BUST ON
PEDESTAL

LATE NINETENTH CENTURY. HEIGHT: 46" BASE: 37" X 31" DEEP

HALL WITH UNUSUAL STAIRCASE

which did not stint on elaboration. The resulting extravagances are much coveted by collectors.

This example, one of the largest, was rescued in pieces in 1962 by a pioneer Illinois collector. The interior was in good condition with its original wallpapers mercifully intact and she took pleasure in furnishing the shell. The house contains only four rooms, on two floors, with a small attic space on the third, but, as its portrait suggests, it is embellished with every spindle, scroll, and spire the most intense admirer of Victorian gingerbread can long for.

When, a number of years ago, it was sent for consignment to The Museum Shop, the elaborate exterior was in such disarray that displaying it for resale seemed an almost insurmountable challenge. There were boxes of parts—columns which had been misguidedly gilded, and multitudinous bits and pieces—an unintentional jigsaw puzzle.

It was difficult to display even for consignment, and the Museum ultimately purchased this mélange and had it restored. A collaboration between the writer and Janis Ernst, a woman of great patience and developing skills (who is not an antiquarian and had never before restored an antique dolls' house), resulted in the quite elegant house pictured. Brass filigree balustrading from the porches to the turrets embellishes the exterior as well as an imposing golden oak staircase in the hall. The brass balustrade above the pedimented entrance frames a balcony which permits the family to take in a breath of fresh air on a warm evening, or to watch a (small) parade, should one be passing. A brass balustrade encircles the porch and matches the brass railings of the exterior staircase.

Although the original wallpaper survived, the draperies were missing. A smaller German house of related vintage provided the pattern and style. Another survivor, mercifully, was the staircase hall,

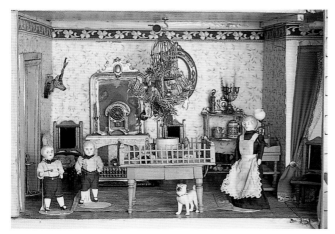

its embossed brass balustrade and matching embellishments in almost mint condition. This hall is possibly the ultimate of dolls' house vestibules. The winding staircase fills the width of the small room, with turned columns framing a built-in projection which serves as a table-top beneath its curve. Embossed brass medallions trim this projection and the columns. A recessed, wooden-bracketed brass embossed strip[1] crowns this extraordinary staircase hall.

Schneegass furniture, described in the firm's catalogue as "yellow cherry," but meant no doubt to resemble the fashionable golden oak of the period, has been provided throughout. In the bedroom, a bed with its original bedding and half tester, is an exception.

An "important" "ormolu" Märklin fireplace with its rare original overmantel mirror has been placed in the dining-room. A hall lamp with its single blown glass white globe hangs in the hall. The dining-room gasolier is by Märklin. (The maker of the parlor chandelier is unknown.) The mirrored ormolu brass étagère displays part of a collection of infinitesimal Vienna bronzes (Golliwogs, penny woodens—here penny bronzes!) from the illustrations of Florence Upton's classic tales. These were found in a London antiques shop many years ago.

An elegant Edwardian family, their servants, and pets are in residence. The pug dog, an inevitable breed for the period, is to be found in many of the houses in this collection, along with innumerable cats.

"Ormolu" étagère
with Golliwogs

1. Similar strips crown the roof line.

A Moorish Revival Shell (with a Swan Gazebo)

Inasmuch as this eclectic piece of Victorian architecture is a shell, withal a complex and sizeable shell, it nearly failed to be included in these pages.

There are neither floors nor rooms within, and it is visibly in need of extensive renovations. What was "renovated"—exquisitely restored[1]— is the gazebo which accompanied it. The gazebo was in pieces—the delicately carved swans totally disengaged from one another. As restored, the swans preen their feathers within the glistening confines of an antique bell jar, on the writer's glazed porch where morning light heightens their presence as part of a small work of art. The "shell," therefore, is shown in the small illustration. The gazebo, all of fifteen inches in height, looms larger.

A number of years ago, I found this most rococo assemblage in a suburban Maryland antiques shop. The only history obtainable was that it had been acquired from a Baltimore dealer who said it had come from France. It had been slathered with green paint, and some gilt, but all four sides are so highly detailed that the eye almost fails to see such defects. There are multitudinous windows, many of stained or frosted glass. Some of them, like the entrance door, are asymmetrical, others are circular or oval, but all are adorned with gingerbread carving, attesting to the skill as well as the patience of an energetic craftsman.

All of this is surmounted by a clock tower with an onion turret not unlike the turret on St. Basil's Cathedral in Moscow. A very similar turret was viewable for generations on a Victorian house in Washington, D.C.

The back and sides of this rococo revival confection are as elaborate as the façade. There is a removable lantern (raised glass skylight) on the roof, a balustrade of great elaboration (some of it

missing), projecting dormers with intricately carved lintels, balconies, rear doorways with removable sets of stairs...very little has been left uncarved or unadorned.

Two substantial flagpole holders may be found on the roof. If only the flags were present the nationality of this extraordinary piece might be confirmed.

VICTORIAN. HEIGHT: 43" WIDTH: 35"
GAZEBO: 15" TALL

---

1. By Janis Ernst, who patiently and perfectly reassembled the swans to ornithological perfection.

A MEDITERRANEAN VILLA

This appealing villa contains every feature a doll living by the Mediterranean Sea at the turn of the century would require. The extensive façade, with the stable at the left and a gated garden on the right, with built-in washing facilities as well as built-in outdoor plumbing in between, is comprehensive, to say the least. Looking upward, there are balustraded flights of stairs leading to balconies which, assuredly, provide splendid sea views.

Unlike the Spanish house, shown on page 228, which is believed to be a one-of-a-kind (or a "one-off" as is more tersely said in Britain), this piece undoubtedly is commercially made, though I confess never to having seen another, or anything remotely like it. It is satisfying that a Barcelona shop label remains on the back. We may not know who manufactured this fascinating piece, but we do know who sold it. [1]

Whether or not it was made in Germany for the Spanish market must be a matter of conjecture. The small classroom on page 377 also bears a label in Spanish. Other old dolls' houses have been known to come from Barcelona, a vast commercial center which is recognized, with its seacoast location, as a hub, with "the merchant shipping of a busy port." [2]

The central portion of the façade lifts off to reveal the four principal rooms—two up and two down. Louvered windows on this central section, and other details—door frames, ceiling medallions and such—are printed on paper affixed to the

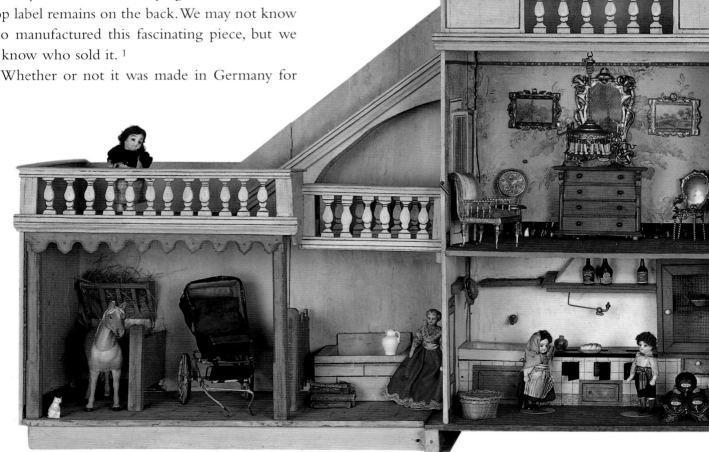

1. Unfortunately, because this lengthy house is difficult to move and was photographed *in situ,* there has been no recent opportunity to read this label.
2. *Encyclopaedia Britannica.*

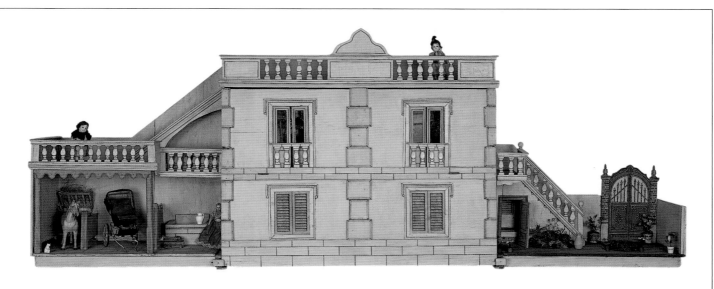

CA. 1890.
EXTERIOR
HEIGHT: 25 1/2"
WIDTH: 67 1/2"

frame. Other details, such as the balusters and the handsome brick-columned garden gate appear to be hand-painted.

There is a pond in the garden at the right encircled with simple greenery which blends with the other plantings, obviously original. (The Vienna bronze potted flowers, always useful in dolls' houses, have been added.) Opening off the garden is the built-in outhouse, and in the hayloft on the left side of the house, there is hay in the rack. (A rare candy-box horse is also an addition.) In the adjoining segment, a pitcher rests on the enclosed well, just filled perhaps by the household member who lingers there.

No furniture came with the villa, but fortuitously, at about the time it came into the collection, I was offered the small family collection of dolls' house pieces by a young Colombian concert pianist. Much of the collection was out-of-scale pottery, but other pieces such as the beaded chandeliers, though perhaps a bit late for the house, lent themselves attractively to these rooms. One of the chandeliers appears to be transitional. A small early electric light bulb in the center is supplemented by four candle arms into which small imitation bulbs have been inserted, suggesting that identical chandeliers were made earlier for candles.

An unusual parlor set of imitation-grained cardboard may be seen in the parlor. There are religious pictures and ornaments in the rooms appropriate to a country predominantly Catholic.

The kitchen is of special interest. What appears to be an open gas jet is suspended from the wall. A substantial cupboard for storing food is built-in along with the sink and the range below.

I'm sure there must be a name (Spanish) for the fitted beverage stand with its triple kegs, [1] and I long to know what it is.

THE KITCHEN REVEALS A GAS JET ABOVE THE OVEN

CHANDELIER MADE IN GERMANY FOR THE SPANISH MARKET

1. There is a similar one in the Spanish house, shown on page 228.

A SEASIDE VILLA

When it first loomed on the miniature horizon, the house alone was sufficiently captivating, a French seaside villa which recalled, to admirers of Jacques Tati, *M. Hulot's Holiday*. Appealingly absurd with its outsize but windowless turret,[1] crowning a steeply gabled roof, and haphazardly punctuated by two rather foolish chimneys and a gilt spire, the only thing missing appeared to be the seaside itself.

It was true that the small house had everything else—even its original furniture—still sewn in. I assumed the French seaside villa was made in

CA. 1900. HEIGHT: 34" (PLUS 4 1/2" SPIRE)
WIDTH: (BASE): 19 5/8"

1. This is removable, evidently for packing.

France.[1] Then, in recent years, other dolls' house detectives got to work, most particularly Evelyn Ackerman, with her splendid book about Gottschalk. I did not give in easily, but ultimately she convinced me—this "French" villa with sewn-in-furniture was indeed made in Germany—a "blue roof" by Gottschalk—for the French market. This type of villa has even been dubbed "Deauville" by collectors, in deference to its similarity to houses in the celebrated seaside resort.

What is not yet certain is whether or not the furniture is indeed French, added when the house

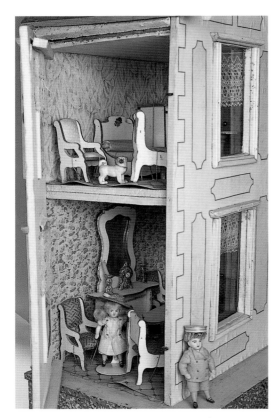

FURNITURE IS STILL SEWN IN!

(and/or room) was shipped to Paris. Until this proof is offered, I shall consider the furniture of French manufacture (see page 251, postscript).

In the past, dolls' house furniture, like other small objects, often was artfully arranged in paper lace-edged boxes and sewn into place. Occasionally today one makes a lucky find, and comes across old dolls' house furniture or accessories still fastened into their original boxes, but years ago, when this house was acquired, I had never before heard of furniture so fastened into a dolls' house. To learn of such a delight might have seemed sufficiently rewarding; to see it (and to acquire it) seemed almost miraculous.

Beneath the blue roof, and within the pale yellow exterior walls on which lavender and aquamarine panels are engagingly lithographed, the sides of the slender house swing open to reveal four rooms containing a total of seventeen pieces of furniture. This is the white-painted furniture so often seen, in various grades and vintages, in French doll rooms. The customary gilt-paper edging outlines the pieces, and the usual, beguiling embossed floral scraps are affixed to table tops, headboards, and other straight surfaces.

The furniture in these four rooms is set off by wallpapers and cardboard "tiled" floors. Pink upholstered chairs and bedding in the bedroom are delightful against a green-and-yellow floral pattern and a red, white, and blue "tiled" floor. The bedroom furniture, incidentally, is so complete that two rooms are required to contain it: the upper-left-hand room with bed, armchair, side chair, round pedestal table, and wardrobe, and the downstairs entrance hall with two more chairs and a dressing table.

With this one exception, the furniture is logically placed, even though it was not expected to remain as, with more luck, it may, till the end of

---

1. In their beautiful book, *The Golden Age of Toys*, 1967, Jac Remise and Jean Fondin, illustrate a row of Gottschalk and Hacker houses, with the caption declaring that "All of them are French." Assuming that this conclusion was reached by studying French toy catalogues, I presumed to say years ago, when writing about similar houses, that they were "probably French."

time. A mirrored fireplace, two armchairs, two side chairs (red-upholstered), and a shaped oval table are in the parlor which is papered in a perfectly scaled pattern of lilacs and green leaves; in an upstairs sitting-room are a sofa and chair upholstered in pale green with a four-legged plant stand. (The chairs are 3 1/4" high.) Red flowers sprout from the mossy vegetation always found in these "ferneries," although sometimes only shreds remain.

As the 1897 French catalogue illustration, shown below, indicates, this type of furniture was referred to as "Louis XVI." The chairs and sofas in the house are of the identical shape and style, but the two tables in the house, one round and one oval (with "turtle" turnings) have more interesting pedestal bases than those shown in the catalogue. A bedroom with a similar type of table, again with the familiar chairs, is shown on page 258.

The rooms are connected on each of the two floors by interior doors which are of lithographed paper-on-wood. The latter has, as its picture shows, the typical Gottschalk metal knob. Identical lace curtains are stretched across the upper halves of the glass windows.

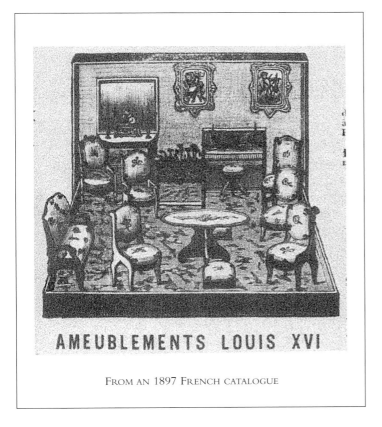

FROM AN 1897 FRENCH CATALOGUE

UNUSUAL MÄRKLIN LAMP
MAY BE LIGHTED WITH "SPIRIT"

A "BLUE-ROOF" GOTTSCHALK

This substantial "blue-roof" Gottschalk was found about forty years ago on the island of Martha's Vineyard. When it was plunked down on a grassy spot and its picture taken, it looked at home despite its Teutonic origin.

With double chimney pots on its two chimneys, half-timbering under the eaves, a third story dormer, and with metal-railed front porch and second-floor balcony, it is a proper piece of German gingerbread and a substantial example of Gottschalk's "blue-roof" genre. All the windows on the front are glazed, revealing their original lace-edged, rose (downstairs) and cream (upstairs) draperies.

The windows on the sides and all other details, except for the wooden exterior and interior doors, and the window and door frames, are of lithographed paper-on-wood. Also printed are the

EARLY 20TH CENTURY.
HEIGHT: 27 3/4" (PLUS CHIMNEYS)[1]
BASE: 26" x 14 1/2"

1. Rare chimney sweep below!

cellar windows on the base.

On this model, the sides of the house swing open to give access to the four rooms. The right-hand pair offers a staircase with a metal railing. The room to which the staircase rises is papered in blue tile, suggesting a sizeable bathroom. The other three rooms are papered with the customary, attractive, Gottschalk bordered wallpaper panels.

In Evelyn Ackerman's excellent book, *The Genius of Moritz Gottschalk*,[1] two smaller but similar houses are illustrated. One opens, as this one does, at the sides; the other opens from the front. However, neither contains the interior staircase such as the one to be seen here, and on both, the dormer detail is lithographed. Here the half-timbering is three-dimensional, of heavy card painted dark brown and applied to the white-painted wood surface. Clearly, this is a more deluxe model. The penciled number on the bottom of the house (for true blue-and-red-roof aficionados) is "3592." The numbers on the houses in the Ackerman book are close: "3580" and "3583." There is approximately a six-inch difference in height between these and "3592."

All three are "blue-roof." "Sometime before World War I, perhaps as early as 1910," according to Mrs. Ackerman, "the roof color of the Gottschalk doll houses changed from blue to red."

The furniture to be seen inside the right-hand wing is, of course, the Gottschalk pressed cardboard furniture. The rare Gottschalk chimney sweep has been added to the exterior.

INTERIOR OF ONE SIDE SHOWING STAIRCASE

PHOTOGRAPHED AS FOUND ON MARTHA'S VINEYARD

A FAMILY IN RESIDENCE

1. Goldhorse Publishing, 1994

THREE MODEST "BLUE ROOFS"

The two smaller Gottschalk "blue roofs" feature identical lithography in two sizes. The tiny one is 10 1/2" tall plus chimneys and retains its original front steps. Both blue wooden rooftops are dominated by projecting dormers of heavy card which look as though they've been chewed by a family dog. (Two different dogs. The houses were found at different times.)

The "big" house is more deluxe than the other two and may be seen in the Cieslik 1907 archive. (Numerically inclined collectors may note that it is #4237.) Though the front door is lithographed and does not open, all but one of the windows are glazed and retain their original lace curtains. There is an upstairs porch, grander than the small sloping roof over the downstairs porch of each of the others. The green Gottschalk fence has been added.

All three of the houses contain typical Gottschalk wallpapers applied in panels and, on each of the two floors, a different floor paper is featured.

LARGEST: HEIGHT: 17 1/2" (PLUS CHIMNEY) BASE: 12" x 8"

SMALLEST:
HEIGHT: 10 1/2" (PLUS CHIMNEYS)
WIDTH 7 1/2"

HEIGHT: 13 1/2" (PLUS CHIMNEYS)
BASE: 7 1/4" X 5"

TWO TRANSITIONAL GOTTSCHALKS

The Gottschalk houses which have neither the earlier "blue roof" nor the later "red roof" are referred to as transitional—with diaper-patterned lithographed paper substituting for paint on some, including this example, which may be found in the Cieslik-Gottschalk archive. Nearly everything opens!—the lower half of the façade, the lower half of one side, the upstairs window, and of course, the front door. Even the turret is removable, should one wish to launder the lace curtain within.

The example shown contains its original, lace-edged rose cotton draperies and/or lace curtains. Even most of the painted muntins, usually obliterated by time, are still to be seen on the biggest of the glazed windows. The original Gottschalk wall-

CIESLIK CATALOGUE ILLUSTRATION,
CA. 1908

CA. 1908.
HEIGHT: 18"
WIDTH: 14"

papers, in the firm's smaller scale, are also intact. The complexity of the roofline with its turret and gables is, in such a small house, impressive. (The finial on the turret has been replaced.) Pieces of Gottschalk furniture in the smallest Gottschalk scale have been provided upstairs and down.

The diminutive gambrel-roofed specimen may

be seen in the 1910 section of the Cieslik-Gottschalk archive. This has a roof painted neither blue nor red, but in an ochre shade.

The original Gottschalk fence (with some finials replaced) adds considerably to its charm, as does the smallest-scale Gottschalk furniture which survived with it these many years.

CIESLIK CATALOGUE ILLUSTRATION, 1910

INTERIOR OF HOUSE BELOW

CA. 1910. HEIGHT: 10 1/2" (PLUS CHIMNEY)
BASE: 9" X 9 1/2"

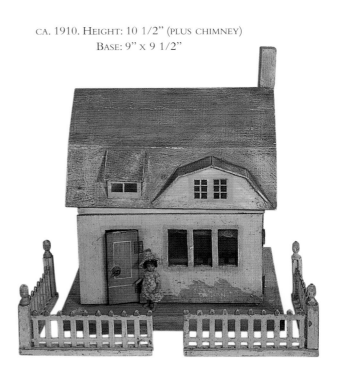

A CASA FROM SPAIN

For years I harbored the impression that this very Spanish casa was made in Germany for the Spanish market.

This was despite the written opinion of the late Colonel Donald Mitchell, the original purchaser, that it was "made by someone with considerable doll house experience and artistic ability." Inasmuch as he restored the house, and many other dolls' houses, the Colonel was undoubtedly better qualified than I to recognize a one-of-a-kind house when he saw one.

CA. 1900. EXTERIOR HEIGHT: 30 1/2" (INCLUDING CHIMNEY)
WIDTH: 28 1/2" (PLUS BAYS)

In a small paperback published in 1980,[1] Colonel Mitchell points out that "the tiles were painstakingly carved into the plank roof" and that "the fancy trim (including wooden tassels) and the wallpaper (are) in distinct Spanish taste." He states that he bought the house in El Rostro, "Madrid's famous flea market, so that its origins can never be traced." On the other hand, when years later we met, (I did not acquire the house directly from the Mitchells) the Colonel mentioned that it, he was told, had been in the Franco family, which is name-dropping of a not particularly informative

1. *Doll Houses. Past and Present*, by Donald and Helene Mitchell. Collector Books. Paducah, Kentucky.

order—but interesting.

Whatever its history, it is rare, and it is exuberant, both inside and out, as its pictures suggest. A confection of pink brick with green frosted-glass glittering behind Moorish-styled bays painted cream (as in whipped), the only solemn notes in color or style are the dark brown double entrance doors and the matching cornice beneath a roof of dark gray "tile," with a curious balustrade in a sort of grape pattern (and a grape color).[1] Those doors which, in their solidity, would do credit to a moated castle, were set into a foundation with spattered dark gray rustication which matches the coigning. Dormer windows at each side of the roof contain the same frosted green glass to be found below, and the central dormer contains a clock. The latter is an actual watch face with moveable hands, which, unless it was added, further suggests that the house was handmade. Its dormer is ornamented with elaborate jig-sawed trim.

The hinged front divides to reveal four rooms of a similarly motley aspect, and unusual architectural elements of their own. As the illustration indicates, the decorative arches which overhang the two lower rooms are supported by columns, and the two upper ones, balustraded in the manner of the early German houses, feature a wooden swag (with wooden tassels) which has no counterpart known to me in miniature or in full size. The bays on the sides of the house are sham and do not open into

1. The left-half of the carved grapelike decoration had to be replaced by Colonel Mitchell and the exterior paint, he wrote, "had to be freshened up to what looked like the typically Spanish color it had been."

the rooms, but the ones on the façade do, and the nooks they form hold small pieces of furniture.

It is largely the wallpapers in the four rooms, and the W. C.[1] tucked into a small cubicle in the kitchen, one step up, with a workable door, which most imply a manufactured piece. Two small windows, wallpaper-framed, are above the door. A floral-patterned paper in the bedroom competes horticulturally with the floral-patterned furniture, but the most remarkable paper is to be found in the adjoining room. In luscious colors, above a papered dado, there are lushly lithographed murals, on the three walls, of children attending what appears to be a very elegant birthday party—in a velvet-curtained room of considerable opulence. Cutout dancing figures, similarly colorful, are applied to the ceiling.

Later, when I met the Mitchells, they told me that the house was empty when they received it. In his book, the Colonel related: "Helene furnished it with dozens of Spanish miniatures, mostly purchased from sidewalk stalls which line the streets of Madrid at Christmas time…These items were not necessarily old. They were just Spanish. Spain and its customs had changed little in several hundred years. All pieces were colorful and exciting and had the feel of the country."

Among these is the bedroom set, a decided crimson, thickly but attractively hand-painted (almost encrusted) with floral sprays. There is one of the traditional stands with three kegs of wine (labeled "Blanco," "Tinto," and "Solera" which appear to be a standard furnishing in a Spanish house of the period. Note: A similar but not identical version is in the house with the Barcelona shop label, see page 216. There is a small wooden casket (for jewels?), a miniature hurdy-gurdy, and castanets….

I've taken the liberty of adding some pieces which are unquestionably antique and almost unquestionably Spanish. These include several unusual dolls (illustrated) and a pair of pictures—Señoritas (in oval frames) which are *surely* Señoritas, or Señoras, page 229.

LUSHLY LITHOGRAPHED MURALS

SPICE CHEST

PERSONAGES GUARDING SPIRITS!

1. It is the overhead tank of this fixture, as well as the style of the wallpapers, which suggest a turn-of-the-century date for the house.

A Beguiling Hacker House

hen this house, rather modest in size, was acquired, many moons ago, I was entranced by the magnificent shop label affixed to the red lithographed brick on its back, and probably didn't notice the Christian Hacker stamp on the bottom. Even if I had, I'd have had no idea in those days, that the logo represented a German maker. The house looked French and the label of "Au Paradis Des Enfants," suggested a French origin.

The small structure was found in almost mint condition. The lace curtains and the satin draperies still appear pristine, and so does the bedroom suite which came, literally, with the second story. The first floor was unfurnished. The lithographed paper-on-wood "tile" roof, typical of Hacker houses, lifts off, and the two stories similarly separate. The bedroom ceiling is charmingly decorated with decals—a delicate ceiling medallion with matching corner pieces.

The upper and lower sections of the façade swing open on hinges, offering two additional options for entering the house. The gilt front door handle and the knocker still glisten. The knocker consists of a clever mechanism which actually per-

CA. 1900. GERMAN. HEIGHT: 19 1/2" WIDTH: 16 1/2"

mits it to knock. Most of the original velvet flowers are still intact in the shallow window box under the four second-story windows.

The bedroom suite, unpainted or stained, is by Schneegass in a small-scale, perfect for the room. The wardrobe and the pier mirror (referred to as a trumeau in the Schneegass 1914 catalogue) bear gilt metal ornamentation in the Jugendstil style. A delicate lace spread over a rose mattress, possibly added by the original owner, matches the rose draperies (with their lace under-curtains) and the

upholstery on the five chairs.

The dazzling label offers a panoramic view of the celebrated toy store as it must have appeared in the 1880's. The Parisian streetscape, with the imposing toy establishment in the background, features horse-drawn carriages, ladies in bustles—even a gentleman riding a penny-farthing bicycle. It is probable that this house is later than the label, and that the latter was re-printed, possibly, over a period of several decades.

UPSTAIRS ROOM

SIZEABLE LABEL ON BACK

A GOTTSCHALK "RED-ROOF" WITH GARDEN

Among the multitudinous houses, stables, and related toys made by Gottschalk of Marienberg, this "red-roof" bungalow is especially beguiling.

With customary Gottschalk ingenuity, a portion of the hinged wooden façade lowers into a garden complete with fence and gate (of the makers' trademark white-pasteboard).

Within the modest width of 25 1/2 inches, the maker has managed to include: (1) a pleasant "all-purpose" room on the ground floor, with a pair of curtained windows and an ornamental staircase, (2) a hinged segment with triple window on the second floor, (3) two porches (one with balcony above), and (4) that garden.

The garden itself is a production, with two well-defined raised wooden flowerbeds. The beds are green—the flowers and accessories to be added. The additions here include potted plants and a stone sundial in the center. A baby in a pram is out for an airing.

In short, a great deal goes on beneath the

EARLY 20TH CENTURY. HEIGHT: 16 1/2" WIDTH: 25 1/2"

swirling gabled roof.

I must confess that I added the Gottschalk furniture to the house years before I knew it was
Gottschalk. It just seemed right and I found out
why: it is, of course, the small-scaled Gottschalk.

The two ladies with aprons and the gentleman,
Gottschalk figures, are exceedingly rare.

RARE SMALL GOTTSCHALK FURNITURE AND FIGURES

RARE GOTTSCHALK CRIB

MORE FROM THE
CIESLIK ARCHIVE,
1914–15

THE BOBLINGEN COLLECTION

In the 1980's a dedicated Museum staffer (and a good friend) came across, in an antiques publication, an ad for a "Miniature doll house, dolls, and furnishings."

This was no ordinary collection. A catalogue was available. When it arrived, the carefully typed listings, with some somewhat blurry black-and-white photographs, specified "771 pieces" and stated that they "originated with a wealthy family near Boblingen,[1] Germany," adding that the family

FURNISHINGS.
GERMANY. 1890's TO 1918.
HEIGHT: 36" WIDTH: 60"

1. This was spelled Boblinger in the catalogue, with an "r" rather than an "n," but an atlas reveals only "Boblingen," near Heidelberg.

name had been lost, but that "the father of the family had traveled extensively at the turn of the century and added to the collection for his daughters."

There was only one remaining bit of background information, presumably furnished by the Mississippi antiques dealer "who purchased it from another dealer in Boblingen in the 1950's." This asserted that "since the dolls served two generations, it is surmised conservatively that most of the pieces were from the 1890's. They were stored in boxes with 1918 newspapers, so some of the pieces came from the first two decades of this century."

Actually, more of the collection, when it arrived, appeared to be from the 1918 period.

However, this was a transitional time and many of the furnishings and the dolls had been made without significant changes, some for more than a decade.[1] Whatever their date of origin, they were in remarkably pristine condition, and it appeared that "the daughters" had played with them very carefully or not at all, and the Mississippi antique dealer had cherished them in the thirty years or so they were in her possession.

The dolls' house dolls, remarkably, remained in their original boxes. (These boxes, alas, reveal no maker's label.)

In any case, the "doll house" was not precisely a dolls' house. The catalogue showed a pair of rooms, stacked upon the kitchen (not shown) and scullery, both of approximately the same width—nearly 41 inches. A smaller room, 17" wide, was placed above those. It hasn't been possible to identify the maker of the kitchen, but the rooms, with their charming balconied and windowed alcoves (one step up) were clearly by Gottschalk.

It was impossible to contain the sizable collection in these rooms, and a number of them have been placed in a house with no façade, but with appealing dolls' house wallpapers and six spacious rooms, shown on previous page. One can only guess where this house, acquired years ago from a Washington D.C. collector, originated. It appears to have been made by a competent carpenter and is, in other words, a "one-off" to employ the useful British term.

One might write an entire book about this

A PAIR OF ROOMS WHICH ACCOMPANIED THE FURNISHINGS

1. A kitchen illustrated in the 1894 F.A.O. Schwarz catalogue was still included in 1918!

collection, and with ease: each category is listed and each item under the category is described—with measurements. There is even a listing of "Miniature Liqueur Bottles," (14 of them) "all still with their original seals." Even the degree of evaporation is noted, for instance: "Amber square. Für Kinder Maggi Suppen u Speisen-Wurze' 2 1/2" tall. 4/5 full."

Much of the furniture, including two Gottschalk bedroom sets, is unexciting, but there is one rare Märklin parlor set upholstered over metal in maroon, buttoned and tasseled.[1] This and some of the dolls have been placed in houses in the Museum worthier of them than are the late

Gottschalk rooms. Re-reading the list, I made a small discovery: a bisque gentleman, 6 1/2" tall, with mustache, "in full dress with black tie, waist-coat, pink cummerbund, folded top hat under arm..." When I reread the latter, I paused. I had not realized till I reread the list that the gentleman had his folded top hat under his arm. Lo! Many years later—I investigated—it is still there! An exciting reminder of sartorial things past.

ROOM WITH WINDOWED ALCOVE. HEIGHT: 11" WIDTH: 17"

HEIGHT: 16 1/2" WIDTH: 40"

GENT IN TUB

1. See *Mystery House*, shown on page 101.

MT. VERNON–ON–THE–RHINE

Inasmuch as Gottschalk seemingly left very few structures of any description unbuilt, it is not entirely surprising that there's a Gottschalk version of Mount Vernon. The architectural references to the original are casual, but the intent is unmistakable. The result was either not very popular, or very few Mount Vernons were made. At least, I have never encountered another.

Where eight columns march across the façade

of the original, the toy version settles for six. There are, however, three dormers, two chimneys and a cupola which would look more at home on the Rhine than on the Potomac.

These words were written before I made an exciting discovery in the Cieslik-Gottschalk 1931 archive—Mt. Vernon, possibly a later improved version of the one in the museum. The round, rather fairy-tale turret has given way to a proper

GERMANY. EARLY 20TH CENTURY. HEIGHT (INCLUDING TURRET): 19" BASE 9" x 21"

cupola. The Museum's example is probably smaller. (No measurements for the catalogue specimen are available.) There are three doors on the façade in the catalogue version rather than one, and two additional dormers—one on each side.

The Encyclopaedia Britannica tells us that till after the Revolution, "The Mount Vernon house was a small edifice of eight rooms." The modest interior of the museum version contains four, anachronistically wallpapered and lace-curtained. It also contains an attic with the central dormer leading out, via a typical Gottschalk door (with typical metal knob) onto a balustraded roof, red, of course. The pierced pasteboard balustrade matches the typical Gottschalk pasteboard mullions of the windows. There are also interior doors between the rooms.

The identical side-porch with balcony above, to be found on numerous Gottschalk houses, was not resisted, however irrelevant, on Mount Vernon.

Unquestionably, a miniature George Washington would have slept here. In this modest version of his beloved residence, we're obliged to settle for him on his horse.

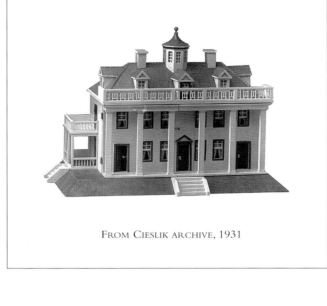

From Cieslik archive, 1931

A Furnished Gottschalk "Red Roof"

This substantial "red-roof" was acquired from its original owner more than forty years ago. It had been given to her, ca. 1921, in her childhood. It had been stored in a rather (then) murky section of Brooklyn and had proved to be difficult to "brighten," for want of a better word, but the wallpaper in several of the rooms is still lively, and the original furnishings and dolls happily survive.

An almost identical model is to be found in the 1923 Cieslik-Gottschalk archive of the remarkable Marienberg firm. The balustraded porches, front and side, are identical, and the third-story access is to be seen in two segments of the gabled roof. The window-boxes, set upon the balustrades, have, alas, lost their flowers, but are in the process of being replaced with vintage blossoms. The only visible difference is to be seen in the window sash—more complex in this 1921 example.

However, it is another contributing structure to the lengthy Gottschalk progression, and if one were willing to repaint it (which I've been reluctant to do), it would be an even more striking piece of miniature architecture than it presently is.

The furnishings which accompanied this house

CA. 1923.
EXTERIOR HEIGHT: (NOT INCLUDING CHIMNEY) 28 3/4"
WIDTH: 32"

provide a time capsule of what was made for dolls' houses—and full-sized houses—in the 1920's.

The furniture is Tootsietoy rather than Gottschalk—the one American contribution to the German house, accessories, and dolls. It is clear that a doting parent took pleasure in embellishing the metal pieces: chairs have been supplied with fabric seats—orange chiffon (another period reference) may be seen in the living-room, and even the metal lamp shades have been crowned with matching fabric.

There are many more pieces than can be shown—but the accessories are a tribute to the

Gerlach catalogue—the waffle iron, the steam iron (complete with plug), the lemonade set, the round fishbowl-on-stand....They are also a testament to the fact Shackman—the celebrated New York novelty firm (still in business)—was nearby.

Particularly satisfying is the presence of the bisque family, in their original clothes. There is one five-inch dolls' house doll—a maid. (The clothes of several others in this series were lamentably savaged, possibly by a young relative.) The five others, which include father, mother, and maid are the 3 1/2" painted bisques with Mary Jane pumps (even the father wears these pumps) but he and the others have appropriate bisque hair-dos. The maid retains her small feather duster.

FROM CIESLIK ARCHIVE, 1923

BAUHAUS BY GOTTSCHALK

When I acquired this very contemporary bit of architecture, and wrote about it in 1974[1], I referred to it as "The International Style."

"With its angular lines and austere practicalities," I declared, "It is the essence of what T. H. Robsjohn-Gibbings[2] termed 'Machine-for-Living Modern,' and a miniature example, seemingly, of The International Style." It is also international in the sense that it is European in origin, but crossed the ocean to the United States where an American child stuck pictures cut from 1920's Christmas cards, and even a Campbell Soup kid, to the walls, possibly to render them less austere.

When it was acquired, several decades ago, the box-like proportions, stucco walls, and metal railings of this commercially made house did not conceal the fact that it had to have been made by the same ingenious manufacturer who turned out the houses in the earlier and more elaborate series which may be seen, for example, on pages 222-223. The curious architectural style of this model, with two front doors, one on each wing of the projecting central section, does not disguise the recognizable pressed cardboard mullions in the unglazed windows and doors, nor the familiar embossed metal "butterfly" handles, both inside

CA. 1930. EXTERIOR. HEIGHT: (NOT INCLUDING CHIMNEY) 21 3/4" WIDTH: 32"

1. *Dolls' Houses in America.*
2. *Homes of the Brave,* Knopf. 1954

and out, which may be fastened when they are turned. There are also the lithographed paper floors in the familiar parquet patterns and the attention to detail which was ever the hallmark of—whoever else—the ubiquitous Marienberg firm of Gottschalk. It seemed more appropriate, therefore, to employ the German term Bauhaus for this small structure.

Inside, though the wallpapers are simpler, The International Style ceases—there is no flow of space, no "living area," but only the conventional number of dolls' house rooms, connected to one another by narrow doors. The "attention to detail" has provided a closet under the staircase, a proper one with a landing, and a "functional" balustrade of solid wood (no balusters to gather dust). But this staircase has a glory of its own, which may be clearly seen on the exterior, as well as inside. This is a "large" stained-glass window (11" by 4 5/8"), which illuminates the stairwell with the light which filters through its red and white geometric pattern. [1] (Frank Lloyd Wright, whose celebrated houses perhaps should not be mentioned in the same sentence with this modest effort, often included a stained-glass window even in his most austerely designed structures.)

Curiously, this glass window, and one next to it in the upper hall, are the only two glazed windows in the house which relate to it in style. The others, of the pressed-cardboard variety already alluded to, are, along with their lace curtains, clearly leftovers from Gottschalk dolls' houses of the past, possibly included as a concession to economy.

The uses of the six conventionally arranged rooms are designated by their wallpapers as well as by the floor coverings. The back of the house has been left open; on the left, the staircase occupies two rooms (up and down) spacious enough to furnish. On the right, tile papers on the walls and tile papers on the floors clearly define the kitchen and bath. In the middle of the house are its two principal rooms, connected by doors to the others. Along with the pictures stuck to the walls, a green wooden one-piece sink with two drain boards and a gilded faucet, probably by Schoenhut, lingers in the kitchen, and, by the same maker, a lavatory with a mirrored medicine chest remains in the bathroom.

THE STAINED-GLASS WINDOW

1. This painted pattern was alluringly applied with a stencil.

Part V

Chambers, Salons, and Such

THE GRADDON FAMILY PARLOR

Although many of the rooms described in near-by pages are French, France did not have a monopoly on the individual room. These papered walls are undoubtedly German. The room was purchased with furniture obviously too large for it and plainly not original, and this was replaced with "French Empire" which the writer originally assumed was French. When Vivien Greene, fresh from her discovery of toy furniture sample books in West Germany, visited the writer a number of years ago, she identified this set as made by the same Waltershausen firm which manufactured the imita-tion rosewood so beloved by those of us who col-lect.[1] Although this furniture is often found with printed embellishment, the set pictured is decorat-ed with metal, a beguiling imitation of ormolu. The legs on table, desk and pier mirror (the latter part-ly hidden by the table) are also of metal.

The set shown here has a history. Almost iden-tical to the one in the South Jersey dolls' house (page 34), this came from New Hampshire in its original paper-covered wooden box, on which fragments of the faded blue-printed paper remain. Inside the hinged lid someone has carefully printed "TOY

MID-NINETEENTH CENTURY. HEIGHT: 8" WIDTH: 17"

1. This was, of course, Schneegass, who later produced the "yellow cherry" furniture found in such quantity. It is now known that Kestner, the celebrated doll maker, also from Waltershausen, made similar furniture. This is owing to recent extensive research by Christiane Grafnitz of Germany.

FURNITURE 100 YEARS OLD—1850," and then handwritten, "in the Graddon family. Please take care of it."

It is interesting to note the few variations between this and a similar set in the South Jersey drawing room. Here the upholstery is of blue silk, where in the South Jersey it is a charming print of birds and flowers in coral, green and blue. The only two structural differences are in the desk which, otherwise identical, has here a green baize panel on its writing surface and a pull-out leaf in front. Since elaboration usually is to be found in earlier pieces, one suspects that this set is older than the more gaily upholstered version.

The carpet has been mounted on cardboard and laid (by a tackless, glue-less method!) over the rather severe, printed "tile" floor.

A Postscript: Concentrating, as I was, on the set of parlor furniture and its history, I did not include in the preceding paragraphs much about the room in which I placed it beyond asserting that it is "undoubtedly German."

Several months after these words were written, my eye happened to fall on a framed catalogue page, mid-nineteenth century, in the Museum, not far from the case containing this very room. Suddenly, after many years, I became aware that the room in the frame was strikingly similar to the room with the Graddon furniture. There were the similar projecting curved cornices over the windows and a wallpaper border of almost identical depth and even style. The window panes—the fenestration—is identical.

In any case, the catalogue illustration is marked "A7495 Nurnbg bei A. Kelb." As a collector of coincidences as well as dolls' houses, I was entranced. (I was not entranced by my dilatory perception process.)

TERRESTRIAL GLOBE,
GERMANY

FROM MID-NINETEENTH CENTURY GERMAN CATALOGUE

A MID-VICTORIAN WEDDING

This unusual parlor is difficult to classify. It is probably hand-crafted and possibly American. The furniture which was unmistakably made for it is hand-carved—the chairs and sofa with faded green velvet seats and backs. There is also a rectangular table, a plant stand (with built-in wooden pot) and a mirrored console table which, along with a strong gilded, bracketed cornice over the lithographed windows, is at the center of the room.

The lithography completely covers the three walls and gives the room its character. These panels are not textured like wallpaper—they are smooth—and informative—and have never been encountered by this collector in any other miniature room or catalogue, but assuredly were printed for the use of mid-Victorian dolls' house builders. The printed panels, two to each side, feature slender, neo-classical urns with delicate floral sprays and greenery, and each rests on a printed shelf with slender tassels suspended beneath. Printed under each of the windows is a bust on a substantial marble pedestal. Two pictures framed in dark wood hang above with printed cords reflecting how pictures were hung at the time. The pictures themselves are typically Victorian. One features a pair of monkey musicians in eighteenth century dress. In the other, a dog is barking at a cat. (The cat does not seem pleased.)

The brown suede pelmets over the windows are themselves a rarity. The scale of the room is somewhat larger than usual, and a larger than usual couple—who appear to be a bride and groom—have been chosen to occupy the premises. An early set of bisque cats, perhaps too whimsically, have been placed upon the extensive train of the lady's dress. Actually, there isn't much space anywhere else.

The parlor has a dream-like quality not found in the commercially-made rooms from Europe.

EARLY BISQUE CATS

CA. 1870. HEIGHT: 13" WIDTH: 26"

A Classical Revival Salon

The klismos chairs inspired by the mid-nineteenth century classical revival (one of several such revivals), and the piano with the black and white keys reversed suggest an early date for this salon in the French style by, as always, alas, an anonymous maker.

It is of interest that the dotted silk crimson fabric on the sofa and chairs, which appears to be original, matches that of the valances hanging from the carved wooden cornices. The gilt paper trim usually seen in such abundance on French-style furniture is limited to a highly embossed oval on the terminus of each sofa arm, and to a narrow pointed striping which binds the upholstery on the three matching pieces. The piano stool contains a wood swivel for raising and lowering the seat. The piano itself is thoroughly gilt—printed in Boule-style motifs on its paper rosewood surface.

The unusual and early chandelier, of heavy twisted copper wire, is an addition, as is the glass-eyed, swivel-necked, Napoleonic-style personage in his tricorne.

A Postscript: At the zero hour, just as these pages were going to press, the "anonymous maker" was discovered to be no longer anonymous and decidedly French! Indeed, there is more than one—with documentation to prove their identity. Through the courtesy of Florence Theriault, editor of *The Encyclopedia of French Dolls, Vol 1,*[1] by Francois and Daniele Theimer, 2003, illustrations conclusively prove that French makers include Louis Badeuille, Victor Francois Bolant, and Choumer & Collet, all of Paris (with addresses given). Pieces identical to ones shown in this section are illustrated. Presumably others will be found in Volume II, not issued in time for this summary.

CA. 1850. HEIGHT: 10 3/4" WIDTH: 22"

1. Gold Horse Publishing.

An Early Louis XVI Parlor

This folding parlor contains virtually the same Louis XVI furniture to be seen in the large-scaled "Paris Salon" shown on next page.

There are six armchairs—no sides—and there are more curlicues on these arms than on the larger-scaled suite, but there is the same deep rose silk upholstery outlined in gilt paper which continues to glitter as new. The rectangular keyboard instrument, with which the earlier of these sets is often supplied, is, except for its diminished size, and its curiously printed keyboard—with black-and-white keys of equal size—similar to the one in the larger set. The center table also differs in design.

The room itself is especially pretty with mirrors at three walls including one over the mantelpiece,

with portraits between of ladies in elegant mid-nineteenth century dress, all framed in the glistening gilt "scrap." The fireplace includes the accessory—actually a convention in these rooms—of a hearth cover, presumably for summer. This one, hand-colored (another clue to vintage), frames a portrait of Madame riding side-saddle on her horse. On the mantle is a pressed-tin clock, attached and obviously original, surmounted by a small woman leaning against a very sizeable wolfhound. These clocks are also to be seen in similar rooms, their paper faces containing the initials "E.P.," perhaps designating the maker of the clock face and not the room itself. For years I've longed to crack this mystery....

Mid-nineteenth century.
Height: 9" Width: 14"

A Paris Salon

Many years ago, in Lahaska, Pennsylvania, there was an antiquarian dealer who told me that on her frequent trips to the Paris flea market, "all the dealers would come running" to her with their dolls and doll-related toys.

From one of these visits, she brought the elegant suite, Louis XVI in style, which is shown in the glazed structure illustrated herewith. Although this set was too large for most dolls' houses, it proved to be irresistible. I brought it home, but it remained in a box till rather recently, when I had, I think, an inspiration:

The curious looking cupboard in which the furniture is pictured was brought to me (also many years ago) by a kind friend who lugged it back from a country sale. If it hadn't been filled with a

(Furnishings: mid-nineteenth century) Height of chair: 6" Case Height: 27 1/2" Glazed base (not shown): 38"

shell collection, both in the upper section, and below, I'd have puzzled endlessly over what this quirky but fascinating piece was all about. The upper half (Height: 28") held what can only be described as a seven-tiered wooden wedding cake, with white paint in lieu of frosting. The shells were displayed around its seven ledges.

It suddenly came to me that with this "cake" removed, the slanted upper section with its tapering mansard shape and surrealistically slanted mullions, might lend itself to the suite. Moreover, aware that rents rise along with roof-tops in Paris, it occurred to me that this elegant apartment would have found its way to an upper floor. It somehow looks French—elegant French—and I hope I may be indulged in this bit of whimsy.

The suite itself includes six side chairs—four more than this setting can accommodate—an arm chair, sofa with two matching pillows, a settee with one pillow, and a rococo standing screen, of black and gold silk, framed in gilt metal. There is also a keyboard instrument, a small rectangular pianoforte with its paper black and white keys reversed, and one often found in earlier rooms of this persuasion. (The Smithsonian, some years ago, reported that all of their pianos with keyboard colors reversed were no later than 1815. Toy versions undoubtedly would have lagged behind.) An upholstered stool is provided for the musician.

Two pairs of crimson silk draperies, still attached to their gilded wood cornices, also accompanied the suite, and one of these pairs lends a pleasing backdrop. Adding a crystal chandelier, a doll, a cat, and a few other accessories of the proper vintage and style, created an ambience which has given much pleasure, at least to its assembler.

The two-handled glass vase with its glass flowers came within its own bell jar, is exquisite, as the detail picture shows, and I like to think it, too, is French. The name "Nevers" glass keeps running through my mind....

GLASS FLOWERS

A RENAISSANCE REVIVAL SALON

During much of the Victorian era, and continuing into the early twentieth century, "France has made a charming specialty of a single miniature room which, as this one does, often folds into a box." I wrote that sentence in 1967, and more than thirty years later, I have reservations about it.

In recent years, some collectors have questioned the French identity of these rooms, and have assumed that, like the French-style houses now known to have been made in Germany for the French market, they, too, may have been imported. Or, as seems quite likely to me, the rooms may have been sent to France and the furniture added there. Until proof is offered, we shall cling to our belief that the furniture is French.

Proof has now been offered; page 251.

In any case, along with the walls (tiny gilt stars on a rich deep ground) and a pair of glazed windows—their green draperies edged in gilt paper with lace curtains beneath—this small salon, whatever its origins, is an ingratiating example of the genre. Two small gilt framed pictures on the back wall and a pair of sizeable gilt paper-framed mirrors are satisfyingly immortalized in their original positions. The box into which these walls fold has a green-patterned base which forms the floor of the room.

Delicately scroll-cut of white wood with fine strips of dark paper applied to resemble inlay, the furniture, in a Renaissance Revival style, consists of an oval tea table, five chairs with fringed uphol-

CA. 1880. HEIGHT: 9" WIDTH: 16"

stered seats, a console table with two shelves, and an imposing cupboard with doors below and scroll-cut shelves above. A more curious piece, resembling a fireplace but revealing shelves when its drop front is lowered to the floor, is covered in the same dark green, leather-like fabric that covers the other chair seats. A matching fabric base supports the attached gilt-metal clock with embossed shepherdess and sheep presiding above its paper face.

A Sevrès tea set, a collection of other miniature French porcelains, and several small books including *Bijou Pictures of Paris* and *Les Rondes de L'Enfance*, the latter with music and illustrations and dated 1895, have been added. Another addition is a rare "ormolu" menu holder (alas, with no menu) along with the lamp, "ormolu" candlesticks, flower-filled vases, and Märklin chandelier.

The two inhabitants, however, are as French as documentation will allow. And one of these has her bilboquet—a rare miniature version (in bone or ivory?) of the classic game of cup and ball.

The cluster of rolls in the cake plate is American, having been baked by Tasha Tudor many long years ago. These rolls, perhaps, warrant more than a footnote.

Many, many years ago my husband and I visited the illustrious author and illustrator briefly at her home in New Hampshire. She showed us her wonderful dolls' house which was occupied by "fashion dolls" (now known, to serious doll collectors, as "fashionable dolls") perhaps twelve inches tall. The

RARE MENU HOLDER

MÄRKLIN CHANDELEIR

rooms they inhabited occupied an entire wall. As a small thank you, I sent her an early porcelain inkwell (with holders for ink and sand) of correct size for her dolls. I had extravagantly admired a loaf of real bread in her scale which she had baked for the dolls. Several slices casually lay beside the loaf.

To my surprise and pleasure, sometime later I received in the mail from "The Shakespeare family," Tasha Tudor's dolls, a tiny Christmas box of assorted breads in my (dolls' house) scale. Showing one of these a year or so later to a visitor, we were startled to see a small "creature" emerge. I embalmed all the loaves with colorless fingernail polish and here—forty or more years later[1]—is the cluster of rolls, seemingly in mint condition.....

A Postscript: Just before these pages went to press, I found in a drawer (of a 28-drawer spool cabinet where small treasures are stored) a true treasure: the one-inch envelope pictured contains a four page letter signed Melissa Crane (the lady of the dolls' house) thanking "the generous giver" for the inkwell, and informing me of the loaves scheduled to arrive. It is dated November 20, 1956. The envelope with complete address was properly affixed, needless to say, with crimson sealing wax, and was clearly written in miniscule penmanship in the early nineteenth-century manner favored by Tasha Tudor in her lifestyle as well as her illustrations.

TASHA TUDOR'S ROLLS AND NOTE

1. More than forty!

TWO FRENCH BOUDOIRS I

Although the French room often folds completely into a box (page 255) it also may be, as this one is, a permanent three-walled unit.

Very pink and white, this room, smaller in scale than the quite similar boudoir, page 258, appears to be an elegant lady's boudoir. Possibly from the 'seventies, its gilded metal candle sconces are attached to the wall—satisfyingly permanent. Such contemporary fixtures, along with the presence, nearly always, of the original wallpapers and draperies, are what make such miniature rooms so appealing from a historical point of view.

A liberty has been taken here, it should be recorded. The room's furnishings having been obviously incomplete, (the round stool beneath the window at the right suggests the former presence of a piano or dressing table), they have been supplemented by a table and cupboard from a set of almost identical pattern purchased long ago in the Paris Flea Market.

The brass album with scenes from the life of Napoleon and the Stanhope (ivory opera glasses) with a view of "Le Monastery" in "Laghet" (Laghouat in Algeria) are among accessories which have been added. The trumpeting page perched upon the gilt clock and his fellow pages at either side comprise a mantle garniture brought together from two sources in one of those surprising reunions so satisfying to collectors.

I shall continue to refer to this furniture as French until proof is found that it is not. It is possible that the rooms were made in Germany for the French market, and sent to France to be furnished. See postscript on page 251.

CA. 1880. HEIGHT: 8 1/2" WIDTH: 16 3/4"

TWO FRENCH BOUDOIRS II

Somewhat larger in scale and undoubtedly later in vintage than the Louis XVI "chamber," page 252, this Louis XVI boudoir is elegant in pink/satin, with delicately-patterned wallpaper and the customary pretty floral scrap pictures applied to the furnishings: table top, cupboard, dresser, and dressing table. One may compare the crimson, carpeted floor edged in gilt paper with the papered floor in the earlier room. The furniture style, of course, is identical. It is the "Louis XVI," so described in the 1897 catalogue of Au Paradis des Enfants, the Parisian department store, page 221.

A few accessories have been added, notably the "dog rug" (a disconcerting concept, in lieu of the customary bear), a soap dish with a blue-wrapped cake bearing New Year wishes, a gilded-lead chamberstick, an ivory clothes brush, and lace-edged handkerchiefs. All of these came to me in a paper-on-wood chest labeled "Chamber de ma Poupèe" and initialed "E.G." There was also a half-tester bed or sofa, similar to the one which came with the room. Bed hangings that were used in France for centuries as a practical way to keep drafts from a bed or sofa survived as an ornamental style in the early nineteenth century—imitated here in the later nineteenth.

The original Paris department store price label appears on this charming chest with its lace-edged interior "Au Bon Marché 10 F 50."[1]

DOG RUG

LATE VICTORIAN. HEIGHT: 10" WIDTH: 19"

1. See postscript, page 251.

FRET-SAWED BEDROOM

In 1953, *The Spinning Wheel* in an article about "Fret Sawed Elegancies," detailed the evolution of the jig saw from the France of Louis XIV to its revival in the New York of one H.L. Wild. Beginning in the 1870's Mr. Wild did a land-office business in fret-saw patterns, the saws themselves, and devices for animating such wooden wonders as steamboats, windmills, and fantastic clocks disguised as churches, workshops, and even locomotives.

For fanciers of gingerbread, there was no jig, jag, or curlicue left unsawed, and it is not surprising that this technique should have lent itself to Victorian dolls' houses and furniture. *The Spinning Wheel* reproduced Wild's line drawing of a fancy dolls' house, ca. 1880, and ten pieces of bedroom furniture.

A few years later, the set pictured below, almost identical to Wild's, was found in an Annapolis antique shop. The chest is two-drawer instead of three, and the design is not identical, but the forms are the same. The pieces are unpainted, of thin basswood about the thickness of popsicle sticks, and since they are fitted together with flat pegs, may be taken apart. The dresser has an oval mirror and brass bail handles on the drawers—accessories also available at Wild's.

An unusual feature of this set is an accompanying room with papered walls which fit ingeniously over the base and are attached by pieces resembling flat clothespins. Fret-sawed window frames in pairs, which are tacked to the walls with a layer of glass between, are the essence of everything a Victorian window should be.

CA. 1880. HEIGHT: 11 1/2" WIDTH: 16 3/4"

A PRETTY PAIR BY GOTTSCHALK

Many long years ago, at an antiques street market in Gettysburg, a dealer from whom I'd bought a few small pieces, volunteered that he had, at home nearby, a piece I might be interested in, and, if I could return after he went home at lunchtime, he'd bring it for me to see.

Needless to say, I did return. When I saw what he had brought, my heart, as the saying is, "skipped a beat." It was, of course, the pair of rooms pictured. There was no furniture, but there were the most elaborate of Gottschalk (the maker unknown at the time) pilasters framing the sides, described in

CA. 1895. HEIGHT: 14" WIDTH: 32"

the catalogue as "fancy" regarding the most imposing stores and kitchens. And there were elegantly framed wallpaper panels.

These charming papers were in excellent condition, but there were no draperies. Somewhat later, I made a happy discovery: There were projecting hooks at either side of the glazed casement windows. In a box in which I store curtain sup-

plies—old laces, ribbons and such—I came upon a pair of antique lace-edged blue draperies attached to a decorative wooden cornice. Two openings in the rear of the cornice exactly fitted upon the Gottschalk hooks! Then, in another storage box, I found two more identical cornices, minus curtains. Draperies made of old fabric have been supplied for these. After these words were written, the

Ciesliks in Germany published their marvelous find of the photographer's plates from Gottschalk's 1892-1931 catalogues.[1] The rooms shown, from the 1895 plates, are identical to these with one minor exception: as their photograph indicates, the window cornices are more elaborate. The ones supplied so enthusiastically by me may have been for kitchens and are similar to ones in the Ackerman (undated) catalogue.

Schneegass pieces, a pair of beds, with their original pillows and lace-edged quilted coverlets, have been placed between marble-topped night-stands in the narrow bedroom.

There are a number of rare accessories in the adjoining parlor. A revolving photo album with ornately framed engravings, mostly of children in peasant dress—one gentleman in knee britches—were part of a collecting discovery even more dazzling than that of the rooms themselves. At a Maryland antiques show (as always, many years ago—such discoveries are rare these days) a Maryland dealer had a most beguiling assortment of "ormolu." This had belonged, she related, to two sisters and therefore there were two of everything

ART NOUVEAU
MIRROR BY
GERLACH

RARE PARROT STAND WITH
VIENNA BRONZE PARROT

1. J & M Cieslik, License USA, Gold Horse Publishing, Annapolis
2. I gave one of the squirrel cages years ago to a friend in a rash moment, and traded, rather recently, a celebrated miniatures dealer one of the two albums for an early electric fan I lacked. (See next page.)

she had—two squirrel cages.[2] (See page 266.) And two revolving albums among them. (In the parlor, a lorgnette rests next to the album for convenient viewing.)

Also rare is the "ormolu" parrot stand. The parrot was missing, but in London, about forty years ago, an antiques dealer had a collection of Vienna bronzes, including a parrot. He was selling the col-

lection at a very affordable price and I, young and foolish, bought only the small pieces, but the parrot was a bit of luck and looks "right," I think, on the stand.

The Gerlach lady, very Art Nouveau, supporting her swirling skirt with one hand and her circular mirror with the other, is less rare, but perhaps similarly intriguing.

VERY FRENCH
PHONE

REVOLVING ALBUM
WITH ENGRAVINGS

EARLY ELECTRIC FAN

FROM CIESLIK ARCHIVE, 1895

A Sizeable Pair of German Chambers

Once upon a time, when F. A. O. Schwarz included an antique toy department, its charming and savvy manager, the late Sally Erath, took me to the firm's warehouse and showed me this mammoth pair of rooms. She told me that it had been given to Schwarz. They did not give it to me! (Though prices were different in those halcyon days—the early 'sixties—and, therefore, perhaps they did, relatively speaking.)

In any case, it needed work. Although much of the oak decor which gave the parlor its character remained, oak moldings which surrounded the windows and doors, and most of the paper border which defined the paneled wallpaper had been ruthlessly stripped away. Fortunately, the outlines of both the moldings and the wallpaper borders were visible, even to the shape of the turned pilasters; and, miraculously, a five-inch segment of the printed border paper remained to be copied.

All of this has been expertly accomplished by a Master Dolls' House Restorer.[1] When a similar, though somewhat smaller pair of rooms appeared in a Sotheby's (London) catalogue in 1998, the success of the process was confirmed.

Height: 19 1/2" Width: 47"

1. Jim Reus. (The title is unofficial!)

For years I tolerated the blemishes, and longed to restore them, but the imposing oak paneling beneath the chair rail which dominates the lower half of the parlor, echoed by the dentilated molding at the top of the room, remained. Also intact was a major feature usually to be found in larger pairs of German chambers ("rooms" seems an inadequate term to describe this imposing pair). This is the parlor alcove, a bay complete with workable casement windows beneath a glazed arched transom. This recess with its decorative oak railing is reached by three oak steps and retains its "parquet" floor paper.

A green velvet upholstered parlor set by Schneegass came with the rooms,[1] along with a

few bedroom pieces by a maker unknown to me. A Märklin brass bed has been added to the bedroom. These beds, which have wire coil springs, are so realistic that more than once they've been mistakenly identified as salesman's samples.

The rooms have been accessorized with many rare "ormolu" pieces, including the cornice and curtain rod in the bedroom, the only one I've ever encountered. Hanging beneath this is a pair of curtains mounted on wood and possibly from a similar room inasmuch as they fitted perfectly beneath the cornice and rod. The hanging birdcage adds to the atmosphere, having been embellished with crimson ribbons. Other "ormolu" pieces include several which came from the dolls'

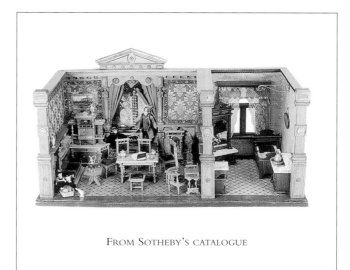

FROM SOTHEBY'S CATALOGUE

BEFORE RESTORATION

1. Similar pieces are to be seen in the rooms sold by Sotheby's and the rooms, therefore, may have been sold furnished.

EARLY PHONOGRAPH

SQUIRREL CAGE

NEWSPAPER
"WAND"

"ORMOLU" BIRDCAGE

house (or houses) of two "little sisters." There were two of each of the rare objects. A Maryland dealer had brought the collection to an antiques show, and I can still remember how exciting it was to come upon them. Two of these, to be seen here, include a phonograph which plays scratchy "music" when its handle is turned and a squirrel cage occupied by a bisque squirrel, a sad reminder of an item mercifully no longer made.

The light fixture with opaline smoke bell, in the bedroom, might more properly hang in a hall but the visibility afforded by a "room," with no ceiling to interfere, suggested the location. I confess to improvising the Wardian case[1] in the parlor, having encountered no miniature example so far. This consists of an "ormolu" table with air fern under a glass bell.

The rooms, which are connected by an oak paneled door, have been supplied with a veritable gallery of those quite irresistible gilt-framed dolls' house landscapes and portraits which reveal the eclectic tastes of the occupants.

After these words were written, I managed to acquire for this room an accessory sought for many years in vain. It is a miniscule newspaper attached to a metal "wand," a vertical post to which the paper could be inserted for relatively wrinkle-proof reading. The paper—here perma-

nently affixed (I've seen others in catalogues) includes an illustrated banner with its name—*Uber Land und Meer*—and, in smaller letters below, *Deutsche Illustrierte Zeitung.* This illustrated German newspaper is indeed illustrated. Enlarged, it is to be seen above.

I do not know which German firm made this imposing pair. For years I assumed it was Gottschalk, but I have been disabused of this notion.

FATHER WITH NEWSPAPER WAND

1. A terrarium invented by a Mr. Ward in England in 1829.

"FURNISHED DOLL APARTMENTS" BY PETER PIA

Many long years ago, the advertisement shown for "Folding Parlor Room, No. 1" was discovered in Montgomery Ward's 1900 catalogue, and the advertisement was duly illustrated in the 1953 and 1965 editions of *A History of Dolls' Houses.* [1]

Some years later, this collector walked into an antiques shop in New York State, and found the most charming of surprises; a similar room, a folding bedroom, rested upon a table, waiting to be "collected." The fragile cardboard walls were intact: The advertisement had promised that the corners, "doubly hinged with book cloth," were "warranted to stay bound." Miraculously, they had.

And every piece of the delicate "white metal furniture" was present and in mint condition—a collector's dream. Fragile prongs still supported the mauve cardboard seats of the rocker and side chair, as well as the card that held the small homemade mattress and pillows on the bed. The easel, with a framed sepia print of cows, continued to work perfectly on its adjustable stand. Most astonishing of all, the "neatly designed mantel fireplace with real glass mirror" still hung by its two prongs to the small openings in the fragile wall.

Somewhat later, I was fortunate enough to find three more of the rooms, also in mint condition. The illustration of the metal chairs and table with its printed cardboard top and plump wooden legs, clearly identified as by Peter F. Pia, provided the final piece to a dolls' house researcher's puzzle. The name Peter F. Pia had been haunting this one's files

DATE: 1900. AMERICAN. HEIGHT OF ROOM: 9" WIDTH: 11"

1. Charles Scribners Sons.

for a number of years. The McClintocks[1] mentioned that Pia had begun making pewter toys in New York in 1848. Because so many tons of "pewter" toys, or "soft–lead" or whatever a layman without a knowledge of metallurgy may choose to call them, were imported from Europe, it was difficult to know which were made by Pia, which by other American makers, and which had come from abroad.

The Ward catalogue also served to identify the maker of ubiquitous metal parlor sets with scenes of Columbus' arrival in 1492, which had, of course, been made for the Columbian Exposition. The table and chairs, in a 1905 issue of *Playthings*, the toy trade publication, were identical to the table and chairs to be found in the parlor.

The illustration for "Furnished Doll Apartments" is from the October 24, 1901 issue of *The Youth's Companion*.

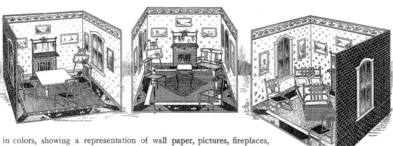

FURNISHED DOLL APARTMENTS.

FOR several years we have searched in vain for a Doll House which would comprise the many desirable features we now offer.

Each Apartment is 11 inches wide, and when not in use may be folded flat and placed away in the usual receptacle for toys. The floors and walls are lithographed in colors, showing a representation of wall paper, pictures, fireplaces, carpets, rugs, etc. The outside of each House is an imitation brickwork, and is also made more realistic by two cut-out windows. We furnish a complete Set of Metal Furniture as follows :

The **Dining-Room** is furnished with a Table, 4 Chairs, an Easel, and a real Mirrored Mantelpiece nearly 3 inches long. The **Parlor** has a Center Table, Sofa, Chairs, Easel and Mirrored Mantelpiece. The **Bedroom** also has an Easel, Mirrored Mantelpiece, 2 Chairs and a Bed. We are confident that no better selection can be made for a little girl than the three furnished Doll Apartments we here offer.

The Three Apartments, with Sets of Furniture, given for one new subscription and 40 cents extra, postage and packing included. Price 80 cents, postage and packing 40 cents extra ; or sent by express, charges paid by receiver. Shipping weight 3 lbs.

DOLL'S GO-CART.

Metal frame and wheels. Very durable. Go-Cart type. Handle two feet high. Suitable for Little Rosebud, or any other doll. Regular price 50 cents. When ordered sent with any other article offered on pages 560 and 561 we will include it for 35 cents. Sent by express, charges paid by receiver.

1. *Toys in America*, Public Affairs Press, 1961.

CHRISTMAS IN JULY

It must be confessed that this charmingly hand-carved case, which hangs in the writer's dining room, is modestly footed, and not meant to hang. Its conversion was inspired many years ago by the acquisition of two pairs of antique curtains and draperies, with gilt scrap cornices. The wall was covered with the one pattern of antique wallpaper then in my possession.

The Victorian furnishings and occupants were then duly installed. The marble-topped fireplace with its flaming metal fire, and filigree surround and fender, was surmounted by one of those perfect "ormolu" Märklin mantel mirrors, usually to be seen attached to a Märklin fireplace. An "ormolu" settee with a gilt-metal mesh back was placed at the left, along with the two lovely silk pillows which had accompanied it to its new owner. A matching gilded brass hanging shelf hangs nearby. It contains the most miniscule of Beatrix Potter creatures in Vienna bronze, including Mrs. Tiggie Winkle, 5/8" tall, and completely recognizable in her cap and "large apron over her striped petticoat."

All of this and more was duly installed and then embellished for Christmas. The feather tree in its red wooden pot is centered in a fenced Christmas garden. A red-striped stocking with a Frozen Charlotte peering from the top was hung from the mantel shelf, and then the family was added.

The children are provided with toys—"The Smallest Farm in the World," as asserted on the lid of the miniscule flats within, which are of metal. Most remarkably, five soldiers remain in their original box, including one on a horse. The touring car, less than 3" long, elegant with a cream chassis out-lined in red striping, has a horn (non-working) attached to the steering wheel, a crank between the headlights in front, and two removable figures—one in front (a chauffeur) and one in back. The spoked wheels turn. This was made by the German firm of Ernst Planck.

In any case, it got to be July before thought of disassembling this Christmas room occurred, and for a number of years now, this small scene has continued as Christmas, in July, August, etc., rather satisfying on a warm day.

TOY SOLDIERS IN ORIGINAL BOX

VICTORIAN. CASE INTERIOR HEIGHT: 17" WIDTH: 21"

METAL CAR WITH REMOVABLE PASSENGER

A Pair of Rooms from Austria I

The folding room, frequently French in style and customarily seen in single form, is here represented in a charming two-room suite. It was found in Vienna, I was told, and later I acquired another pair, pages 272-273, also "found" in Vienna. Even though two pairs cannot be said to constitute a trend, I've wondered if such pairs may have been an Austrian specialty.

Certainly this prettily lithographed apartment on heavy card is very different in character from the rooms of wood which were manufactured in

Germany. With one wall besprinkled with lilies of the valley and the other with parrots and pansies, and with crimson silk draperies crowned by gilt fringed cornices at its glazed windows, it has more in common with the delicate French salons and boudoirs which, like this pair, fold into their boxes. In the absence of hard evidence, "from Austria" as identification will have to suffice.

Considerably more sedate than its setting, the fret-work furniture was with the rooms when they were acquired. These are meticulously dovetailed

and more delicately wrought than the fret-work-revival pieces made in such multitudes in the United States in the 'eighties, page 259. There is a curiosity in the form of a sewing machine with workable treadle and an imposing sideboard which totally overwhelms in scale the other pieces, but there are some charming surprises. Four wooden pegs in one of the twin cupboards hold miniscule hats, and the shelves of all the cased pieces are laden with piles of tiny linen, tied in the crispest of narrow blue ribbons. Many of these are embroidered and initialed with an infinitesimal "E."

Alas, we'll never know who the careful seamstress was, the creator as well, undoubtedly, of an exquisite blue silk bedspread and pillow with lace appliqué and a dressing table draped to match, with matching pin cushion.

Two quite elegantly gilt-framed mirrors, visible between the windows, and two similar frames with pictures, were fastened quite firmly to the walls. These are more in character with the elegant rooms, and I was emboldened to place all of the fret-work furniture in one of them, and furnish the other with a more rococo suite upholstered in silk seemingly more suited to the delicate decor.

LATE VICTORIAN.
HEIGHT: 15"
WIDTH: 35 3/4"

A Pair of Rooms from Austria II

This pair of rooms, similar in several ways to the more elaborate duo on pages 270-271, came with the information that it had been found, as that pair had, in Vienna. These rooms are somewhat smaller, and less elegant, but they are a pair, and they were accompanied, when they crossed the ocean, by furniture and dolls, presumably original.

Whether either pair was manufactured in Austria must be a matter of conjecture. Unlike the German rooms with solid wood bases and walls, page 264, these are of heavy card and, like many of the French rooms[1], fold into their original boxes.

These are divided into a parlor and a bedroom. The parlor furniture is upholstered in checkered

1. There is, as these words are written, as yet no matching catalogue or ad to reveal whether these are French or German.

velvet and includes a piece described in a 1914 German toy catalogue as "a sofa with top." This piece, with infinite variations, is an almost ubiquitous presence in German parlor sets. This one features not only the attached mirror across the back, but a small storage cupboard at either side, with a niche above each as well.

The six dolls include three generations. A gray-haired lady in rather tatty attire in the bedroom has

an eye on a tot on one of the beds. In the parlor, a man in a black hat is either coming or going, and there appears to be a controversy of some kind. A gentleman with sideburns and an old-fashioned style of dress (suggesting that he is earlier than the others), a woman in an apron, and another, more elegantly garbed, complete the group.

LATE VICTORIAN.
HEIGHT: 12 1/4"
WIDTH: 30 1/2"

A Bedroom On the Bedroom Wall

Collectors, as we all know, are compulsive. This one felt obliged to hang the bedroom pictured on her bedroom wall. Above it is a framed lid from a box of Bliss bedroom furniture; alongside it a large sheet of bedroom furniture vividly litho-graphed in 1892 by F. Cairo of Brooklyn. (The latter, in an elaborate frame of proper vintage, is part of a sizable collection of paper furniture.)

Judging by the furniture with its metal embellishments, the room appears to date from the early

GERMAN. CA. 1910. HEIGHT: 12" WIDTH: 23 "

twentieth century, and to have been re-papered in the 1920's. (There is dark green paper beneath the 'twentyish layer.) A metal medallion against the back wall, of the type from which a hanging lamp was extended, and a rather primitive light switch on the left wall allude to early lighting, alas departed.

A far more interesting furnishing fortuitously remained in the room. At each of the four windows the curtains are hung from rare brass curtain rods.[1] These extension rods are accompanied by the essential hardware which holds them but—most intriguing—the curtains themselves are held by miniscule brass clamps with infinitesimal springs—which still perform perfectly.

It might not have been possible to identify the rare "ormolu" piece on the washstand (left) if the original sponge had not remained suspended from one of its two arms, and the original washcloth from the other. This came with the room, along with an ornately embossed metal towel rack (with towel) on the wall, and a circular metal washstand with jug and basin.

The assorted French-type, glass-eyed occupants have been rather arbitrarily added.

EVEN A METAL RACK FOR
SPONGE AND WASHCLOTH

BRASS EXTENSION ROD WITH
TINY BRASS CLAMPS

1. A footnote to these curtain rods—and a word about the affinity between cats and dolls' houses—and their owners. One evening the owners of Sadie, a young, foolish "tortoiseshell," returned home to discover that the room on the wall, protected (but evidently not very well) by Plexiglas, had been invaded. One pair of curtains was off, the lamp with its delicate opaline shade was leaning at a precarious angle, and the dolls were laid out like little corpses on the floor. Presumably Sadie, who favors height, was on her way to the top of an adjoining six-foot highboy. We were never quite sure of her escape route.

A PARLOR FOR MIGNONETTES

This small lithographed paper-on-wood salon is perhaps more distinguished for its company than its décor. It was probably made in Germany, but the petite bisque mignonettes[1] (2 1/2" tall) are as French as the Louvre, even though one is garbed as a Scotsmen, and one chap with a military look and a walrus moustache is Oriental in appearance. This motley assemblage includes two other members of the military, complete with swords, a Judge dressed as though he just stepped out of a Daumier print, and a gendarme. Their hostess stands aside in some bewilderment, but a Red Cross nurse is nearby if there is a problem.

The pretty furniture which came with this room, and probably originated with it, is of a similar lithographed paper-on-wood construction, and it is of a genre to be found in several sizes and numerous patterns. [2] The latter are often horticultural, with such useful additions as clock faces and insects! (One pattern includes a large, quite gorgeous black beetle.) The maker is unknown to me.

LATE NINETEENTH CENTURY. HEIGHT: 6" WIDTH: 11"

1. The name in France for little dolls.
2. The chair-backs are of card as is the table top. (The latter, of a more geometric pattern, is a substitute for the one missing piece.)

A Christmas Room from St. Louis ca. 1900

A festive sticker on the box-lid says "A Merry Christmas." One on the wall inside says "A Happy Christmas." Whether these are original to this room-in-a-box is difficult to say, but with the decor of the red-and-green printed carpet on the floor and the printed red-brick fireplace, this very jolly parlor exudes Christmas.

The ten pieces of wood furniture which came with this setting are off-hand, to say the least. The furniture is of thin stained wood, cut simply. If the glue showed, no one seemed to mind. But, somehow, this merry suite captures the essence of Christmas, and the simple shapes manage to express turn-of-the-century Arts and Crafts decor.

The box itself is printed with latticed windows which open. The evergreen walls with oak wainscoting are a perfect foil for the furnishings, originally sewn into the box. (The framed picture on the wall is still attached.) Even though there is absolutely no logical spot for the fireplace with its glistening built-in mirror above, and its printed roaring fire below, and the top of the sheet music ("Mooning" is the title) is bent over and glued to the top of the not very grand piano, the room is a remarkable capsule of its style and era.

The company which made this cheery ensemble proudly put its initials "WLDR"[1] and its St. Louis trademark on the box label, and given the fragility of the whole, it is doubtful if another complete example exists. It very nearly qualifies as ephemera.

CA. 1900.
BOX: 15" x 5" x 12"

1. Wilder Manufacturing Company.

ROOMS WITH A CONSERVATORY, 1912

In 1912, when this set of rooms was made[1], the trellis-trimmed space one step up on the left may have been referred to as a "sun room." However, Gottschalk has provided it with such an assortment of the company's well-known pasteboard trim, here mostly in the form of lattice, that "conservatory" may be an appropriate term.

The trellised balustrade at front and side is further framed by a cornice of some elaboration above. An even more intricate pattern is pressed against the three wood pilasters which define the rooms. The conservatory and the right-hand room each contain a casement window from which

original white silk curtains hang, harmonizing with delicate floral-printed Gottschalk wallpapers of the period.

An early wicker chair, possibly from Madeira, may be glimpsed in the conservatory. A rare set of metal filigree furniture (I've never seen another) consisting of a circular table, six chairs, and a settee, appears to be of a sufficient lightness to relate to the conservatory, though most of it is placed in the adjoining room. There is a bird in a small crimson cartouche on each piece, but what is perhaps most unusual are the pair of tasseled projections at the front of each seat, with a matching pair dangling

1. The identical piece may be seen in the Ciesliks' catalogue compilation (which provided the date). Of course it may have been made for more than one year.

delicately from each chair back. Miraculously, of this delicate trim, only one metal tassel has been lost.

This suite is in contrast to the large German early 20th century pieces nearby. These, of a red-dish wood with black-painted trim and gilt metal

embellishment, are by an unknown (to me) German maker.

The wax parrot clinging to his gilt metal ("ormolu") circular perch is early for this setting, but parrots are known to live for many years!

RARE FILIGREE PIECES LATER
PLACED IN ROOM BELOW

FROM CIESLIK ARCHIVE, CA. 1912

CA. 1912. HEIGHT: 12" WIDTH: 29"

A FOLDING BEDROOM

The bed lamp hangs from the wall rather than from the bed, but for those of us who remember those long ago days, the style of this lamp effectively places this room in the 1920's.

The light and airy room, which folds neatly into the base—its lithographed paper-on-wood box—came fully supplied not only with furniture but with two bisque-headed, glass-eyed dolls, a young lady, and a lad in a sailor suit. There are plants in the window box, oddly situated inside the window. There are two portraits of "beautiful ladies" and one of a saint, framed in gilt scrap, and affixed to the wall.

The furniture is painted quite charmingly. A sea view is lavished on the two chair backs. Roses dominate the other pieces, including a towering mirrored armoire.

The room looks French, but I dare not say that it is, having been tripped up in the past by French style interiors later found to be German. This room, however, is of a very different genre, and I am willing to go out on the limb a modest distance.

CA. 1920. HEIGHT: 8" WIDTH: 13"

A WASHINGTON, D.C. "LIVING ROOM"

The "parlor" of an earlier era had become the "living-room" by the time this piece was created. When it was acquired, furnished, with a Gottschalk set from Germany, the bold paper strip declaring its Washington, D.C. origin was firmly in place above the fireplace, and beneath the lush cabbage-rose border.

The four landscapes, printed and paper-framed, were also firmly glued to the walls, and it is possible that one of these is a segment of the Potomac River, and another, a view of Great Falls in nearby Virginia. There is a wallpaper textured carpet which exactly fits the deep room, suggesting a commercial origin. Inasmuch as the Gottschalk fireplace and matching console mirror on the right side are firmly attached to the walls, perhaps the room came with the furniture from Germany and was embellished in D.C.

The very complete suite is in the largest scale which Gottschalk made, a very large scale indeed.

The console mirror rises to the edge of the room cornice; the piano is 8 1/2" tall. The sofa, "easy chair," piano bench, arm chairs, and desk chair are all upholstered in a dark floral green fabric. There are so many pieces in the set that, even in this large room, the cupboard has to be displayed outside it.

An unusual gilded metal lamp with a workable wick and a crepe-paper shade (which has survived a predictable conflagration) is on the center table. A bisque gentleman with nothing to smoke stands disconsolately next to his handsomely-turned wood smoking stand. The lamp on the desk is quite Art Deco with its triangular stitched-parchment shade. A desk set from the Museum's display of miniature writing equipment, in perfect scale and style for this desk, has been borrowed for the illustration. (It came originally from F.A.O. Schwarz, a gift from a friend's 1920's dolls' house, possibly only a trifle late[1] for this house.

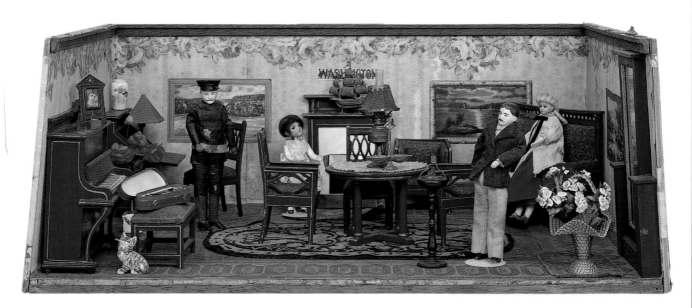

EARLY 20TH CENTURY. HEIGHT: 10" X WIDTH: 24 3/4"

1. The Lord Dolls' House, 1908-9, in The Boston Children's Museum (*Dolls' Houses in America,* page 57) contains identical Gottschalk chairs, and it is likely that this Washington room is no later in date than the 'teens.

A Set of Bauhaus Rooms

This sizeable set of Bauhaus rooms came to me unfurnished. A set of windows on the left wall, a small window in the right-hand room and glazed doors between the rooms, are the only architectural features, but the vintage and style are unmistakable. Even the built-in wooden curtain rod above the set of glazed windows bespeaks Bauhaus. Two separate groupings of Bauhaus furniture have been placed within the papered walls. One of these sets consists of only three pieces and a clock but is of remarkable quality with its highly polished tiger maple finish.

The credenza on the left wall of the middle room, contains, along with a section for holding suspended goblets, a truly modern innovation: Inside the right-hand door a phonograph lurks. This, of course, can be extended and there are sections beneath it for storing records.

There are sliding glass doors on the cupboards in both sets. The dressing table in the bedroom with its triple adjustable mirrors is properly unframed. Although Bauhaus has come into its own in full-size, I prefer it in miniature.

CA. 1930. GERMAN. HEIGHT: 11 5/8" WIDTH: 55 1/2"

CREDENZA WITH EARLY
RADIO AND PULL-OUT
PHONOGRAPH

GLASS CONSERVATORY

A dolls' house collector willing to compromise doesn't always require a dolls' house. The glass shelter pictured herewith was, according to the dealer who sold it, the top of a street lamp from Hanover, Pennsylvania. With a Plexiglas circle to support it, and a wicker smoking stand beneath it, the globe seems an appropriate domicile for the 1920's wicker it contains.

One piece in this set, the fernery with bird cage, resembles an adjacent full-sized fernery on the writer's glass porch. The miniature fernery retains its original foliage, though, alas, the bird has flown. Rarer still, perhaps, are the six glass spoons still intact in their striped iced tea glasses. The tea,

or lemonade, may be poured from the "hammered" silver pitcher which is a miniature version of a full-sized example my mother filled on summer days in the 'twenties.

The 'twenties lamp, clipped to an appropriate battery, is lightable. A white metal smoking tray-with-match-holder resembles a brass ashtray fitted to a second full-sized wicker smoking stand on the same glass porch. Undoubtedly there was such a fitted fixture on the wicker stand which supports the group.

The golfer, in his felt plus-fours and checked bisque cap and socks, is rare.

BISQUE GOLFER

FURNITURE: 1920's.
GLOBE: UNDOUBTEDLY EARLIER. HEIGHT: 13" WIDTH: 13"

AN ATTORNEY'S OFFICE

Inasmuch as it is not antique, this lawyer's office was nearly excluded from these antique-oriented pages. I assembled it for my husband's law office in Washington, D.C., approximately two decades ago, using materials of the time, both hand-crafted and commercial.

Most proudly, the room highlights the artistry of Carol Boyd, formerly of Virginia, who retired years ago from the making of her wonderful, sculpted dolls. Her white-haired attorney, presiding here, attests to her art.

When my husband retired, I brought it home and placed it in an obscure corner. It has been rescued herewith, and though it bears no resemblance to my husband's former office which did contain mostly antique furnishings, it does reflect the roll-top desks, office safes and water coolers which furnished numerous offices of the past.

Newspapers, which supplement the law books, predictably include *The Wall Street Journal, The New York Times* and *The Washington Star.* On the latter, dated September 19, 1979, one may read wistfully, the headline: "Sadat Hails Peace Progress."

MODERN LAW OFFICE WITH CAROL BOYD LAWYER.
CA. 1980. HEIGHT: 9" WIDTH: 22"

Part VI

Kitchens, Plumbing,
and a Dentist's Office

EARLY NUREMBERG KITCHEN I

To prove that educational toys are not in the least modern and the meticulous German hausfrau not in the least accidental, we submit the Nuremberg kitchen which, agleam with rows of brass pans, pewter plates, and copper pots, has traditionally instructed small German daughters in the household arts.

"Eighteenth century," the designation applied to the specimen pictured, is unquestionably broad, but kitchens, even more than dolls' houses, possibly because metal is so much sturdier than wood, tend to become accumulations of objects handed down mixed with later additions. Dating them becomes hazardous, but I venture to say "ca. 1800" of this one after studying a picture of a kitchen so dated at Augsburg. Several important utensils are common to both kitchens.

All early Nuremberg kitchens have the inevitable hooded oven with a chimney to carry off the smokey fumes. Charcoal used for cooking on the brick hearth was stored in the opening

CA. 1800. HEIGHT: 17" WIDTH: 36"

below it—concealed in our photograph by the handsome copper fire screen. The latter was set on the hearth to protect the person revolving the spit from the heat of the fire. This screen is identical to the one pictured in the Augsburg kitchen, and so is the copper vessel with the hinged lid suspended between two metal brackets above the open fire on the hearth. The position of this imposing utensil assured a continuous supply of hot water all day long. The lidded copper jug beneath the scales, used to carry the water, is also identical to the one in the Augsburg[1] kitchen, and there are numerous other similarities.

Matching copper pots in graduated sizes, hanging by their own brass rings, are lined with tin. Such cooking pans were popular for genera-

tions, but "in spite of the highly attractive appearance of a polished and gleaming batterie-de-cuisine of this metal," say *The Connoisseur Period Guides,* "the 1850's saw the introduction and acceptance of the more hygienic and more easily managed enameled iron."

In the left foreground, an early, finely handcrafted pewter porringer may be seen. Also of special interest, on the hearth, is a tin lamp which burned fat in the cup beneath its lid, a wick emerging from its spout, and with a saucer base to catch the drippings.

The crèche figure is an addition of the correct scale and—hopefully—aspect. She adds a needed dimension to a splendid reflection of the culinary past.

FAT LAMP

COPPER VESSEL WITH
FIRESCREEN BELOW

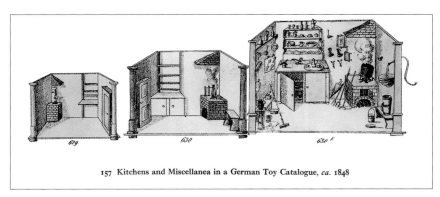

157 Kitchens and Miscellanea in a German Toy Catalogue, *ca.* 1848

1. Evidently these resemblances were no accident. The late Dr. Lydia Bayer, whose charming toy museum in Nuremberg, was well-known, wrote that this should be identified as an Augsburg kitchen, and that Kitchen II, shown on next page, may be correctly identified as from Nuremberg. However, though it is fascinating to learn that these kitchens can be pinpointed to a particular town or region, the term was used here in a generic sense, and the heading, for this reason, has not been altered.

EARLY NUREMBERG KITCHEN II

Even though comparisons are said to be invidious, it is difficult to refrain from observing that this eighteenth century kitchen, given the complexity and multiplicity of its accoutrements, is even more remarkable than Kitchen I, shown on previous page.

These kitchens were, of course, handed down in German families, from daughter to daughter. It is clear that the family in which this remarkable specimen descended took exquisite care to keep it intact for many generations. Regrettably, its provenance is forever lost.

One might write a fulsome essay on the variety of objects, dominated by a dazzling array of

EIGHTEENTH CENTURY. HEIGHT: 16" WIDTH: 32 3/4"
THE MARIONETTES AND CRÈCHE FIGURE ARE ADDITIONS.

early pewter, to be found in the small, beshelved rectangle. Heavy brass skillets flank the traditional hooded oven, hanging above skewer racks (complete with slender skewers). These once supplied a turnspit. Customary metal rings for lighted charcoal and surface cooking are implied by black painted circles on the oven surface. A harshly realistic accessory is a poultry coop, on the right, where the unfortunate occupants, it was said, were fattened on kitchen scraps. (A cheerier theory is that the egg supply was maintained within the hen.) A copper kettle stands on a tin brazier, here placed on top of the oven. Next to it is a stacked quartet of pewter hot dish carriers, bound together with a leather thong of which a counterpart, we are told, is still in use in India. On the wooden tres-

MARKED PEWTER CHARGER

RARE PEWTER FISH STEW PAN
AND FOOD WARMER (CENTER),
PLUS SPICE BOX (RIGHT),
AND EGG RACK (LEFT)

tle table, the oval fish stew pan is one of several handsome pewter pieces with mushroom finials on their lids. A matching rectangular sectional container with sliding top, probably for spices, is on the left-hand counter. Next to this is an egg cooker, a two-tiered multi-holed rack in which eggs might be uniformly immersed for boiling.

The decorative detail with which many of these small pieces are made is most alluring. A delicate leaf pattern which appears to be hand-wrought embellishes a pewter salt box, while nearby, a pair of embossed pewter birds build a pewter nest with pewter twigs on the upper side of a fuel carrier. Minute brass appliqués ornament a set of graduated tin colanders.

The crèche lady is an addition. Of the correct scale, and approximately of the correct vintage, she adds a touch of vivacity to the proceedings.

NUREMBERG KITCHEN COOKBOOK

Even if only the cover of this small cookbook with its informative illustrations had survived, it might have been considered a treasure, but it is intact, faded and a bit wrinkled, like an elderly cook, and weathered by the heat of the oven and possibly a little gravy.

Printed in Nuremberg in 1858, the title page informs us in German that this is a "Little Cook Book for the Dolls' Kitchen," or "First Instruction for Cooking for Girls 8-14 Years of Age." So worded, this inscription is an explicit corroboration—if more is needed—that such toys were educational toys, specifically intended for instruction as well as for play.

The small treasure was found with Nuremberg Kitchen II, shown on pages 290 and 291, a mid-nineteenth century addition to its hoard of pewter and copper of considerably earlier date.

It is of interest to note that in the illustration on the cover, a stove of the same 1858 vintage cook book stands on the floor between the two girls and beneath the classic eighteenth century kitchen above it. The latter, similar to the eighteenth-century kitchens shown on pages 288-291, was possibly a family heirloom, cherished, as these toys were, and displayed, but supplemented by the later metal stove with chimney. Such stoves with their

brass-rimmed stove pipes, made in an infinitude of variations during the second half of the nineteenth century, were lighted with "spirit."

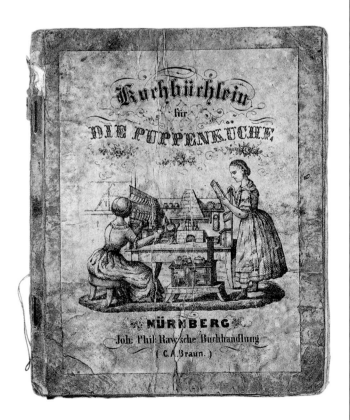

COOKBOOK DATED 1858. SIZE: 4" x 5"

EARLY NUREMBERG KITCHEN III

This relatively modest kitchen (modest in comparison to the two which precede it) was the first "early" [1] Nuremberg kitchen found by this collector many long years ago. Judging by the style and the contents—the heavy pewter pieces, especially—I have believed it to be late eighteenth century. It is assuredly no later than early nineteenth. Though the fireplace hood is a bit off center, and the construction of the whole is somewhat off-hand, there are proper upright wooden pegs on the top right-hand shelf to hold the pewter hot-water jugs in their places, and helpful wooden ledges on the shelves to keep the substantial pewter plates from crashing down on the cook.

There are later nineteenth century additions (there usually are) and we long to know how many generations were instructed in cookery by this appealing teaching toy.

CA. 1800. HEIGHT: 9 1/2" WIDTH: 17 1/2"

1. "Early" is, of course, a vague but highly serviceable term which can be applied to eighteenth or nineteenth century objects, depending upon which century appears to be nearer the mark.......!

TIN KITCHENS

A traditional Victorian toy, the tin kitchen, usually stenciled or embossed, with a stove in the center and a workable pump on the side, was manufactured with infinite variations both in the U.S. and abroad, and numerous examples survive.

Although these are often found with the original utensils replaced, and in varying stages of peeling paint, bent tin, and general disarray, the kitchen shown below, which came out of an old store, was believed to be intact, with its original pots, molds, and scoops still hanging on its small hooks or perched on its metal racks. I accepted the antique dealer's statement that the kitchen was intact when I acquired it many moons ago, but looking at it now, with an older and, possibly, wiser eye, I wonder about a few things. For instance, where is the

tea kettle? How could such a standard item be missing?

While the range in this kitchen is topped with a stove pipe, the example, shown on next page, retains the hood found in earlier kitchens. The latter resembles the specimen to be seen in Althof, Bergmann's 1874 catalogue. It includes the hood as well as the arched opening below for wood. On the other hand, the Stevens & Brown illustrated price list of almost the same date (1872) shows the stovepipe top and the workable oven door below. Almost every toy catalogue of the period pictures at least one tin kitchen, available in assorted sizes, and with many variations.

The pump-on-the-side was a convention to be seen in toy kitchens as early as the mid-nineteenth

A Stevens and Brown kitchen. Second half of the nineteenth century. Height: 9 1/2" Width: 17 1/2" (plus pump)

ALTHOF, BERGMANN KITCHEN. SECOND HALF OF THE NINETEENTH CENTURY HEIGHT: 7 1/2" WIDTH: 10 3/4" (PLUS PUMP)

century. The German catalogue illustration ca. 1848 shows such a fitting. However, this kitchen is probably not of tin.

The miniscule example, shown below, is early and rare. In a four-inch width, the maker has managed to include a hooded oven (with a workable door) and a full complement of racks and shelves. Even a cookpot has survived. It stands proudly, withal lidless, on the stove.

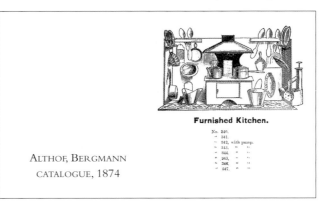

Furnished Kitchen.

No. 340.
" 341.
" 342, with pump.
" 343, " "
" 344, " "
" 345, " "
" 346, " "
" 347, " "

ALTHOF, BERGMANN CATALOGUE, 1874

A TINY EARLY EXAMPLE, PROBABLY GERMAN. HEIGHT: 3 1/2" WIDTH: 4"

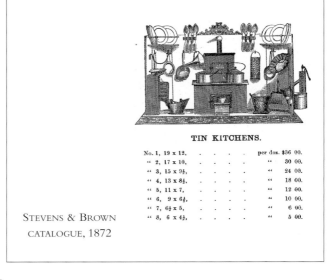

TIN KITCHENS.

No. 1,	19 x 12,	.	.	.	.	per doz.	$36 00.
" 2,	17 x 10,	.	.	.	.	"	30 00.
" 3,	15 x 9½,	.	.	.	.	"	24 00.
" 4,	13 x 8½,	.	.	.	.	"	18 00.
" 5,	11 x 7,	.	.	.	.	"	12 00.
" 6,	9 x 6½,	.	.	.	.	"	10 00.
" 7,	6½ x 5,	.	.	.	.	"	6 00.
" 8,	6 x 4½,	.	.	.	.	"	5 00.

STEVENS & BROWN CATALOGUE, 1872

A GARGANTUAN KITCHEN

The expert who replaced a few missing shelves in this kitchen found structural evidence to suggest a reason for its gargantuan width: two kitchens, he thought, had been combined. I am not as positive. It is possible that, for ease of construction, the two sections were built separately and then joined together. A built-in cupboard on the left-hand wall of one seems always to have been there, along with a matching built-in cupboard with drawer on the right. The matching plate racks in both sections and the set of drawers, appear to be original. It is clear that the impressive result has undergone, as similar household toys often do, assorted alterations in its long history. Just as dolls' houses were updated for younger sisters and, ultimately, for succeeding generations, this kitchen has had its share.

There is evidence here that the stove replaced an earlier oven, possibly with a hood. There is also an indication, where a strip has obviously been torn away on an inside wall, that a poultry coop adjoined a low shelf still present. Like the kitchen itself, the kitchen range may also be described as Gargantuan (13" wide plus water reservoir with faucet at the side), one of the most sizeable of the genre. With its brass bun feet, [1] the stove is supplied with blue enamelware pots and matching tea kettle. It is provided with the usual interior removable

GERMAN. MID-NINETEENTH CENTURY. HEIGHT: 15" WIDTH: 46"

1. Two ranges with bun feet (smaller than these) may be seen in the magnificent 1875 Rock & Graner catalogue and it is possible that this kitchen was made by the Biberach firm.

wicks for cooking: when "spirit" was ignited beneath the burners, it was possible to cook actual, withal miniature, food.

A number of the accessories in the 1875 Rock & Graner catalogue as well as the 1895 Märklin catalogue are to be found on the shelves. Of tin, the spoon holder, spice box, "coffee filter machine," and a splendid glazed lantern are to be seen in both catalogues. There are copper molds, one fish-shaped, and brass ladles, as well as an imposing wood and metal chopper for dealing with the blue sugar cones frequently found in grocer's shops of the period. (See page 324.) The extensive white porcelain tea and dinner service

ca. 1895 which lines the racks may have replaced pewter.

A brass mortar is missing its pestle. Curiously, I had always taken for granted a similar miniature mortar (and pestle) with matching candlesticks which had stood in my mother's Washington, D.C. kitchen, and then in mine, for two generations, but which I knew had been brought to this country in the middle of the nineteenth century from Germany, by my maternal grandmother, Bessie Hepner, born in 1839. When writing about this small brass mortar in 1999, belatedly, it dawned on me that, unknowingly, this had been the beginning of a substantial collection of miniaturiana—my own.

MÄRKLIN LANTERN

BUTCHER'S BLOCK

A VICTORIAN KITCHEN WITH PANTRY

When this colorful German kitchen with its adjoining pantry was acquired years ago, three of the original wood fixtures were affixed to the back wall. These, painted ivory with blue trim, were the decorative shelf, supported with porcelain tacks, the utensil rack (the missing wood handled porcelain potato masher, skimmer, etc. have been added) and the lid rack.

It was one of those coincidences so gratifying to collectors when somewhat later, I came across the lid rack—identical except dark oak—part of a matching set of kitchen pieces. There was a table, salt box, dough tray, dish cupboard, pie safe with stiff cloth mesh for ventilation, and a spice rack with five labeled drawers. The pot-lid rack was missing one side and is not shown here, but it was

GERMAN. MID-NINETEENTH CENTURY. HEIGHT: 12" WIDTH: 24 1/2"

clear that this set would be very much at home in this kitchen.

The most complex piece, which came with the group but was not originally part of it, is the popular ice box by Schneegass. This, with its elaborate hinges, pierced brass circular vent, wire racks and lift top, reveals two bottles of wine on most realistic ice. (The ice is original.)

The appealing "Blue Onion" Meissen patterned wall paper above a blue and white "tile" dado and, in the adjoining pantry, the red paper sprinkled with tiny gilt stars, provide a cheerful background for the oak furnishings. A toast rack with the original toast is on the tea table, probably unnoticed by the miniscule Vienna bronze mouse nearby. A chef with his molded-on hat may be too splendid for this nice middle-class kitchen, but he is, somehow, presiding.

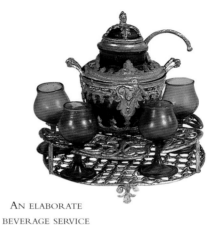

An elaborate
beverage service

Lid rack

Fruit rack (left)
and knife rack

A LATE VICTORIAN GERMAN KITCHEN

The variety of miniature kitchens made during the eighteenth and nineteenth centuries is astonishing, from the early Nuremberg examples with their lovely hand-wrought copper and pewter implements to the ones manufactured in quantity until as late as World War I. That the latter ones could be as elaborate as the most choosey small cook could wish is thoroughly demonstrated by this sizeable German specimen with its splendid clutter of furnishings and utensils.

The tin stove which has an alcohol trough beneath, can actually cook a (very) small dinner. [1] The curious, red-painted "Eismachine" with its white porcelain finial will not only make real ice cream but also has recipes, in French and German, on a page rolled up inside, for making several flavors—enough for several large dolls! A printer's symbol for 1894 on this sheet helps to date the whole.

Most of the plenishings came with this kitchen

1. The writer once attended a luncheon actually served from a considerably larger version of this stove. The hostess was obliged to refill the roast frequently from a larger pan in her full-sized kitchen, but the toy stove served to keep the small portions warm.

"Eismaschine" for
making actual
ice cream

and probably originated with it. Some pieces of enamelware of blue, white, and granite have been added to similar pieces, and there have been other additions, such as the tin icebox and the rack for "Sand, Seife, and Soda," a trio meant for scrubbing German tile floors (in this kitchen represented by a lovely stenciled pattern on varnished wood.) The chair which converts to a ladder is a combination often used for library steps. A tin rack labeled in German, with specified hooks on which to hang towels for glassware, silver, and china, harks back to an era of more meticulous and careful housekeeping than most of us have time for today.

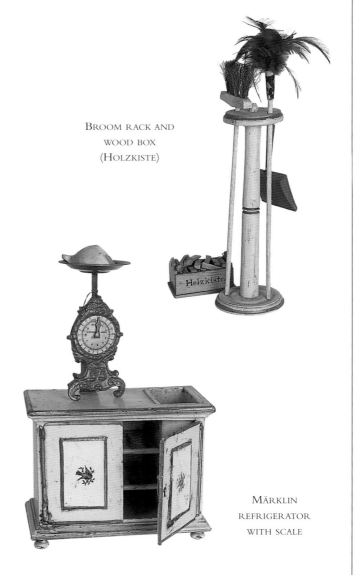

Broom rack and
wood box
(Holzkiste)

Märklin
refrigerator
with scale

CA. 1895. Height: 15" Width: 36"

A GOTTSCHALK KITCHEN

It is always gratifying for a collector to discover a piece in one's collection illustrated in an old catalogue or other publication. A smaller and possibly later version of this Gottschalk kitchen is shown in the black-and-white photograph from the December, 1923 issue of *House & Garden*. Considerably smaller (eight inches less in width) it lacks the window at the back [1] which considerably enhances the larger example, but contains some of the same furnishings, including the very "Gottschalkian" tall cupboard with its white pasteboard latticework.

The simpler stove in the *House & Garden* example may be later, or merely indicative of a less costly kitchen. The retail price of the H&G kitchen was $6.25 in 1923. The caption describes an "attractive blue and white kitchen," similar to our version. However, it lacks the casement window at the back, and such elaboration as the deep wallpaper border, very Dutch, with wooden shoes (on small girls) and windmills much in evidence.

There is a similar chair and side table and the identical enameled tin lavabo in both kitchens. Each includes a wall shelf. The larger kitchen has two, and the shelves on the one on the left are edged in lace, possibly added by the proud young owner.

HOUSE & GARDEN, 1923

EARLY 20TH CENTURY. HEIGHT: 15" WIDTH: 27"

1. There appears to be a smaller window on the side wall at the right, with a lace curtain. There are typical Gottschalk hooks for a curtain in the Museum's kitchen.

TWO ART NOUVEAU KITCHENS BY GOTTSCHALK

Both of these kitchens—the one-walled version, with its clock imbedded in the ultimate Art Nouveau setting, and the room-sized example, are to be seen in the Cieslik-Gottschalk 1905 archive. Each of the two is shown in five sizes.

The one-walled specimen came with its original tin stove (stovepipe top replaced) and assorted implements, not all original. The larger, room-sized kitchen has the rather over-sized service table built-in. The only accessory that remained with it when acquired was the chopping block and cleaver, to be seen in the catalogue illustration, but the built-in shelves with their swirling Art Nouveau brackets define their style and their era.

1905. ONE-WALLED VERSION. HEIGHT: 11" WIDTH: 16"

ROOM-SIZED VERSION. HEIGHT: 11" WIDTH: 22"

A Rare Kitchen by Converse

Inasmuch as it happens so seldom, it is gratifying when a toymaker of the past puts his name on his products.

I dislike referring to this rare and informative kitchen by Converse as a "product." It is quite charming with its china cabinet, window with potted plants and figured wallpaper, all lithographed on tin in a sunny palette of canary yellow and brick red—the latter matching the brick oven behind the kitchen range.

This, however, is a tin kitchen with a differ-ence: it is a tin-and-*wood* kitchen. The floor consists of incised strips of blonde and red wood. The sides are framed by a pair of round, typically Converse wood pilasters.

Most satisfying, however, is the silvery tin range built into the wall with "Converse" emblazoned on one of the lithographed doors. Two handled, lidded pots which came with the kitchen, fit over the two openings on top. A tin coal scuttle, which also accompanied the kitchen, is somewhat irrelevant inasmuch as

CONVERSE KITCHEN. CA. 1900. HEIGHT: 7 3/4" WIDTH: 17"

UNMARKED TIN KITCHEN.
CA. 1900. HEIGHT: 5 1/8" WIDTH: 10"

another is lithographed on the wall, reinforcing the fact that this is a coal-burning range.

The smaller kitchen, shown above, is entirely of tin but appears to be related though there is no reassuring maker's name to be seen on the lithographed "iron" range—only the stove's name: "My Pet." Again, there is a lithographed coal scuttle nearby.

A LARGE KITCHEN WITH PROVENANCE

In 1973 I received a letter from a Mrs. Muriel Fox in Schnecksville, Pennsylvania. The land in her area was soon to be flooded and she wanted to find a home for her childhood toys.

There were dolls and a few miscellaneous tea sets and such—and this enormous kitchen. She sent pictures, and after I journeyed to Pennsylvania

and acquired the collection, she wrote: "I know how important the history can be...." She offered information every serious collector longs for: her maiden name (Muriel Josephine Wall), her birth date in 1916 and her birthplace, East Orange, New Jersey. She had received the kitchen "at about age eight." It is, probably, by the ubiquitous Gottschalk,

CA. 1924. HEIGHT: 22" WIDTH: 45"

and inasmuch as she was born in New Jersey, it is likely that the kitchen was purchased in New York at F.A.O. Schwarz.

In any case, the kitchen speaks for itself. Although the metal stove and the Arcade refrigerator (the latter obviously an addition) are underscaled and dwarfed by the assortment of splendid wooden kitchen cabinets and other furnishings, the effect is imposing. Of the plenishings, nothing is omitted, from the cereal sets to the dish towels.

The cereal sets, one of tin, and one of German porcelain, are complete. (The latter contains such unusual labels as "gruel" and "gravel.")[1] There are foods both packaged and tinned, and prepared foods on the German cardboard plates of the period. There is an iron meat grinder and a tin oil lamp with reflector. There are strainers and graters and ladles. This was a kitchen for serious cookery, and there is an 8" glass-eyed doll in an apron to do the cooking.

IRON ARCADE ICEBOX

1. The latter absolutely defeats me. There was no "gravel" in my German dictionary. In Webster's it is predictably a mixture of sand and pebbles.

A TIN BATHROOM

From time immemorial, bathing the baby has been an important and essential aspect of doll play, it is not surprising to find the plumbing-conscious twentieth century provide a complete bathroom in miniature—with running water.

This liquid, the one full-sized element always in proper scale, is supplied, as in generations of the kitchens before it, in small tanks above the basin, tub, and commode. Turn the basin tap, which swivels, and there is a wonderfully realistic plug with a chain to detain the precious fluid. There is also a roll for the bathroom tissue, a towel rack complete with towels, and that memento of a more precise era, the bath thermometer. With even more realism, the shower head has a pump arrangement on the back which once provided at

GERMAN. EARLY 20TH CENTURY. HEIGHT: 7" WIDTH: 13"

least an unsatisfactory shower, and the commode has a pull handle attaching to a tank above which, for all we know, may still be workable.

It is of interest to note that this "imported bathroom," to be had in "beautiful pink or blue shaded enamel finish," was pictured in the 1922 catalogue of F.A.O. Schwarz at a selling price of $6.00.

It may also be of interest to note that this

example nearly failed to be collected: years ago, in Rhode Island, on our way to the Newport ferry, I stopped at one last antiques shop. On a table, with a price tag of $5 (!), was the quite irresistible specimen pictured. No proprietor was in view.

"Hello!" I called. "Hello!" There was no reply. More "Hellos!" Time to reach the ferry was becoming shorter. I suppose I could have put down a five dollar bill and left with my prize, but, somehow, I could not bring myself to do so.

With a number of other "Hellos!" and a final unanswered "Hello!" we got back into our car and headed toward the ferry. As we passed the antiques shop, sitting on their lawn, there were the proprietors, chatting with friends. I made my purchase and we reached the ferry in time.

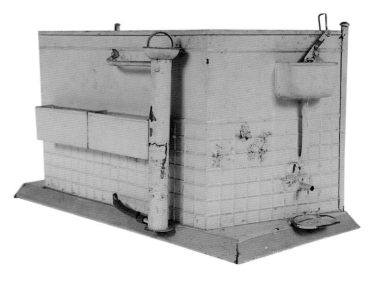

BACK OF BATHROOM

A Very Small House—An Outhouse

The makers of miniature wares not only provided indoor plumbing (when it became available) but they did not entirely neglect outdoor facilities. This small tin painted outhouse is rare. At least it is the only example that I've encountered. Inside, there's a hook for hanging a garment, and two shelves on the hinged door with circular openings, presumably for rolls of paper.

Ornamentation has not been omitted. A decorative pierced strip crowns the door with its workable knob. On this knob, a mere half-inch in diameter, a friend with an eye more discerning than my own discovered in raised lettering, and under a coat of yellow paint at that, the whole story: "MADE IN U.S.A." on the inner circle and "MERIDEN, CT." on the outer. There are also the initials of the manufacturer, which were not readable. I had thought the piece "probably German," and this was a discovery. Underneath the base is written in a florid turn-of-the-century hand: "Compliments of A.E.Lamb, October, 1903."

The front and sides of the small structure include small diamond-shaped openings for ventilation. The corrugated roof is painted a sky blue within, and the projecting tin base is a grassy green.

AMERICAN. DATED 1903. HEIGHT: 6 1/2" BASE: 4 1/2" SQUARE

AN ARCADE BATHROOM

The name of "Crane," a manufacturer long celebrated in the world of full-sized plumbing, is printed on the bath rug in this folding cardboard bathroom. The fixtures themselves are considerably more substantial, painted cast-iron toys made by the Arcade Manufacturing Co. of Freeport, Illinois as faithful imitations of full-sized furnishings for all the rooms of a house. Included were diminutive versions of the products of major manufacturers of the 'twenties and 'thirties—"Hot Point" stoves, "Thor" washers and other well-known names in kitchen and laundry appliances, so realistic in appearance that they are likely to be mistaken for salesman's samples in uninformed circles.

Dining-room, living-room, and bedroom furniture, also copies of manufactured pieces, must be rather uncomfortable in cast-iron, even for dolls. They, however, are assiduously collected—by full-sized collectors, and, for those who have the space, a huge house to contain all of them occasionally can be found.

AMERICAN. 1926-34. HEIGHT: 12" WIDTH: 10"

AN IMPORTED DENTIST OFFICE

Perhaps this toy was meant to placate young patients who were unenthusiastic about visiting the office of their full-sized dentist. The dentist here is celluloid, hardly threatening, but the instruments of torture are all too realistic.

These metal fittings, painted in cream, include the dentist chair, with head and foot-rest, the patient's basin, connected by a pipe to the wall and, most importantly, to a tray with cups and a highly visible and moveable drill. Like the tin bathroom, shown on page 308, a tank on the rear of the right-hand wall leads to a pedestal sink where a faucet may release real water. The latter may be, if need be, retained with a small plug on a chain. (The legs of the young celluloid patient are too short to take advantage of the foot-rest.)

PROBABLY GERMAN. CA. 1920. HEIGHT: 6" WIDTH: 11"

Few details have been neglected. A metal rack for patients' garments is attached to the wall. Also on the wall are a metal-framed mirror and, most importantly, a framed certificate on which the word "college" can be distinctly read. Another patient, this one of bisque, has been added to the improvised "waiting-room" along with a bench for her comfort (not shown).

This dentist office bears a strong resemblance to the tin bathroom, shown on page 308, described as "imported" in a 1922 F.A.O. Schwarz catalogue. Here, for a reason difficult to account for, the walls are not of metal but of heavy cardboard, but they are obviously original. Perhaps, following World War I, metal for such purposes was in short supply.

It is possible that this toy was not particularly popular. I have never seen another.[1]

PROBABLY GERMAN. CA. 1920. HEIGHT: 6" WIDTH: 11"

1. It rarely fails to happen: a few months after writing these words, I was able to acquire a dentist office identical to the first, shown above, with two exceptions: the walls, as speculated about above, are indeed metal, though, sadly, with considerable paint loss, and several major fittings are incomplete or missing. I considered moving the mint-condition fittings into this scruffy shell, identical in size and openings, but could not bring myself to do so.

PART VII

Shops: Mercantile History

in Miniature

A Rare Toy Stall

One felt indeed a serendipitous moment when this rare—perhaps unique—toy and sweet stall found in Zurich[1] revealed its enchanting secret. Its stock, about seventy miniscule toys and sweets, had been described by the London dealer who sold it as "of wood and plaster." However the delicately molded fruits and figures appeared to the touch to be of a more delicate substance. It was fortuitous that one tiny cupboard arrived broken, for a bit of paper neatly folded inside it reminded a momentarily distressed collector that this damaged treasure had to be of gum tragacanth, a substance which early-nineteenth-century pastry cooks combined with meal and

CA. 1800 HEIGHT: 11" WIDTH: 8"

1. Undoubtedly, however, made in Germany

sugar, molded into charming novelties with mottoes inside, and then painted. Printed in old German, the motto placed perhaps two centuries ago inside the ancient tidbit discovered here, is as fatuous as most "fortune cookie" messages, but a treasure for all that. It led to the writing of *The Toy Shop Mystery*.[1] Gröber, the German toy historian, relates that the little figures were "for the most part edible" and became at their best an imitation of porcelain.

Among the meticulously fashioned articles in this assortment are bowls of fruit, a boy on his hobby horse, a mask for a masquerade, and the cuirass from a suit of armor. The wooden toys include checkerboards, bayonets, hobby horses, tenpins, whips, and tiny musical instruments— horns, drums, and lutes. The booth itself, which has a door in one side, is painted a rusty sienna on the outside and a faded blue inside and is presided over by a beautifully carved wooden proprietress whose face, alas, is missing.

FROM AN EARLY NINETEENTH CENTURY GERMAN CATALOGUE

GUM TRAGACANTH ITEMS WITH MOTTOS FROM SHOP

GUM TRAGACANTH FIGURE

1. Flora Gill Jacobs, Coward-McCann, 1960

AN EARLY GENERAL STORE

ound in Zurich along with the toy stall shown on pages 316 and 317, this appealing general store may be of the late eighteenth century, and is no later than early nineteenth. The paper labels on its sixty small drawers with bail handles are in German. A few are missing, and some are illegible. Figs, almonds, lentils, marjoram, caraway, candles, sago, and anise, at random, give a key to the type of merchandise they represent, and an expert in such items might write a learned treatise on the total.

There is a slot in the counter leading to a money drawer below, and glass doors enclose dis-

CA. 1800. HEIGHT: 19" WIDTH: 27"

play shelves behind the counter on which bead necklaces hang in profusion. A net bag of attractive ceramic fish may be seen on the counter near one of two handsome baskets for sale with their original price tickets. Bundles of candles, a basket of coiled wax tapers, and jars of candy "pills" with stretched paper tops are among the stock. Fabrics were obviously a specialty of the shop. (Perhaps there was no mercer in the neighborhood.) There are shelves of tiny bolts of fabric, and although a museum authority on textiles has told us that they, actually cards of ribbon, are from the 1870's, considerably later than the shop itself, many are embroidered in lovely old colors and patterns and are late but delightful additions to this rare piece, one of the earliest in the collection.

CERAMIC FISH IN MESH BAG

SLOT IN COUNTER LEADING TO CHANGE DRAWER BELOW

An Early German "Handlung"

"Early" is a reasonably vague dating for a toy establishment I believe to be from no later than the first half of the nineteenth century. Like the early nineteenth century general store shown on pages 318 and 319, there is a slot in the counter to the cash drawer below—the only two shops in the collection with this primitive predecessor to the cash register.

This large and beautiful "Materialwaren-Handlung" is hand-painted, and is so early and pure that I have resisted adding anything whatever to the relatively few accessories which accompanied it. These include a brass scale on a heavy iron frame, a brown-painted barrel with matching pair of canisters, and a painted tole urn which is for kerosene. (Shown elsewhere, a similar example which appears to be later, is labeled "Petroleum."[1]) Lacquered in tan with black striping, this fascinating object, as the detail illustration on the next page shows, features a glass protuberance encased in black-painted metal with a cock above and a workable faucet below. (A small lid is missing from the top.) There are movable wire handles. This vessel accommodated the fuel for the lighting used in the shop.

On the decorative bar across the top, there are five small pegs. From one of these the only other accessory is suspended. This consists of a set of six paper bags with printed labels, attached as a group with thread which is clearly original. In varying colors, two of these are marked "Kaufhaus zum sussen Männlein," and two are marked "Bezug zum guten Engel." These and another marked "Max & Moritz" bear a small, identical trade mark of a stylized bird.

Height: 17 3/4" Width: 28"

1. Shown in *Doll Kitchens*, Eva Stille.

The remaining bag, with a different trade mark, is printed "Geschwister Klein."

These grocery bags must have been placed in the shop at a later stage in its history. Max and Moritz were the stars of a celebrated early twentieth-century German comic strip and, assuredly, this store is considerably earlier.

There is a total of thirty drawers, one set of which is placed vertically between the two pairs of glazed cupboards, and there is a double row across the base. It is of interest to note that there are no labels on these. In the early-nineteenth-century shop, shown on pages 318 and 319, labels were pasted on, and perhaps that procedure was intended here.

To summon the shopkeeper, a cord outside the right-hand window is attached to a brass bell within. The painted detail on the sides includes arched windows with painted panes which match the glazed pair on the façade, and coigning. One longs to know who the maker of this rare piece was, and when it was made.

SIDE OF "HANDLUNG"

THIS "GROCERY STORE" WAS UNDOUBTEDLY MADE BY THE SAME GERMAN MAKER FOR THE AMERICAN MARKET
HEIGHT: 9" WIDTH: 10 1/2"

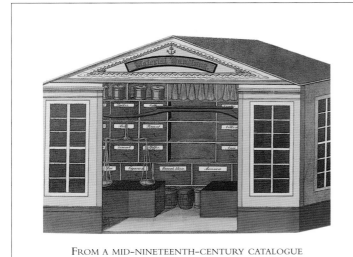

FROM A MID-NINETEENTH-CENTURY CATALOGUE

KEROSENE
DISPENSER

"BULL BUTCHER"

Why the butcher shop should have an appeal in miniature that it conspicuously lacks in full-size is demonstrated in this especially charming example with its quite uncharming sign: "Bull Butcher." The many little cuts of meat, realistic in shape, are quite unrealistic and chaste in material. The small roasts, sausages, and slabs of bacon are uniformly of oak (bearing that patina so desired in antique furniture!) which banishes all thought of gore and reveals them largely as exquisite little objects. Especially appealing are two strings

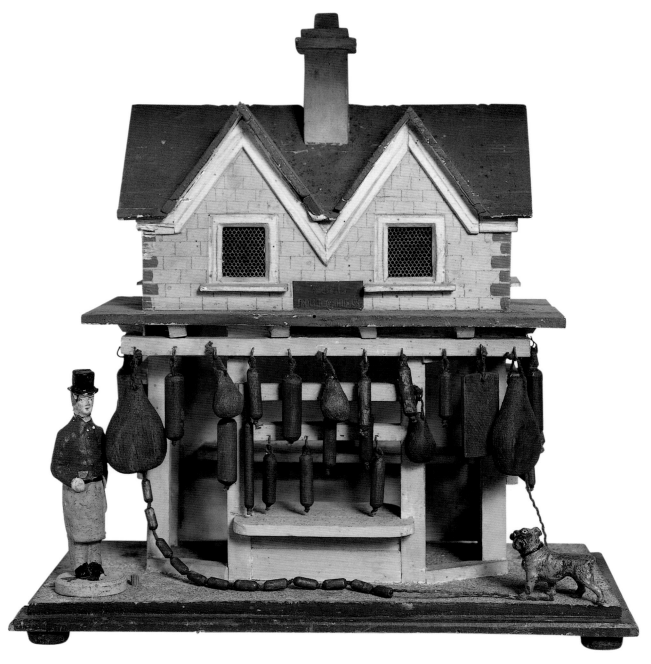

CA. 1850. HEIGHT: 13" BASE: 11" x 6"

of link sausages. The meats, perhaps thirty-five in all, are hung by stout threads, darkened with age, on delicate hooks.

The value of old toy catalogues is well-illustrated, literally, in the case of this shop. Some thirty years ago, the catalogue illustration shown below was discovered in a ca. 1848 German toy catalogue found in Copenhagen. This was a heady discovery to one who had almost the identical butcher's shop in her collection. (Naïvely one learns quite a lot during the course of half a century of collecting.) I'd thought the sign "Bull Butcher" necessarily referred to a toy made in England where butcher shops were popular toys.[1] I soon realized that this shop and many others were European, labeled in various languages for export.

As one can see, with the exception of a few bits of trim, the sausages, and the butcher, this shop and the one in the catalogue are nearly identical. (The butcher is a replacement—a lucky find. The late Patrick Murray, Curator of Toys at the Toy Museum in Edinburgh, explained, when he came to dinner years ago, that British butchers wore bowler hats—not top hats, which German butchers wore, as this one does.)

In the shop, the sand is on the floor, and there is a peg on which the butcher stands. The footed base of the structure supports the yellow building with its red brick coigning and dark green roof. Stiffened net, covering two windows in front and one at each side, presumably prevents flies from invading the proprietor's lodging upstairs. The meat, of course, is not so well protected.

FROM A GERMAN CATALOGUE, CA. 1850

1. And where elaborate models of such shops, not necessarily made as toys, were often to be found in the windows of full-sized butcher's shops, usually with an endorsement by the Crown.

A CHRISTIAN HACKER GROCERY

This appealing grocer's shop was found in a remarkably unblemished state, with the unfortunate exception that its counter was missing. Fortuitously, the drawer from the counter survived and Jim Reus, restorer par excellence, recreated the counter, incorporating the drawer and the painted details of the desk in the proprietor's office. The pattern for the counter was borrowed from one in another store of similar style and vintage.

The striking feature, of course, is the proprietor's office, separated by its own door and provided with a gleaming brass bell which rings clearly when the wooden handle in the shop is pulled. Also present is the proprietor himself—a bearded chalk figure—as well as a group of blue sugar loaves (of wood) and a variety of wood canisters with such arresting labels as "Prussian Snuff."

The five drawers across the back bear the gilt and "rosewood" lithography which is similar to that on Waltershausen furniture. The piece, however, with its charming decals of ivy trailing down the pilasters, is not from Waltershausen. It bears the paper label of Christian Hacker, the Nuremberg maker who is also responsible for many exquisite dolls' houses including "The Queen Anne Mansion" (page 212).

PAPER LABEL ON BASE

CA. 1880. HEIGHT: 19 3/4" WIDTH: 20"

"Gertrud's Store"

Although the two stenciled labels proclaiming that this was the "Kaufhaus" of "Gertrud" are an addition, and the exterior of her shop regrettably was repainted, the interior is virtually in mint condition, suggesting that its young owner was careful with her toys.

The sixteen drawer-fronts with their imitation wood veneer and brass labels proclaiming the usual staples, and typical of the manner of Christian Hacker, are like new. I long to remove the yellow paint with its red trim from the exterior, but with its handsome glass windows at front and sides and its scroll-cut embellishments, this is as appealing a doll's shop as one might wish to see. And it is not every day that one finds such a piece with its owner's name, a personal link, however anonymous, to the past. (It would seem almost an affront to remove it.)

The staples and spices, like Gertrud's name, are in German. Among them are "Biscuit" and "Salz,"
"Safran" and "Anis," and "Lorbeerbl.", the latter an abbreviation, I learn, for "bayleaf." With its four iron weights, the brass scale is a mammoth object which is attached to the counter and virtually covers it.

A pair of hinged, painted tin cake boxes, several tea canisters handsomely decorated with scenes of life in the Orient, a few pieces of stoneware and glass, and the visible assortment of porcelain jars are among the shop's varied containers. Half a dozen plants, as fresh as daisies, and some of the other fittings, are undoubtedly additions.

FAÇADE SECTION
SWINGS OUT

BY CHRISTIAN HACKER.
CA. 1880.
HEIGHT: 18"
WIDTH: 23"

STIRN & LYON GROCERIES

If the two Stirn & Lyon "Combination" Dolls' Houses shown on pages 98-100, are charming and unassuming, perhaps it is fair to say that this Stirn & Lyon "Combination Grocery Store" is comely and imposing. It is assembled in very much the same tongue-and-groove, peg-and-dowel manner as the two houses, and is of the same unpainted wood with pressure-printed lettering and decorations. It has beams and other accents in the bittersweet red which adds so much decorative warmth to the houses, but it has considerably more personality.

Like the two houses, its parts fit into a wooden box which becomes the foundation when beams, walls, and other segments are "combined." Like them, its lid is covered with a lithographed label bearing an idealized and ornamental portrait of a Victorian grocery plus some basic information:

DATE PATENTED: 1882. HEIGHT: 21 3/4" WIDTH: 18"

BOX LID
HEIGHT: 9" WIDTH: 18"

"Manufactured by Stirn & Lyon N. Y. Patented April 11, 1882." The label also offers the names of groceries one might expect to find in such a store at the time, and even some trade names which may very well be useful to future food historians—who are unlikely to find a more vivid or concise memo on the subject. It is of interest that these products pictured on the box label differ almost entirely from the ones inside, a discrepancy which suggests that the toy was made by Stirn & Lyon, but that the lithography may have been done elsewhere.

Some of the products mentioned are possibly still available—Royal Baking Powder, for instance. A specialist might write a monograph about these "classics," and those no longer familiar—"Washington Mills" on a barrel, "Morgan's Hand Sapolio" on a case. And was Sudsine H. B. & F., as it sounds, a laundering agent? What about "S. K. Mumm Extra Dry 12450"—we wonder if this was the delectable vintage its name evokes?

There are many others, none of them the same as the stock inside. The stock on the shelves consists of the same wood to be found in the store itself, unpainted or stained with that marvelous shade of red, but made in blocks, rectangular or square, embossed with the names (though not the shapes),

of the products they represent. We'd suspect, even if the manufacturer's name were not available, where he was located, from such labels as "N. Y. State All Cream Factory Cheese" and "Pride of Jersey Tomatoes." There are also such exotic imports as "Jamaica Allspice," but the implication is clear.

The clock over the counter ungraciously states "No Time Here," but even if "Cash & Co" did not give credit, it undoubtedly gave pleasure to the young shopkeeper who played with this engaging establishment.

The steps across the front of the store, made with treads which fit into grooves (as are the narrower flights on the Stirn & Lyon houses), resemble the wide steps one used to see in front of old country stores. "Mr. and Mrs. Lehmann Walking Down Broadway" may be seen, with their dog. This early Lehmann toy relates to an astonishing coincidence. I had placed this appealing tin couple—their dog missing—in front of the store. Then Madame St. Quintin's dolls' house came to me. In the large mélange of unsorted furnishings was Mr. and Mrs. Lehmann's tin dog. (Part of a toy made for the American market by a German company in an English house.) There was an emotional reunion.

Mr. Lehmann's cane, alas, is still missing.

A DELICATESSEN BY GOTTSCHALK

The heading here might read "Before" and "After." The small black-and-white photograph illustrates the appearance of this Gottschalk general store when it was acquired years ago. It also may serve as an illustration of the possibilities of sensitive restoration.

The counter had been heavily over-painted. For some fortunate reason, the "fancy columns" (as described in the catalogue) which guard the mirrored door in the central alcove, and the simpler pilasters on the front, were left alone. An ebony elephant placed between the two finials presented a challenge. Under this, "W. D'Oliphant" was rather casually hand-lettered, and one suspects that this store was a display piece in a full-sized Dutch delicatessen, and the ebony elephant a visual pun, perhaps relating to the owner's name.

Clearly this store was made for the Dutch market. The familiar metal ribbon labels remain untouched on the drawers and those include "HARING" and "RAGOUT VON TONG." (The latter sounds tempting, but I, as they say, haven't a clue.) The sizeable assortment of tins are also labeled in Dutch. The thimble-sized tins

CA. 1892. HEIGHT: 15" WIDTH: 22"

include such delicacies as "ASTRAKAN CAVIAR" and "APRIKOSEN," the latter two reasonably identifiable without a Dutch dictionary, unlike some of the others—"WARDBEYSEN-SAP," for instance. Unfortunately, many of the tins were silvered in a stubborn paint which has resisted all efforts to remove it. Even the blue sugar loaves were silvered, but on these wood loaves, the silver was removable.

The original Gottschalk wall phone, unmistakable with its pair of dangling receivers and white-painted transmitter, remains hanging in the alcove.

This clearly was made as a "delicatessen," as the original lithographed strip beneath the molded central ornament states. The molded ornament, of course, replaced the elephant, and the substitution is an educated guess. It is possible, judging from similar but not identical Gottschalk stores, that the original may have included a clock.[1] In any case,

I've presumed to have the ornament to be seen at each side duplicated. The latter was molded and painted by Jim Reus who sensitively restored other areas, especially the counter, which had been unnecessarily and mysteriously, redecorated.

ORIGINAL GOTTSCHALK TINS LABELED IN DUTCH

PHONE ORIGINAL TO SHOP

SHOP BEFORE RESTORATION

FROM CIESLIK ARCHIVE, 1892

1. There was indeed a clock. Early in 2001, Marianne and Jurgen Cieslik discovered a complete set of catalogue photos (original negatives on celluloid) of all Gottschalk products between 1892 through 1931. They found these in a closed down printing company.

A photograph of this very delicatessen was among the illustrations from the year 1892. It is possible that this shop was also made earlier. There are two examples shown and this is the larger of the two.

AN ELEGANT GOTTSCHALK MILLINER'S SHOP

Like the magnificent stable shown on pages 360 and 361, this elegant milliner's shop is one of the deluxe productions of Moritz Gottschalk. Its German origin belies its Parisian appearance.

As though the pristine condition of its mirrored cabinets, its blue cream and gilt decor, and its beguiling accessories were not disarming enough, this lovely toy bears a further collector's delight— its original label. When the celebrated New York toy seller F.A.O. Schwarz helpfully affixed his name and address, the latter was "West 23rd Street," the firm's location between 1890 and 1910. Although

CA. 1900. HEIGHT: 18" WIDTH: 27"

a twenty-year span will seem rather wide, it is relatively specific in the dating of designs which frequently were repeated for several decades.

The styles of the merchandise—the straw and felt millinery, beflowered and beplumed, may be a bit later. Presumably all the merchandise came with the shop, but some additions are possible.

The counter, a pair of wide drawers behind it, and the elegant pair of console mirrors at either

side which hang upon the delicately papered walls, are movable. Other original accoutrements include the delicate metal hat display racks, weighted and gilded, an ivory hand mirror, and a standing wooden rack. The bisque clerk, the lamp, customer, a cash register (National), and the gilt metal "bentwood" furniture with wire mesh seats have been added. So, too, has the charming spool rack on the counter. The latter was made about half a century ago by a retired textile manufacturer, the father of Elizabeth Zenorini, a New Jersey dealer from whom this lovely shop, the Tiffany House and other treasures were acquired. It is one of three reproduction pieces in the collection. The lithographed clock which presides over the shop is, alas, only a pretty face, which says, 1:27—presumably for all eternity.

Soft-lead German cash register with workable mechanism

Gilded metal hatstand with original millinery

A "FRENCH MILLINER'S SHOP"

It is disconcerting that I can't recall where this attractive piece, entirely of mahogany, came from, or anything about its past. When the Museum opened in 1975, it was provided with a sign designating it as "A French Milliner's Shop," from information undoubtedly supplied by the seller, but I cannot guarantee its nationality.

With sets of drawers flanking a vertical mirror, and shelves below, it is assuredly meant for a custom milliner. Feathers, straw, and other materials are still to be found in the drawers.[1] There is no counter, possibly lost before the piece came into my possession. Two sets of bentwood tables and chairs have been supplied, along with a clock and a fashionable customer. In any case, it is part of the Museum's "Shop-windowful of Shops" in which the individual establishments—butcher, grocer, etc., are arranged on elevated rectangular plinths, a display adapted from a full-sized shop window in an early photograph.

HEIGHT: 14" WIDTH: 20"

1. There is a recent discovery—penciled writing on the back of most of the twelve drawers, barely decipherable, which suggests that at one point in its existence, the milliner's shop may have held foodstuffs—spices perhaps. The words appear to relate to food—"chicory," sucre (sugar?), and such. I do not choose to take them seriously...

A GROCERY BY BLISS

Instead of "R. Bliss" on the door of this small grocery, there is a sign saying "Fresh Dried Beef."

There is no Bliss name elsewhere either, but because the grocery store was a peculiarly American establishment, it had always been clear that this miniature example was made in the United States. The presence of an American flag in the hand of the small boy in an upper window only underlined this realization, but it was not till the store was discovered in a 1901 Bliss catalogue that its maker could be positively identified.

The grocery had been patented in 1895 and had been "materially improved for the year 1901." Perhaps the patentable features were the awning, braced by a movable wooden bracket on one side, and the double cardboard dormer which fits an opening beneath the folding roof (exactly as it does on the unmarked Bliss house on page 113).

The Bliss lithography is as usual, imaginative, and it is also—to students of inflation—informative. In a window showing numerous cuts of meat, there is a barrel of apples with a sign: "15¢ a peck." Pickles are "10¢ a doz." Along with sacks of flour and tubs of butter and lard, there are several items which were staples then which are no longer to be found on grocery shelves: stove polish and bottles of blueing.

A cake of lithographed paper-on-wood soap glued to the counter, and several wooden bottles and barrels appear to be original.

FROM BLISS 1901 CATALOGUE

Patented March 12, 1895.

CA. 1895. HEIGHT: (NOT INCLUDING CHIMNEY) 9" WIDTH: (INCLUDING EAVES) 9"

A VICTORIAN BUTCHER

Although this butcher's shop was made in Germany for the British trade, butcher's shops were almost as traditional a plaything in England as the toy theater.

I so described this one in a book[1] more than thirty years ago, and I was a bit startled some years later when Evelyn Ackerman asked to illustrate it in her splendid book about Gottschalk.[2] She identified it as Gottschalk primarily by the brick, windows, curtains, and other printed details. And of course it has a blue roof. However, many German companies were turning out similar toys, and it is known that there were common sources for such printed papers. Mrs. Ackerman may be correct that this is a Gottschalk piece, but, in labeling this, I shall be conservative and wait for more comprehensive proof to come along.

This shop, like "Bull Butcher" shown on pages 322 and 323, has the addition of the butcher's living quarters above. The butcher, a chalkware chap, wears his top hat, as a proper butcher should, but his cleaver is missing, an absence indicated by the empty scabbard at his waist. We know that he's been standing in the same spot for well over a century inasmuch as he fits on a peg near his doorway. Little was left to a child's imagination in Victorian days, but antiquarians may rejoice here at the permanence of a position as well as an object.

Examples of great elaboration crammed with roasts and haunches in which hardly a rib or vein is left undefined, were often to be found in the windows of full-sized butchers' shops. These are quite beautiful examples of Mr. A.C. Benson's theory quoted elsewhere in these pages, that "there is great beauty in smallness...the blemishes and deformities (of similar objects) in full size...all disappear."

CA. 1880.[3]
HEIGHT: 16" WIDTH: 19"

1. *Victorian Dolls' Houses*
2. Ibid
3. An educated guess. Nothing similar is to be seen in the Cieslik-Gottschalk reprint which does not begin till 1892. However if this was made for the British market (as the Empire furniture is believed by many to have been made in Germany for the French market), these may have been shown in a separate archive or in no catalogue at all.

AN UNUSUAL "AMERICAN GROCERY"

The oak strip affixed to the top of this small oak place of business leaves no doubt as to its purpose. With calligraphic flourishes, the sign proclaims: "American Grocery." I do not know who made it, and I have seen only one other, advertised in 1995 by a New Hampshire antiques dealer in the indispensable *Maine Antiques Digest*.

The example in the *Digest* lacks several pieces to be seen in the Museum's version—a matching oak floor which offers a base for the counter and a two-poled object (not shown) where possibly a billboard would be posted, but with nothing to suggest where the two tall supports would be placed. The front closes.

Both examples include identical iron scales, of a rather unusual style, and even a few of the same groceries, e.g., Uneeda Biscuit.

The New Hampshire dealer for some reason chose to label it a "Toy Country Store." Our dating, "ca. 1900," purports to be an "educated guess."

CA. 1900. HEIGHT: 8" WIDTH: 11"

A Cartheuser "Grocery Store" from Stuttgart

The paragraphs to accompany the photograph of this attractive store had been written, and the store identified by me as German…"assuredly made for the English market by one of the numer-ous German toy makers in Saxony, the Rhone Valley, or elsewhere…" Then I made a significant discovery. In my collection of antique toy cata-logues which had been mislaid, there was one with

Turn of the century. Height: 15" Width: 28"

an illustration of the identical "laden."

(To a toy researcher, this was like discovering America.)

This is the largest in a series of shops pictured by Carl Cartheuser of Stuttgart, a firm founded in 1846, and identifying itself in several languages as a "Manufacturer of High Class Toys." Unfortunately

the catalogue is not dated, but appears to be from the turn of the century or before. [1]

Like the earlier mid-nineteenth-century butcher's shop shown on page 322-323, this store was made in Germany for the British trade. The labels on the drawers are in English, and the store had been part of an English collection of toys and games assembled in the early years of this century, and packed away till about thirty years ago when I acquired it, curiously enough, from an English antiquarian bookseller.

There has been a recent tendency to associate most German toys of this type with Gottschalk. This one is, as can be seen, very different in character, and as mentioned above, I made the assumption before rediscovering the catalogue that this was by one of the many other German toy makers. Unlike the metal labels on the drawers of Gottschalk shops, the labels here are of porcelain. [2] They mention "Candy" as well as such foodstuffs as "Flour," "Rice," and "Cocoa." The two metal urns in niches alongside the drawers and the wooden kegs in a rack on the floor suggest beverages. Appealing items on the shelves, clearly added

SHOP BELL

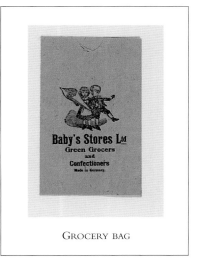

GROCERY BAG

1. After these words were written, this very store was discovered in a 1902 Gamages trade catalogue where two sizes were described as "strong oak grocery stores." One of these, "complete as illustration" was for sale at "15/6" and the "large size" at "27/6."
2. It should be noted that in the Cartheuser catalogue, most of the shops appear to have porcelain labels, but the catalogue does include one substantial shop, and several counters with drawers, which have metal labels similar to the ones on Gottschalk pieces. This reinforces a further theory that these accessory pieces were not necessarily made by the factories which did the woodwork, but were acquired elsewhere, from other companies which specialized in porcelain or metal fitments.

after the store crossed the channel, include a wooden case imprinted "Boot Buttons Penny Per Box" and a sponge with a price tag marked 7d. A wooden rack on the counter may once have held an account book.

The style and detail of the dark woodwork suggest an earlier date than the likeness of Edward VII on an attractive red, gold, and blue tin canister, or even that of Her Majesty, Queen Victoria, on an embossed tin would suggest. Such accoutrements are, of course, often added for or by a younger member of a family.

A few bits of trim are missing, and the only clue to the original vivid blue pattern of the wallpaper, now faded brown, is to be found inside a hanging shelf on one side. Perhaps the most distinctive feature of the shop are the roll shutters which still glide smoothly outside the glass windows.

A rare, workable metal shop bell, shown on the counter of the previous page, is an addition and so, of course, is the Märklin hanging lamp. A scale similar

to the one shown in the catalogue is a substitution.

A Postscript: at almost the zero hour, as these pages were completed, it was discovered that a less imposing but most appealing grocery store had somehow never been photographed. It proved to be another grocery by Cartheuser. A very similar example, perhaps produced in a different year, may be seen in the catalogue shown on next page.

Because "Grocery Store" appears on the decorative sign upon the crest, this piece appears to have been made for the American market. (If, for the British, it might have said "Grocer.") As in the big example from Britain, the porcelain drawer labels are in English—"Raisins" and "Sugar," though the maker, not in complete command of English nomenclature, included "Hirse" (the German for Millet) and "Caffee." The counter has a marbleized top and a stenciled front. I've chosen to furnish it more as a general store, with pairs of (metal) rubbers, lanterns (containing their original candies), and pottery jugs.

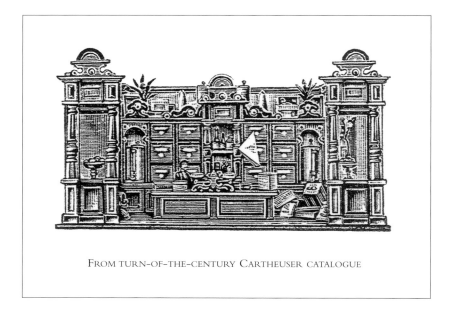

FROM TURN-OF-THE-CENTURY CARTHEUSER CATALOGUE

ANOTHER "GROCERY STORE" BY CARTHEUSER

This relatively modest grocery store was found many years ago in virtually mint condition, its papered walls and floors unblemished. There were no groceries save for those implied by the drawer labels.

The items which have been installed are in the nature of ones to be found in a general store, except that full-sized lanterns do not, as these do, contain (the original) minuscule pink and white candies. There are also multiple pairs of rubbers (another contribution from early crackerjack boxes) and labeled bottles of Port, nearly evaporated, alas, on the mirrored shelves behind the counter.

The clerk is also an addition. Her fabric clothes cover a well modeled plaster figure, and she has a small metal hook in her white cap, suggesting that she was once a marionette, but she looks very much in charge.

When I discovered the big Cartheuser Grocery Store shown on pages 336 and 337, in my Gamage's trade catalogue, I had not noticed this smaller example lurking on a previous page— nearly identical to the illustration. The exception was "Material Handlung" rather than "Grocery Store" on the sign. For years I'd assumed it was a Gottschalk piece.

There are porcelain labels on the eight drawers in lieu of the more usual metal "ribbon" ones to be found on Gottschalk drawer-fronts. These define such essentials as "COFFEE," "SUGAR," and "RICE." There was some slight confusion in language with two: One says "HIRSE" which translates to "MILLET," and one which says "CACAO."

CA. 1900.
HEIGHT: 9 1/2" WIDTH: 15 3/4"

TWO GOTTSCHALK BUTCHERS' SHOPS

About forty years ago a number of small butchers' shops were found in mint condition by a Baltimore antiques dealer. The smaller of the two shops shown here was one of these.

At the time their Gottschalk origin was undiscovered. In more recent years, the stenciled counter and pilasters, and the wallpapered interiors clearly identified the maker. The wooden counter and the realistically molded and painted cuts of meat which hang suspended on brass rods across the back, and from simple hooks on the side walls, were the only contents. From the same old store stock, small tin scales were found in quantities and one was placed in the shop. (The butcher and the customers are other more arbitrary additions.)

The (considerably) larger of the two shops contains an additional counter, a more elaborate scale, and more numerous cuts of meat. The wallpaper border with its landscaped series of houses is more elaborate than the simple strip at the top of the small version.

EARLY 20TH CENTURY.
HEIGHT: 6"
WIDTH: 13"

EARLY 20TH CENTURY.
HEIGHT: 10 1/2" WIDTH: 22 3/4"

A "Lost" Japanese Porcelain Shop

The shop itself was lost. The contents, mercifully, were not.

This beguiling assemblage was sent, in 1909, by a lady in Kyoto on her wedding trip to her little sister in Washington, D.C. It was purchased from the little sister, then elderly, about thirty years ago.

It seems almost a sacrilege that the multitudinous tea sets, saki sets, covered bowls, and ginger jars, to name a part, are here displayed in an old wooden Coca-Cola case, but all of the pieces are so exquisitely wrought that nothing can detract from their delicacy and beauty.

The tea sets, in various scales, were made both for export, with handles on the cups, and for domestic use, without the handles. Some are glazed; most are unglazed. One ceramic pattern which features alternating panels of cream-dotted coral and floral blue, is found, though rarely, in early Victorian dolls' houses. Such a tea set came with the mid-Victorian Pennsylvania Cupboard House, suggesting that the contents of the lost shop may have been antique when purchased in 1909, or, like many porcelains in full-size, were repeated over a period of years. In the collection, there are tea sets in this appealing pattern in various sizes. There is an infinitesimal tea set with a ceramic side handle on one pot and a conventional diaphanous wire handle on the other.

CA. 1909. CASE: HEIGHT: 12" WIDTH: 18" (CASE NOT ORIGINAL)

(Somewhat larger teapots in various patterns have actual wrapped handles in raffia, or a diminutive equivalent thereof.) Also to be found in the coral and blue paneled pattern are ginger jars, pitchers and a most unusual three-tiered covered casserole.

There are many pieces in blue and white, including attractive covered (rice?) bowls with blue striping, and rectangular flowered platters with canted borders. A teapot in deep green is set upon a matching hibachi. In the same deep green, a bowl, with a swan incredibly molded within, is accompanied by tiny serving dishes, similarly molded but with a pattern too diminutive to discern. There is more. Much more.

What must be said is that to find such a treasure as this is almost improbable. In various illustrated books about Japanese miniature pieces in recent years, I have seen only one porcelain shop, and the contents were totally different in concept. (Mostly vases and other larger pieces were represented.) An expert in Japanese ceramics could undoubtedly produce a learned and lengthy paper on the contents of this remarkable collection. Perhaps one day one will.

Another remarkable miniature object came with the shop contents which is unrelated, and is added here as a sort of postscript: it is a miniscule "doctors' doll,"[1] 1 3/8" long, of ivory, fully articulated and so detailed that even the thumbs are defined. Its comparably miniscule wooden box is also, needless to say, a treasure. (The emperor and empress have been added.)

PORCELAIN JAR AND BOWL

DOCTOR'S DOLL

1. This, of course, was taken to the doctor by its owner, who modestly pointed to the affected member on the doll rather than on herself.

A GOTTSCHALK FOOD STORE

Like our milliner's shop shown on pages 330 and 331, this attractive Gottschalk general store has the additional allurement of an F.A.O. Schwarz label on its underside. The address printed thereon, "Fifth Avenue at 31st Street," was Schwarz's between 1910 and 1931, later than the one on the milliner's shop.

In surprisingly good condition, with its metal drawer labels bright and its canned goods in abundant supply, an ingratiating feature is the paper labels on the cans—pretty fruits in color with no lettering to impose a language difficulty upon miscellaneous importers. Painted molded insets embellish the stenciled counter and shop frame.[1]

A grocery store which is nearly identical, differing only in minor, mostly decorative details, is shown in F.A.O. Schwarz's 1910 Christmas brochure. This has an extra row of drawers at the top, instead of the open shelves, and shelves at the back, instead of the door. This was evidently a popular item; in the 1913 Schwarz catalogue, nine different styles were available in various sizes and styles ranging from a simple affair twenty inches wide at $1.75 to a twenty-eight-inch emporium "very complete" at $16.50. A grocer dressed in a dark business suit is shown in the illustration of, presumably, the latter store.

It is interesting to note that this same store (with only one apparent variation, two counters instead of one) was still to be seen in the 1920 Schwarz catalogue—a significant comment on the number of years almost identical toys were often made and the difficulties of dating them precisely.

EARLY TWENTIETH CENTURY. HEIGHT: 16" WIDTH: 28"

1. Identical molded insets are to be found on the frames of similar stores in the Cieslik-Gottschalk catalogue, pubished after this summary was written.

A Gottschalk Sweet Stall with Awning

In a book published in 1967[1], I described this beguiling piece as a "sweet stall." It came to me only with its workable awning and with no supplies. It seemed to lend itself to bakery products and a tea room ambience. I provided antique cakes and pies and a few cafe-style bentwood tables and chairs for visitors who might stop for a casual cup of tea and perhaps an iced cake.

When I supplied a color transparency of this treasure for Evelyn Ackerman's Gottschalk book, she reproduced alongside it "an artist rendering from a department store catalogue, ca. 1913," unmistakably of the same piece, but she referred to it as a "general store," in which "the drawing clear-

CA. 1910.
HEIGHT: 20" WIDTH: 17 3/4"

1. *A Book of Dolls and Dolls' Houses,* Tuttle, Japan, 1967 (Reprinted in *Victorian Dolls' Houses.* Washington Dolls' House & Toy Museum. 1978)

ly illustrates the original provisions to be tins of food, sugar cones, and boxes of tea."

The usual metal ribbon-shaped labels are on the drawers both in the "rendering" and on the actual example. The labels cannot be read on the rendering, but those on the actual piece are of a tea room aspect: sugar, tea, coffee, chocolate, macaroons, raisins, and figs.

As we know from the catalogues, Gottschalk structures, like those of other companies, were made in several sizes. Perhaps, I mused, these stalls were also made for several purposes. Although the two shown have the same number of drawers, the example from the catalogue, for which no measurements are given, reveals one less row of shelves and is probably not as large as the one in the photograph.

There is also an example, unmistakably smaller, and less complete, in *The Universal German Toy Catalogue,* 1924-1926[1], where these were referred to

as "shop window stands, with blinds and equipment."

In any case, I was prepared stubbornly to continue referring to this charming stall with its mirrored counter and its blue-and-white striped awning as a sweet stall when suddenly my stubbornness was justified. There in my own library, I came upon *Gamagés Christmas Bazaar,* 1913, with an illustration of, clearly, the identical stall shown in the "artist's rendering" and labled, by the English establishment, as "Sweet Stalls." The price of the example pictured was five shillings and eleven pence. Undoubtedly the Museum's example, assuredly larger, would have been more pricey.

A scale of the proper vintage and style has been added, along with the "sweets." So, too, have the bentwood chairs and tables, in deference to those confectioner's shops—tea rooms—which provide refreshments on the premises.

FROM *GAMAGÉS CHRISTMAS BAZAAR,* 1913

1. Hobby House Press, Cumberland, Md. 1985 (English edition).

A CASS GROCERY

American toy makers of the nineteenth and early twentieth centuries were almost pathologically modest and, except for Bliss, Converse, Schoenhut, and a very few others, did not trouble to put their names on their toys. Therefore, it was gratifying when this Cass grocery loomed on the miniature horizon, offering a name known to collectors, but a toy previously uncountered, at least by this one.

It was also of particular interest to discover that the N.D. Cass Co. of Athol, Massachusetts, was still in business and, having been established in 1897, celebrated its one hundredth anniversary in 1996.[1]

Unfortunately, of the few catalogues remaining in the firm's files, in 1972, when I visited the company, the earliest is from 1922, and no grocery stores or dolls' houses are shown. Curiously, a lone photograph filed with the lot was of this very grocery—undated and, unfortunately, unblemished by any identifying word of any kind. I was about to settle for "ca. 1915" as an approximate dating for the store when a muddily printed inch in a Butler Bros. reproduction catalogue caught my eye. There, listed under "Toy Grocery Stores," was the very model, and since the catalogue was from 1912, a dating of "ca. 1915" seemed a trifle conservative.[2]

The small store, which is of heavy cardboard with wooden shelves (a quarter inch thick), includes a counter mounted on a solid block of wood, with a cardboard counter top lithographed to represent graining.

According to the 1912 Butler Bros. catalogue, the stock of the Cass store included "10 facsimile pkgs. staple groceries, some filled." The groceries in this store, and in a larger and more costly "Little Toy Town Grocery Store," also illustrated in the Butler advertisement, contained "real groceries guaranteed under pure food law." (The pure food law had been

passed only six years before, and this was a prompt reference.) "Some" of the packages in the Cass store were filled, according to the advertisement, but the eight surviving staples to be seen in the photograph appear to be dummies, including the square of Fleishmann's Yeast, which is filled with wood, and with the possible exception of the outsize tin of Royal Baking Powder, marked "Free Sample" and still sealed. Empty cardboard containers include two kinds of Educator crackers—chocolate and oatmeal. (Although I had never heard of this brand, a 1910 periodical lists twenty varieties.)

The fragility of the stores may account for their rarity, but it is also possible that they were manufactured for a relatively short period, although there is a recollection at the factory that these were made from about 1900 to 1920.[3]

In any case they provide a glimpse of foods and their packaging at the beginning of the twentieth century.

CA. 1912. HEIGHT (INCLUDING SIGN): 9" WIDTH: 7"

---

1. *Antique & Collectible Dollhouses,* by Dian Zillner & Patty Cooper.
2. This toy was made for at least three years; it was later discovered in a 1914 Butler Bros. catalogue.
3. In a 1918 *American Made Toys Trade-Book,* Cass advertised "grocery stores, doll furniture, kitchen cabinets and doll trunks." The kitchen cabinets—a similar line was made by Converse—contained related groceries.

A Toy Shop from F.A.O. Schwarz

F.A.O. Schwarz sold not only a series of "mystery" houses but, more modestly, a series of "mystery" shops. These, advertised in a 1918 Schwarz catalogue were, of course, considerably later than the houses, but the mystery is similar: who made them?

All evidence points to an American origin, and it is known that Schwarz had "exclusives" provided by American sources. Two kinds of stores, grocer and toy shops, were available, with one door or two, in various sizes and price ranges. Though relatively recent, they are rare and, inasmuch as they are advertised in the 1918 and 1919 Schwarz catalogues, but are not to be seen in the preceding or succeeding issues, it is likely that relatively few were made in this short span.

The Strong Museum has examples of both toy and grocer's shops, and it is owing to the presence in the latter of such uniquely American products as Kellogg's Krumbles, ZuZu Ginger Snaps, and Uneeda Biscuits that an American origin is suggested.

These are also totally different in concept from the European stores. The toy shop pictured below, is a small example ($6.50 for this model) with one

PROBABLY AMERICAN.
CA. 1918. HEIGHT: 14"
WIDTH: 12 3/4"

ERZGEBIRGE TOYS

door rather than the pair to be seen on larger versions, but all the appealing features are present: the large shop window with "Toy Shop" in stylized gold lettering outlined in black and accompanied by matching stylized flourishes is one. The larger models had an "address," a single number "six" or "eight" on the doors, and a pitched roof. The model shown has the flat roof, and is open at the top.

The latter feature permits a full-sized hand to arrange with ease the merchandise on the shelves within and the merchandise on the counter. The latter is attached to the façade and serves as the display window. Dolls may enter through the glazed door. The decor within is simple, with a stylized two-inch strip of wallpaper bordering the interior. On the exterior, lithographed red-brick paper is framed in well-designed, cream-painted wood panels. Across the top of the façade, undoubtedly to let more light into the interior, there is windowphanie[1] of an amorphous pattern.

Our toy shop was empty when it arrived and several types of merchandise have been supplied which appear to be correct in vintage and scale:

There are painted soldiers to be seen through the window. Inside, there is a supply, in mint condition, of the small one-inch German dolls in crocheted clothes which also populate the Museum's hotel shown on page 389. A sizeable collection of the small Erzgebirge wooden toys with their miniscule wooden personages has been drawn upon as well.

VIENNA BRONZE FIGURES

A FOOD STORE FROM WÜRTTENBERG

This sizable food store was acquired years ago, empty. There was not so much as a can of beans, but it was impressive with its glazed shop window at either side and with its twenty-four drawers, each with porcelain label. And, as the illustration suggests, it did not remain empty.

An almost identical store was pictured in a 1927 feature about Württenberg toys in a German toy trade publication, *Deutsche Spielwaren Zeitung*. In a 1929 issue of the same publication,

a Württenberg manufacturer, Carl Gross, advertised a smaller version, unmistakably of the same construction.

The porcelain labels are in English (two obvious replacements are in German) identifying such staples as flour, tea and rice, and other more diversified foodstuffs—including vanilla, raisins, currants and, rather surprisingly, laurel.

A profusion of comestibles, both German and American, have been added. Baskets of wonderful

CA. 1920's. HEIGHT: 16" WIDTH: 37"

wax vegetables, placed within the two shop windows, may be Italian. A number of tins which appear to be of proper scale and vintage are American. A rare miniature version of Log Cabin Syrup has, alas, sprung a leak during the course of the years it has remained affixed on an upper shelf of the shop, and may remain there, of necessity, through all eternity. Miniscule dark blue bottles of Vicks drops with metal caps which readily unscrew mingle with these tins. Nine tins of "Runkle's Pure Breakfast Cocoa" offer, in triplicate batches, a nice display. There is one tin of

"Wild Cherry Snuff," a substance not readily to be found these days. A couple of the small German triangular grocery bags made for miniature stores such as this one, contain (for one illiterate in German) one unmistakable word—"delicatessen."

A metal till brimming with infinitesimal German metal coins,[1] a brass scale, also German, and a rare tin hanging lamp with glass shade and workable wick, suspended above the counter, are other additions. Another American intruder is the coin "counter mill" shown in Arcade's 1902-03 catalogue and described as "an excellent representation of the groceryman's grinder." It retailed at 10 cents.

WAX VEGETABLES

TIN LANTERN

METAL MILK BASKET

1. These are embossed. One miniscule copper coin, more legible than the others is for "1 pfennig" and, like the others, is embossed "DEUTSCHES REICH" and is dated "1910." A coin collector could undoubtedly write a fulsome essay on the lot.

A 'Twenties Food Market

No maker appears to be identifiable with respect to this unusual store, though it has a French look to it which goes beyond the French labels on the packages.[1] Even the proprietress with her 'twenties flapper bob, her 'twenties dress, and even her strapped pumps with Cuban(?) heels seems straight from Paris.

The term "FOOD MARKET" is used advisedly, inasmuch as the premises appear to feature cuts of meat and butchers' paraphernalia, but the packages which came with the store suggest a variety of comestibles, and so does the most striking feature of the whole—the luminous lithography behind the counter. The upper half of the two deep sections which the artist has chosen to divide this space continues the butcher's shop theme. Behind the projecting metal rack from which hang painted cuts of meat, there are pictured, ready to be cut for the gourmet customer, garlands of sausages and tempting wedges of cheese and patés. There is a decorative mound of butter which I could not have identified but for its small placard: "Beurre. 3.75." The patés are another hint of French origin.

For the lower lithographed section, the artist has provided a veritable still life of vegetables, freshly arrived, surely, from the French countryside—bunches of carrots and spring onions, a basket with one splendid cauliflower...Even a tall sack of potatoes is an attractive contribution to the picture.

The drawers which flank this vivid paper fantasy are of metal with matching bins for more provisions below. The counters are of wood, and it is clear that they once were tied into the lavender paper tile floor—a bench is still knotted in place. It is of interest that these pieces fold into a four-inch depth when the back of the store is lowered.

The meager assortment of provisions on the shelves were possibly added by the original owner. There are two chocolate bars, still packaged and still edible (?)—"Chocolat Morand" and a reminder in French that the chocolate is "Extra Fin." Other packages are empty but decorative: "Petites Patés pour potages LA LUNE" embellished with cheery-looking "men-in-the-moons." There is even a tin of metal polish: "MIROR."

POSSIBLY FRENCH.
HEIGHT: 12" WIDTH: 18"
DEPTH: 16" (WITH FRONT EXTENDED)

1. I say this despite having been trapped more than once with an incorrect theory, withal many years ago, with the very Gallic-looking milliner's shop, page 330, which proved to be Gottschalk, and the Empire style furniture with "ormolu" trim which turned out to be Schneegass.

PART VIII

Assorted Structures: Churches,

Stables, Firehouses, Etc.

HABITATION FOR HORSES:
A MISCELLANY OF GOTTSCHALK STABLES

Unlike a car, needless to say, a horse cannot be parked in front of one's house. Because in the carriage era, horses, along with their carriages, had to be housed, full-sized stables abounded and, as our sampling suggests, their toy counter parts abounded as well. In addition to the two sizable examples, shown on pages 360, 361, and 363, one of them American (Bliss), and one German (Gottschalk), we offer an assortment, all by the ubiquitous Gottschalk.

The most imposing of these, No. 2557, shown on page 359, is 25" tall and 22" wide. It is a relatively early example. The hoist above the hayloft has had to be replaced, but everything else has survived—the wagon, a hanging ladder, even the hay in the metal feedrack. The flocked horses also remain, though they, poor things, have seen better days.

It was gratifying to find the penciled number 2646 under the largest of the three "blue-roof" stables—exactly corresponding to the number in the late 19th century Gottschalk catalog (reprinted previously by Evelyn Ackerman). Made, as usual, in several sizes this specimen is 18" tall and 17" wide. Like the previous stable, it retains its wagon, its horses, and its supply of hay. The coachman's quarters has glazed windows (sash bars repainted) and there is a wooden manger below the feeding rack beneath the hayloft. The smallest shown below left on next page, "blue-roof stable," No. 2392, retains its hoist (oddly

HEIGHT: 13" WIDTH: 11 1/2"

GOTTSCHALK CATALOGUE NO. 3256
HEIGHT: 10 1/2" WIDTH: 9 1/2"

GOTTSCHALK CATALOGUE NO. 3266
HEIGHT: (PLUS CHIMNEY) 16 1/2"
WIDTH: (AT BASE) 17 3/4"

GOTTSCHALK CATALOGUE NO. 2392
HEIGHT: 11 1/2" WIDTH: 11 1/2"

GOTTSCHALK CATALOGUE NO. 4189

not supplied with the more imposing example shown above it).

The smaller of the two very crimson stables, shown on page 356, numbered 3256 is 10 1/2" tall and 9 1/2" wide. Oddly, the larger example to its left, 13" tall and 11 1/2" wide, has no number, though it contains its wagon and two perfect flocked horses. (They retain not only their bridles, but their ears!) Both stables have metal feed-racks and identical lithography.

The remaining Gottschalk stables include the smallest shown on next page, top, 8" tall and 7 1/2" wide, numbered 3254. Then there is the rather decorative number 4189, shown on page 357, with green shutters at the windows. The final "blue-roof" specimen number 3266 is considerably larger: 16 1/2" tall plus chimney, 17 3/4" wide at base. This includes not only a metal-railed balcony on its upper story, but opening doors at both front and side. Adjacent to this, the façade segment to the coachman's quarters swings open. There are twin metal hay racks below and a white platformed horse which appears to be original. (Because there are eight stables herewith, they are offered together including their catalogue numbers.)

GOTTSCHALK CATALOGUE NO. 2646
HEIGHT: 18" WIDTH: 17"

GOTTSCHALK CATALOGUE NO. 3254
HEIGHT: 8" WIDTH: 7 1/2"

GOTTSCHALK CATALOGUE NO. 2557
HEIGHT: 25" WIDTH: 22"

A SPLENDID GOTTSCHALK STABLE

This splendid "blue-roof"[1] stable is assuredly one of the earlier and more deluxe productions of the German Gottschalk firm. Evelyn Ackerman titled her excellent book about the German maker *The Genius of Moritz Gottschalk* with logic. Her title is clearly meant to encompass not only the wide-ranging variety of the Marienberg artist and his company, but probably to include what this stable exemplifies: an attention and devotion to detail which rises almost to an art form.

Only thoroughbred horses should occupy this splendid structure. The ones which inhabited it originally are probably deceased. (Those which remain do not appear to have the correct bloodlines.) However, they'd have been the gilt on the gingerbread.

The clock beneath the highly ornamented roof says "1:23" and one needs time to study all the detail which has been incorporated into this architectural fantasy. Spires, columns, highly ornamental vergeboards under the eaves, pierced metal railings on the stalls, and every conceivable finial and bracket are among the embellishments. At each side of the central stall is a handsomely turned wooden coach lamp. The stable doors swing open upon elaborate metal strap hinges. There is a typi-

cally lithographed Gottschalk floor within. The central section above, with its trio of glazed windows, is similarly hinged to reveal the coachman's quarters. Metal chains service the pulley to the haylofts. Metal chains also protect the lower stalls.

If it does not seem sacrilegious to say so, and if an anachronism may be indulged, this stable is worthy of the Nativity!

ELABORATE
GABLE END

1. Per Mrs. Ackerman, the blue-roof structures continued till approximately 1910. Then the "red-roofs" took over. The transitional lithographed roof may be seen on houses in the Cieslik–Gottschalk archive as early as 1907. (See pages 226–7.)

CA. 1885.
HEIGHT: 23 1/2" WIDTH: 27"

A SIZEABLE BLISS STABLE (AND TWO OTHERS)

When the splendid stable on the next page was acquired, it appeared to be in almost mint condition. Alas, there was one noticeable exception—the central turret was missing. It could be visualized, but not precisely.

Years went by, and there was always the hope of seeing a similar stable, somewhere, with the turret in place. There were numerous smaller examples with small turrets, but not one of this rare size. Then one day early in 1999 an auction catalogue arrived in the mail with the very stable. The missing turret was measureable and copyable,[1] and now this imposing toy may be shown complete.

In 1965, I had wondered in print if this stable might be a Bliss. The 'sixties were still, in many areas, the dark ages of toy research. Later, I realized that there was a considerable clue on each side of the lavishly lithographed stable which, lacking,

apparently, a sufficiently eagle eye, and information, I had dismissed as decoration. As the illustration shows, on each side of the stable, above the stall, a bit of lithographed embellishment contains an "N" at the left, another in the center, and a "CO" at the right. If one looks at these entwined (almost hidden) letters with the proper spirit and a degree of information, these clues become clear. The Library of Congress does not (or did not at the time) possess the first four years of *Playthings*, the toy trade publication. The National Novelty Corporation, until later, had eluded this researcher. In any case, Bliss was a member of a "toy trust" which flourished for a few years (1903-07) and Bliss was one of the members. Combined with other clues (such Bliss numbers as 624K and 624E near the base—the model numbers, plus the letters to guide the proper lithographed segments to their

A CURRY COMB

OCCUPANTS

HEIGHT: 16 1/2" BASE: 7 3/4" x 12"

1. The improvement in color xeroxing has made it possible to repair many an antique toy which has been wounded but is worthy of salvage. As long as it is explained, this process has been welcomed in antique toy circles as a legitimate method of restoration.

proper locations) this was unquestionably a Bliss piece.

The most substantial clue of all, of course, is the stable shown on previous page. When this was later acquired, it not only was virtually the same stable, though of diminished size and diminished details, but the Bliss name was clearly lithographed above one of the two stalls. This stable, like the big one,

was in mint condition—and complete with turret and similar lithographed paper-on-wood posts.[1]

The third stable, with turned posts, may be earlier but again its turret was missing, though its hoist and railing chains had managed to survive. The turret and its varnished finial have been replaced. (This stable is 19" tall.) It may be seen on Bliss Street, shown on pages 110 and 111.

CA. 1895.
HEIGHT: 27" BASE: 23 3/4" X 9"

1. The rare curry comb is an addition. The horse shown on previous page has his back turned for a reason: he is a candy box and his head is missing!

FARM PROPERTY BY CONVERSE

The "Roosevelt Stock Farm," shown below, especially the deluxe example shown here with its three-inch peg-in-wood foundation, is more subtle in coloring, but the "Red Robin Stock Farm" boasts its own "Live Stock Express Co." freight car.

President Teddy Roosevelt seemed to inspire toys. The Teddy Bear, commemorating an incident during a 1902 visit to Mississippi, created a vogue during the years of his presidency which had an overwhelming revival a century later. Another, representing his African safari, by Schoenhut, is the epitome of the toy as a work of art. The "Roosevelt Stock Farm" by Converse is a more modest example.

From the manner in which the two barns pictured are pressure-printed—directly on wood—with diverse colorings as well as style, one might not immediately suspect that both were manufactured by one maker. It is when they are examined carefully that it becomes apparent that the "Roosevelt Stock Farm," which is not marked, as well as the "Red Robin Farm," which is, were both by Converse of Winchendon, Mass. Although

ROOSEVELT STOCK FARM. HEIGHT: 16" (PLUS CUPOLA) WIDTH: 19 1/2"

both were made in several sizes, the two models shown have identical measurements. (A three-inch foundation printed with windows and stone, on the Roosevelt, pegs into the base and came with the "deluxe" model only, to be seen herewith.)

As the illustrations suggest, the "Roosevelt" barn shown in the photograph is the same as the one labeled "Red Robin Stock Farm," in the 1913 Converse catalogue illustration. The windows are of the same latticed design; and there is the same arch, near the roof line, with sliding doors.

Farm animals, poultry, and a horse and wagon, all printed on wood, accompany the Stock Farm. ("Reuben," presumably the name of the horse, is printed in red on the wagon.) A catalogue issued by the John M. Smyth Co. of Chicago, circa 1907, shows Roosevelt Stock Farms in two sizes, at 44 cents and 88 cents.

For the "Live Stock Express Co." car, Converse forsook its usual blue for a shade of apple green. This piece is an eight-wheeler, with sliding doors and unmistakable provenance both front and back. The 1912 printed on its sides is clearly the date of its origins. With "M.E.C. & S."[1] on both front and back and "Converse" on both ends, no magnifying glass is needed to track down the maker. A printed label exhorts: "RETURN THIS CAR TO RED ROBIN FARM." No one would dream of doing otherwise.

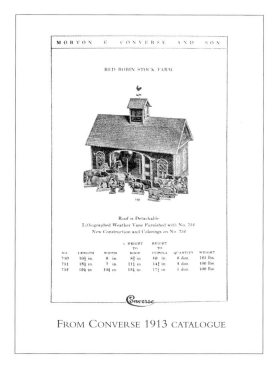

FROM CONVERSE 1913 CATALOGUE

RED ROBIN FARM.
HEIGHT: 13" (PLUS CUPOLA)
WIDTH: 19 1/2"

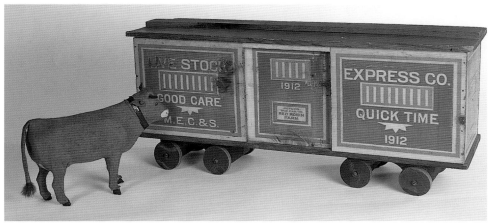

LIVE STOCK EXPRESS CAR.
HEIGHT: 9" WIDTH: 19 1/2"

1. Morton E. Converse & Son

A BLISS WAREHOUSE

It was necessary, when it was found years ago, to go out on a limb only a short distance to identify this warehouse positively as Bliss. Although, at the time, there was no absolute proof, it bore all the earmarks of the Rhode Island maker's style: the familiar lithographed paper-on-wood, the Bliss-type cardboard dormer, the same sort of wooden barrels—and even the typical, obscurely placed model number.

This identification was verified when a 1901 Bliss catalogue was discovered and two similar warehouses were advertised. Cissna of Chicago, a faithful seller of Bliss products, advertised the identical warehouse in 1898: "It has four double doors, large platform and office, pulley and ropes for hoisting cases from one floor to the other. A large wagon 12 inches long goes with every warehouse." (The price to the retailer for all this was $4.75 per dozen.)

In its 1901 catalogue, Bliss described similar features and boasted: "The modern warehouse is thoroughly represented in the construction of this toy."

CA. 1895. HEIGHT: 15" WIDTH: 12"

TWO BLISS "FORTRESSES"

In 1905, *The Youth's Companion* advertised this small stronghold as a fortress. Since it resembles the armories still to be found in considerable numbers throughout the United States, it may be considered authentic American "architecture" despite its somewhat misleading label. Undoubtedly "fortress" was a more comprehensible and glamorous term to soldiers under ten.

After the larger of the two examples pictured was acquired, the smaller version was found. These and the one illustrated in *The Youth's Companion* are the only "fortresses" I've seen, but many more have been made and sold—and given away. Given away almost literally, because in 1905 *The Youth's Companion* was offering the fortress plus a small Bliss stable for one new subscription.

It is true that the *Companion's* fortress was advertised as eleven inches tall, and if this figure is not in error, theirs was a smaller model than the larger one pictured. Even so, the offer was impressive—the fortress came complete with soldiers, cannon, and flag.[1]

Our smaller version is only nine inches tall, so perhaps three sizes were made. Where the large fortress contains only lithographed paper in a wood pattern inside, the smaller version, when the hinged façade swings open, contains a charming surprise. Typically Bliss—at their most imaginative—there is, as the detail illustration shows—a brightly lithographed scene on the interior of the back wall, and on the interior of the hinged facade. "The Battle of the Toy Brigade" is the title of the interior scene. "On Guard," depicting a toy soldier and an American flag with six stars is printed on the inside of the lithographed façade.

HEIGHT: (INCLUDING TURRETS) 8 1/2"
LEFT TURRET MISSING

CA. 1905.
HEIGHT: 15" BASE: 8 1/2" X 14 1/2"

1. Our soldiers, of metal, unfortunately, are not original, and our flag is a substitute.

TOY CHURCH ARCHITECTURE BY BLISS

Because it is composed of blocks, the Bliss church is toy architecture rather than doll architecture, but with its lithographed paper-on-wood construction and architectural aspect, it bears a distinct kinship to other Bliss structures shown throughout this book and on pages 366 and 367.

This is a "Sunday Toy" in the most convincing sense of the term. Children in deeply religious families who were permitted to play on Sundays only with toys of a religious nature, could hardly be denied this one. Arranged within the base of the building are two dozen shallow blocks, lithographed on one side with a Biblical text, and on the other with a picture interpreting the text. "The Parable of the Two Debtors," from St. Luke VII is illustrated

with one debtor wringing his hands and one covering his eyes in shame, with St. Luke between the pair, presumably offering comfort. "Daniel, the Captive Prince" (Daniel VI) is shown calmly seated on a boulder with two lions, actually rather cheerful looking, at either side. On each block is printed: "Look in your Bible for this beautiful story."

The church was complete and in excellent condition when found, with one small exception: the small wood finial was missing from the spire. Some months later, in another antique shop, there was one block for sale: it was the spire with the finial intact! To one who doesn't necessarily believe in such, this was a miniscule miracle, most appropriate to a toy of an ecclesiastical nature.

CA. 1895.
HEIGHT: 20 1/2" WIDTH: 12"

CHURCH ARCHITECTURE BY REED

Two Reed churches may be found in the Museum's "Sunday Toy" exhibit. One is of lithographed paper-on-wood. The other is printed directly on the wood. The lithographed "Cathedral" is so similar to the Bliss church shown on previous page, that it makes one wonder…The Reed is a few inches shorter than the Bliss, but in both the box provides the base. The construction is similar, with turned wood finials of a similar shape to surmount the gables. Where the Bliss church contains blocks with Biblical text, the Reed contains blocks which include A Book of Prayer and the story of Noah's Ark.

A lithographed clock beneath the Reed spire has a black face reminiscent of the ones on early New England churches, though this one is late Victorian. (The Bliss congregants aren't given the time!) Both are late nineteenth century.

The printed-on-wood Reed church is labeled "Reed's Sunday Toy" on its lid, leaving no doubt as to its purpose. "Church and Sunday School" is printed as well. The Ten Commandments and The Lord's Prayer are printed within the blocks which form the sides. The illustration is from *The Youth's Companion,* October 30, 1890 issue.

CA. 1895.
HEIGHT: 16" WIDTH: 9 1/2"

CA. 1895.
HEIGHT: 17" WIDTH: 12"

A PENNSYLVANIA COUNTRY CHURCH

This country church, found in Pennsylvania many years ago, was clearly fashioned by a skillful hand. The proportions, the construction, and the design appear to be professional. Unfortunately the history of the piece is unknown, and to date it "early twentieth century" is only an educated guess, but it is certainly no later.

The "stained glass" windows are courtesy of windowphanie, a product described in a 1910 *Ladies Home Journal* as "a thin translucent material which makes stained glass out of plain glass." *The Journal* further pointed out that this was "appropriate for doors, transoms, windows in houses, churches, hotels, etc."[1]

There are double doors, both front and rear, through which the doll members of the congrega-

tion may enter. The rest of us, to view the interior, must be content to lift off the roof. Nevertheless, this is clearly a toy church, not a model. There are half a dozen upholstered pews inside, actually imported dolls' house settees of a suitable simplicity.

When rung, the bell in the imposing steeple chimes impressively.

EARLY 20TH CENTURY.
HEIGHT: 28 1/2" WIDTH: 16 1/2"

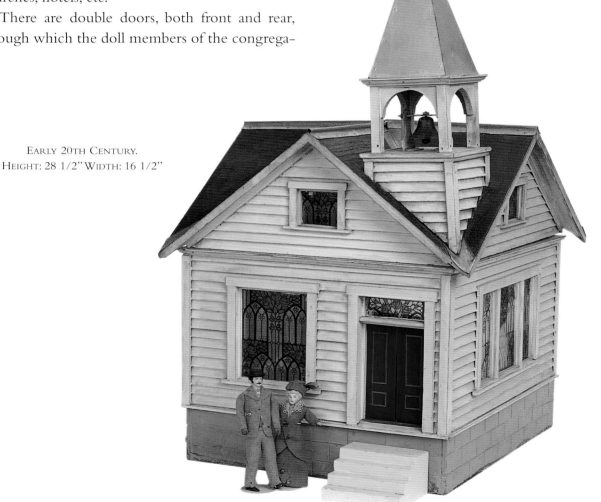

1. See also pages 74 and 325 (Gertrude's House and Store).

THREE FIRE STATIONS BY BLISS

No microcosmos would be complete without a fire engine house; the peril of miniature conflagrations to miniature houses can never be far from mind. R. Bliss advertised three fire houses in its 1901 catalogue, in 25, 50 and 75 cent sizes, and the larger one shown is the most "expensive" model.

Lithographed on the upstairs windows ("hanging" inside) are such appropriate items as firemens's helmets, boots, outercoats, and even a speaking trumpet. "Through" the downstairs windows, the same round steam boiler may be seen that is more three-dimensionally represented on the rear of the toy fire engine standing in front of

CA. 1900.
HEIGHT: 19 1/4" BASE: 10 1/2" x 8"

CA. 1900.
HEIGHT: 17 3/8" BASE: 9 1/8" x 7"

the station. This friction toy (not shown), an addition, shoots sparks and makes siren sounds as it races across the floor. With its 1912 license, it is later than the fire house. The leather Dalmatian with glass eyes is also an addition, but, of course, a traditional one. He has been given the metal fireman's hat.

For a toy otherwise made with so much detail, it is amusing to discover, when the building front is swung open, a conventional two-room wallpapered dolls' house interior within. There is not even so much as a brass pole for a fireman to slide down.

A smaller but similar Bliss firehouse in the collection—perhaps the medium "50-cent" size, is shown on previous page. We are informed by a lithographed sign above the left-hand lower window of each firehouse that both are "No. 2", but other lithographed details vary. The original gilded wooden bell hangs in the belfry of the smaller version. The metal bell in the larger model is a replacement.

Another Bliss firehouse, totally different in construction from "No. 2", and smaller, shown below, features a lithographed clock above the belfry. All of the details are lithographed, including the doors, which may be opened. The company economized by placing identical horses in each of the two windows, facing them in opposite directions.

CA. 1900.
HEIGHT: 12 1/2" WIDTH: 10"

BALTIMORE SCHOOLHOUSE NO. 63

When this schoolhouse appeared many long years ago, I phoned my octogenarian Baltimore cousin and told her we'd just acquired "Baltimore Schoolhouse No. 63."

"No. 63!" she exclaimed. "In the Walbrook area?"

"That's what I was told."

"I attended Baltimore Schoolhouse No. 63!" She was astonished and, as a collector of coincidences as well as dolls' houses, I was delighted.

This very sizeable schoolhouse is made in sections. If assembled, it would occupy considerably more space than the Museum could afford. Only the façade has been displayed: the sides, with their matching windows, the back, and the roof are necessarily in storage. Lights have been installed behind the façade, to enliven the colorful stained-glass windows (both arched and rectangular), and a bisque teacher and a few of her bisque students gaze from a few of these.

This is a substantial and typical piece of late Victorian schoolhouse architecture, with an incised "brick" façade, with applied wood ornamentation, and with a dentillated molding under the eaves. There is even a proper vestibule with glazed inner double doors, and basement windows covered with wire screens.

Dolls' houses are sometimes erroneously described as "play houses" which more usually are child-sized structures. This one might qualify as a playhouse. When full assembled, several small children would fit into it, at least snugly.

EARLY TWENTIETH CENTURY.
HEIGHT: 40" WIDTH: 39"

A Schoolhouse from Ohio

It always seems essential to confess that I furnished this schoolhouse, which came from Ohio minus furnishings and students, with the contents of what I believed to be a French schoolroom—including the students.

It came via a Cincinnati dealer, who believed it may have originated in southern Ohio. Whatever its origin, it authoritatively represents that nineteenth-century American institution, the one-room school house.

The bell in the imposing belfry may be rung by a "rope" suspended in the classroom.[1] The casement windows may be opened or closed. The blackboard, which extends the width of the room, may be written on. Two clock faces surmount the belfry, one on the front and one on the side, in perpetual disagreement (11:45 and 12:50), but it is always satisfying to see time suspended, no matter how.

An opportunity came soon after the schoolhouse was found to acquire the contents of what I believed to be a French schoolroom, in perfect scale for this. Included were desks, maps, a terrestrial globe, an abacus, four school girls, and one teacher. Visually, at least, the combination appeared logical. It was not until this volume was virtually ready for publication that I discovered in a 1914 Schneegass catalogue the identical desks, abacus, blackboard easel, and terrestrial globe, even to the pattern of the desks—in a simple schoolroom. Only the students and the teacher were not shown. (I like to think that the latter were added in France!)

In any case, I'd added a hanging lamp, some miniature books, a tin wall clock, a framed portrait of George Washington, and an American flag (imported contents notwithstanding.) And, needless to say, a cat. At the right, a tall and most architectural flight of steps, which is portable, fits alongside the door. An arch beneath the landing duplicates well-designed repetitive arches which ornament the base of the small structure. The degree of detail suggests that the schoolhouse may be a copy of an actual one, and one with some architectural pretensions.

CA. 1900(?) HEIGHT: (INCLUDING BELFRY) 38 1/2"
WIDTH: (INCLUDING EAVES) 27 1/4"

FRENCH SCHOOL-
GIRL WITH ABACUS

---

1. For almost three decades, it has been rung frequently by young visitors to The Washington Dolls' House & Toy Museum.

SCHOOLROOMS: A QUARTET

Of this modest quartet of schoolrooms, one appears to come from France, one from Spain, and two from Germany.

The example, below, which *appears* to be from France is part of the controversy which has been addressed re: French rooms, shown on page 251. Whether these were made in Germany for the French market, or whether partly made in Germany and finished in France, I long to discover. In any case, this schoolroom is a charming lesson in French geography: On its walls are affixed delicately colored maps of four French departments with sketches of scenic and historic attractions surrounding each. In the department of Ille-et-Vilaine, we are shown the tomb of Châteaubriand, the Cathedral at Redon, and the Hotel de Ville at Rennes; in the department of the Basses Alpes, the ruins at Digne, among other sights, and the departments of Yonne and Drome, similar wonders.

This schoolroom is in the style of all rooms which do not fold entirely; with its folding floor flap, it becomes part of its own deep box for storing. A metal clock marked "H.H. Paris" has been substituted for a wall clock missing when it was acquired. Additional liberties have been taken with the addition of such non-French but appropriate accessories as a German atlas with colored maps of the continents, red "school-bags" containing notebooks with realistic black-and-white marbled covers, and cardboard slates with crumb-size sponges attached. The well-varnished school desks with lift-tops and attached seats, and the blackboard which shows signs of thorough use, are original. The small French or French-type, glass-eyed students are an additon.

★ ★ ★

The folding cardboard walls, printed with two simple windows, fit into slots in the wooden boxlid of this German schoolroom, shown on next page. The blackboard and desks with attached benches are, like the schoolmaster's bench and stand, of painted wood.

HEIGHT: 8" WIDTH: 18 1/2"

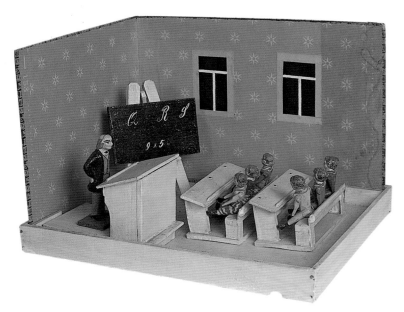

BOXED TINY GERMAN SCHOOL CONTENTS.
HEIGHT: 4" WIDTH: 6"

GERMANY. LATE VICTORIAN.
HEIGHT: 8 1/2" WIDTH: 12"

Himself of painted composition, the gray-haired plaster (?) schoolmaster teaches an intriguing group of students, all of whom are carefully carved of wood with their clothes and features attractively painted. The girls wear matching cotton skirts below their wooden blouses. Both girls and boys have jointed wooden arms and legs, the latter with black boots painted on. Each literally sits on a tack, a small prong in the figure's posterior, which enables each to sit or stand.

★ ★ ★

The second German schoolroom, shown below, appears to be a teaching tool, or, assuredly, it has been converted into one. The lap of each of

EXTERIOR

GERMANY. HEIGHT: 6 1/2" WIDTH: (EXTENDED) 10"

the twenty-three plaster students, seated on wood benches, contains an open plaster book, and to many of these a paper letter of the alphabet has been affixed. Others are missing.

The girls are clad in long skirts, the boys in long trousers, suggesting a relatively early date (ca. 1870?) for the piece. The possibility of such a date is reinforced by the printed presence, on the plaster professor's desk, of an ink bottle and a sand container—the latter, needless to say, a predecessor of the blotter.

The simple room itself is wallpapered, with printed windows applied to the wood walls inside and outside.

★ ★ ★

A nun presides over this small schoolroom from Spain, shown below. It is a portable schoolroom and, when folded and fastened, it is contained in its own case. The four students, still attached to the floor, are dressed like their teacher in black and white—white collars, white aprons, and white bows in their dark hair.

A printed label on the back offers disappointing information. I had hoped this label would offer a clue about the maker. However, it contains such words as "impuesto lugo a metalic," "Parmiso," and "Facture," (sic) and there are numbers, all of which appear to relate to patent or tax.

With or without the label, however, this is an appealing toy.

SPAIN. HEIGHT: 6 1/4" DEPTH: (OPEN) 12"

"DOLLYVILLE:" BY BLISS

When Bliss patented this informative and appealing toy in 1895, the company might well have called it—in lieu of the name they gave it— "Main Street." Those of us who are engaged in attempting to reflect architectural and social history in dolls' house terms are not likely to find a more striking illustration of an 1890's cityscape in the space of thirty inches.

These small lithographed buildings, which peg together, represent a virtual city block, with a grocery store, a market, a drug store, a bakery, and—of most interest—an opera house and bank, a rare pair to be found in miniature.

Behind the vivid façades of these buidings, are the similarly vivid interiors, all in the colorful, imaginative lithography of the firm founded by

Rufus Bliss in 1832 in Pawtucket, Rhode Island. Perhaps this Main Street is a reflection of Pawtucket at the turn of the century. By the time it was produced, "R. Bliss" was deceased and it is not known who designed the wide range of highly imaginative Bliss toys which were produced

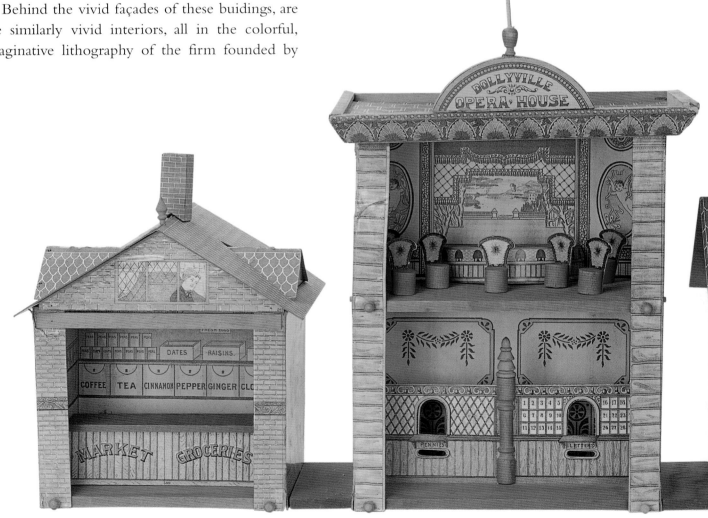

PATENT 1895. HEIGHT: 16" WIDTH: 30"

before and after the turn of the century.[1]

There are faces in the windows of the lithographed buildings and, not surprisingly, all of them are children. The drug store has a sign for "Chocolate Seegars" and "Goo Goo Chocolates." Inside, such products as "Jack and Jill Liniment" are to be seen on the thoroughly printed surface, along with, for some odd reason, shelves of "Crackers"—to soothe, perhaps, the cries of small hungry customers? "Dr. Pill" is the name of a side door printed on the façade adjoining the drug store.

The grocery store has the always amusing (to current shoppers) prices on its signs: "Potatoes 10 cents a Peck" and "Milk 6 cents QT." There is a sign for "Stove Polish," a product no longer in demand.

Cut-out windows within the interior of the

bank and post office have cut-out slots below each, one labeled "pennies" and one "letters," slots large enough to accommodate a very small letter—or penny.

But perhaps most appealing is the Opera House with its oval stage and seven seats. The latter, on red wood bases, are elegantly lithographed in blue, but their cardboard backs somehow are not lithographed and need to be faced in the wrong direction to look their best—the only omission by a Bliss designer I've ever encountered.

As the catalogue illustration, below shows, a number of accessories came with "Dollyville." It is merciful that the opera house chairs, the donkey cart, and another cart[2] survive in a rare toy which is in almost mint condition. An antique flag has been supplied by the proud owner.

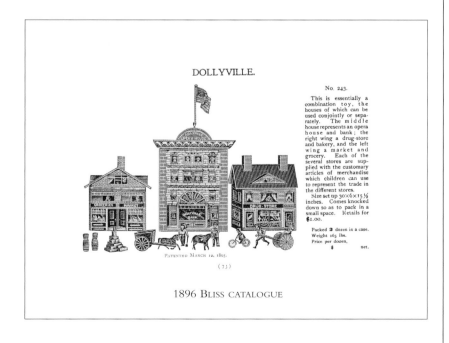

1896 BLISS CATALOGUE

1. The late Blair Whitton, who researched the history of the Bliss Company, noted that a patent for a folding dolls' house was issued to Vincent W. Wilson of Pawtucket in 1895—the same patent which covers many of the toys, including this one.
2. Not illustrated.

AN IVES R.R. STATION
PLUS A "PLAYSKOOL PULLMAN"

With its splendid glass shed, this Ives Station has sheltered many an earlier train than the Standard Lionel shown pulling into it herewith. The latter, from the 'thirties, is late for this handsomely lithographed tin depot of which Ives, of Bridgeport, Connecticut, began a series circa 1905.

The vivid lithography informs us that this is "Union Station" and that it contains a "Ladies Waiting Room" as well as a "Men's Waiting Room." The two chalkboards, labeled "Ives R.R." display the trains' schedules.

It is irresistible to include here the "Playschool Pullman," shown opposite, lower right, manufactured in Milwaukee, Wisconsin in 1932 (by the *Play School Institute*).

This charming toy offers a very complete interior of a Pullman car, including the protective curtains, the bedding, and even the painted-bisque

CA. 1905. HEIGHT: 10" WIDTH: 22"

occupants. The entire piece resembles, with its leather handle, a lunch box in shape and size.

The newsstand did not accompany either the Ives Station or the Playschool Pullman, and it is German, but its inclusion here with these very American objects seemed quite appropriate. Amazingly, it still contains its original German language newspapers, neatly folded. Very Art Deco, it is, at least, of the proper period.

GERMAN NEWSSTAND BY CARL HILPERT.
HEIGHT: 4 1/2" WIDTH: 5"

PLAYSKOOL PULLMAN.
HEIGHT: 9 3/4" WIDTH: 11 1/2"

A 'TWENTIES FILLING STATION

Shortly before this compilaton was completed, *The Antique Toy Collectors of America,* whose catalogue reprints have greatly assisted dolls' house and toy researchers over the years, distributed to its members a reproduction of an undated brochure from the "Gibbs MFG. Co." of Canton, Ohio. Inside, there is not only an illustration of this very 'twentyish filling station, "No. 80," but another rendering, with several other Gibbs toys, is on the cover.

There is no date given, but the brochure points out that Gibbs Toys "have been the backbone of thousands of toy departments for 30 years" and this one is clearly from the 'twenties. It "is an exact duplicate in miniature," the brochure proudly continues, "of a gasoline filling station, complete in every detail—station in imitation stucco and red tile roof." More impressively, "the gasoline pump has a rubber hose (alas, ours is missing) and gauge

that can be operated by a child and registers one to five gallons." The garage was constructed of metal and wood and was "ornamented" in seven colors.

The one thing Gibbs failed to provide was a sign with the price per gallon. That would have been of particular interest.

No. 80 Gibbs Filling Station

An exact duplicate in miniature of a gasoline filling station, complete in every detail—station in imitation stucco and red tile roof. The gasoline pump has a rubber hose and gauge that can be operated by a child and registers one to five gallons. Strongly constructed of metal and wood and attractively ornamented in seven colors. Length 15 inches, width 9 inches, height 7 inches. Packed, set up ready to sell, one toy in box.

FROM A GIBBS BROCHURE

AMERICAN. HEIGHT: 7" WIDTH: 15"

"A MODEL COTTAGE HOSPITAL"

Inasmuch as it is occupied by three dolls, it is tempting to refer to this unusual structure as a "dolls' cottage hospital."

However, hand-lettered provenance on a shade in a side window identifies this extraordinary piece as "A Model Cottage Hospital and Equipment Designed and Made by Agnes Gilruth Pringle of Broughty Ferry."[1] During a visit to Scotland a number of years ago, this was a surprising discovery in an Edinburgh antiques shop.

The three dolls consist of a nurse and two patients, the latter in sad shape, swathed in bandages and beset with splints. One has a bisque head (suprisingly undamaged in what may have been a

nasty motor accident!). The other has a wax head. A small printed sign on this one warns: "Press chest very gently." When one does, an astonishing thing occurs: the small wax mouth opens and closes! (In a manner which resembles artificial respiration.) The nurse, also of wax, is a giant in this setting—13" tall. She is tending patients whose multiple problems are listed, each on a small card, Patient No. 1 with "Fractures" and Patient No. 2 with multiple "Wounds."

There is a fireplace, befitting the climate and the period, and shelves containing innumerable bottles of medicine, fresh bandages, and other medical necessities. There is even a tent-like device placed over the feet of one patient, to relieve pressure, possibly?

The exterior is indeed designed like a cottage, with a balustraded porch and a pitched roof crowned with two chimneys. Alas, it is clear that two chimney pots once occupied each of the latter, removed perhaps to fit into the crate when this was shipped across the ocean so many years ago.

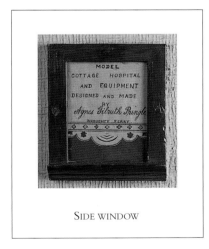

SIDE WINDOW

SCOTLAND. EARLY 20TH CENTURY.
HEIGHT: 24" WIDTH: 35"

1. In the county of Angus

Part IX

Arts & Leisure: Theaters,
Zoos—Even a Houseboat

A GOTTSCHALK CARAVAN

Leaving no possible habitation unbuilt, Gottschalk outdid itself with a caravan—a predecessor to the modern mobile home.

There was a motorized version in the 'twenties, but the example pictured with a chain at the front was clearly an earlier vehicle—to be pulled by horses. A small porch with flower boxes could be enjoyed when the caravan was parked, with a small flight of detachable steps. These steps are contained in a hinged storage area when the caravan is in motion, and may be hooked to the front when it is at rest. Embossed brass balusters on the porch establish this as the Rolls-Royce of caravans. Swing open the façade and inside there is a surprise: the original furnishings, still sewn in! This furniture, of the unmistakable French genre, was probably added to the caravan in France, along with the lace curtains. German doll makers often sent dolls to France to be dressed; Gottschalk probably sent this charming vehicle to Paris to be furnished.

It is of interest to note that the furniture is identical—though in smaller scale—to the furniture in the house to be seen on page 219 (see also postscript on page 251). Curiously, the furniture is also still tied in—never played with—for reasons we shall never know. The dolls, cat, and plant have been added. Unless it was lost over the years, no horse was supplied with the caravan.

A miniscule version of the caravan, fashioned by the gifted Lew Kummerow of California, is one of only two reproductions in the collection.

CARAVAN OPEN

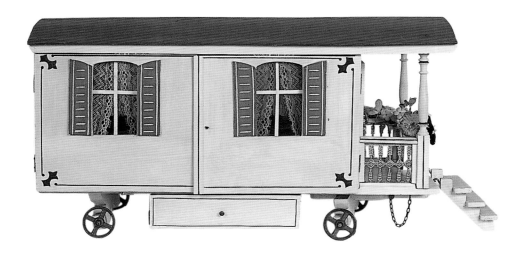

CA. 1900. LENGTH: 16" (PLUS STEPS)

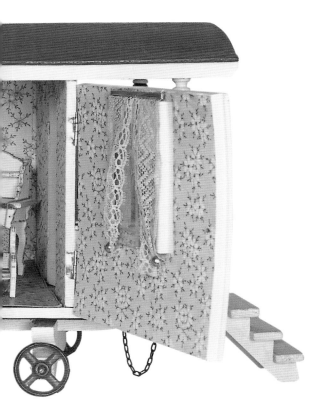

MINIATURE VERSION BY LEW KUMMEROW.
LENGTH: 2 1/2" (PLUS STEPS)

A PAVILION DATED 1889

Usually one knows the purpose of a small structure (a house for dolls, for instance). Here we have a date, 1889, prominently displayed but lack knowledge of the purpose for which this charming pavilion was made. It came, many years ago, from an auction in Skaneateles, New York where it may or may not have originated. It is substantial, nearly four feet tall including its attractively fenced base, from which it may be lifted off.

There is a hinged door on the rear of the pitched roof. A small, circular opening in the tall chimney descends to the interior. Two circular metal-framed glass slides, one green and one crimson, attached to circular windows on each side of the deeply pitched roof, as though an electrical display, possibly added later, was intended. There are arched Moorish-style windows, unglazed, on both front and sides.

But perhaps of most interest here is the presence of a decorative built-in fireplace against the back wall, logically placed inside beneath the tall chimney outside.

Webster describes a pavilion as "a light, usually open building used for shelter, concerts, exhibits, etc., as in a park or fair. The fireplace in this one suggests that this pavilion was in use in winter as well as summer.

In England, years ago, suspended across an antiques shop window in Bath, was a vision—the assorted personages to be seen here in their vivid costumes. They still retain small wires—perhaps they hung on a Victorian Christmas tree, the angel on top.

Here they are shown taking their bows in a traditional Christmas pantomime—with the arched entrance of the pavilion serving as a narrow but properly shaped proscenium arch.

Accordingly, I have borrowed, from the Museum's annual Christmas exhibit, this small, obviously gifted company of performers.

AMERICAN.
HEIGHT: (PLUS CHIMNEY) 41 1/2"
WIDTH: 25 1/2"

A New Jersey Hotel (?) Dated 1903

If the heading to these paragraphs had been written in 1965 when this six-story building was acquired, it would unhesitatingly have read "A New Jersey Seaside Hotel."

The dealer who sold it was relatively specific.

He had been told that it was a dolls' hotel from New Jersey—he thought from Asbury Park. We now offer this seaside aspect with a question mark. Unfortunately, there was no documentation, and only one fact was positive, the date, 1903, unmis-

Height: 33" Width: 33 1/2" Depth: 16 1/2"

takably placed, in metal numerals, on the cornice. The condition of the small building was sadly rundown indeed—as rundown as the original may well be, or may have been, if it has not given way to the wrecker's ball, or to some other catastrophe.

But even disrepair could not dim the vitality of this small structure with its imposing cornice, balustraded roof and balconies, positive coigning, and multitudinous windows.[1] The interior, with a grand staircase leading to the top story, is equally imposing, and especially appealing is the fact that this is clearly a building for dolls, and no mere model.

There are rooms opening off each side of the central staircase on each floor, and the back of the hotel opens in three hinged sections to give access to these.

A small circular opening in the base, beneath the front, suggests that there was, originally, an extension—a garden?—which pegged in. (Forever lost, alas.)

When first this charming puzzle was acquired, no formal efforts were made to learn which Asbury Park hotel it might be. Asbury Park post cards were sought out at antique shows, New Jersey visitors to the Museum were questioned.

After a slide program in Connecticut in which I projected a view of the structure, two listeners volunteered information, one mentioning an Asbury Park hotel on the boardwalk which had been torn down a few years (now more than a few) before; one describing an off-the-boardwalk hotel still, at that time, standing. Both promised to send further details. Neither did.

Appealed to, the State of New Jersey Library pursued many possibilities. The Archives and History Bureau made "a thorough check" of all their publications of the Atlantic City and Asbury Park areas, and they checked their post card collection of Jersey shore resorts. "Actually, we spent some time with the people of the New Jersey State Museum, and even consulted a local architectural historian in discussing this interesting problem," Mr. David C. Munn, the archivist, wrote. "Although we can offer nothing definite, I thought you may be interested in what the consensus opinion was."

This opinion sent the building detectives off into a new direction: "We thought," Mr Munn continued, "that it was the model of an apartment house rather than a hotel, that it was most probably from an urban area, and would not have been

A BRIDE AND GROOM

1. In all 85, 76 rectangular, 9 arched. Some are glass, some are mica. The numerous casement windows, which swing open, have metal frames.

found in New Jersey resort communities. At the time this building was erected (1903), the big hotels at Asbury Park, Atlantic City, and Cape May were frame. Masonry hotels began to appear in the teens and 1920's."

The white building with green trim has been restored, and the search for its identity, amended and considerably widened, goes on.

There are curious framed rectangles on the interior walls of the small building—possibly to resemble windows when seen from the front. Within these frames, some rather stylized strokings with a paint brush have led some viewers to conjuncture that these frames may be intended to represent paintings hung on the walls rather than the windows, but this theory is suspect. An old lighting system, contemporary with the building, would have served to illuminate these.

Because the ceilings are a mere six inches tall,[1] locating furnishings of a proper midget scale was essential. The small "bronze" pieces marked "Made in France" proved to be ideal for this purpose. I started collecting the beds—having begun when the conviction that they were to furnish a hotel was unquestioned. One of the beds is pictured—the hotel now contains twenty-six! These are not only of the proper scale (length: 2 1/2") but of a suitable vintage. They were advertised in 1911 in a *Baltimore Bargain House* catalogue, and David Pressland, in his excellent book abut penny toys, has identified the maker, Simon & Rivollet, and the material as a painted lead alloy.

SIMON & RIVOLLET.
METAL BED. LENGTH: 2 1/2"

There are also matching tables, chairs, settees, and pianos. These pieces are usually gilded and occasionally painted a soft green. They are also made in a larger scale. Many years ago, F.A.O. Schwarz's antique toy department (long gone) had for sale a set of this filigree furniture still sewn into its original box. The clock was the same size as the piano.

The hotel guests consist of a number of tiny (one-inch plus) German bisque dolls of the variety always found in crocheted outfits. A bride and groom, clearly on their wedding trip, may be seen looking out of a window. (Not every bride has a crocheted wedding dress.)

During "The Season," a bit of boardwalk is extended at the side of the hotel and the very rare straw rolling chair with its small bisque passenger is placed upon it. A china lady in yellow boots, attached to the chair and, seemingly, original to it, is pushing the chair, presumably with a view of the ocean.

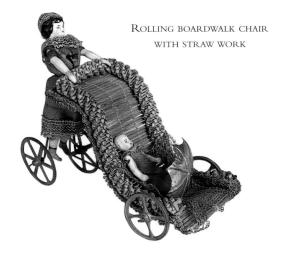

ROLLING BOARDWALK CHAIR
WITH STRAW WORK

THE DATE ON THE FAÇADE

1. On the first and top floors. On the other floors, they are a bit lower.

TWO SWIMMING POOLS

In 1928, *The Scientific American* reported the manufacture of a dolls' swimming pool which contained among other amenities, a dressing-room, a diving platform, and a shower. "The shower has a miniature pump, operated by a lever," the report continued, "which lifts the water from the main basin up to the shower head."

The larger pool shown here may be the very one described. The miniature pump to be seen on the right, when supplied with water, lifts the water to the shower head. And it *is* a head—a gilded lion's head which serves, delightfully, as the spout.

There are two dressing rooms with build-in benches and clothing hooks, though the small bisque bathers which came with the pool are not dressed. There is a sundeck with a removable opaque glass canopy and a diving-board and a ladder to a lower diving-board on the side from which a swing is suspended. There are stairs protected by decorative railings at all (presumably) slippery levels. The guard rails which rim the pool are a further protective touch.

The small bisque diver in pink-edged trunks is an addition.

The smaller pool, very different in character, is clearly by another maker, not yet identified. The attached, workable pump is similar to ones to be found on numerous fountains and related toys, and is made in Germany.

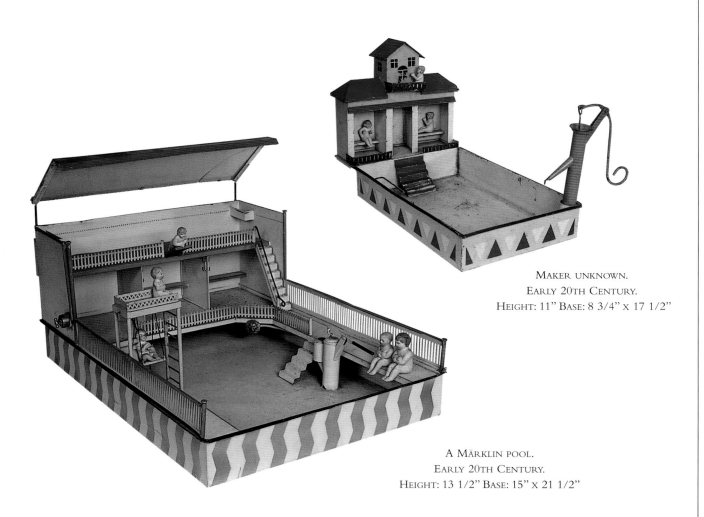

MAKER UNKNOWN.
EARLY 20TH CENTURY.
HEIGHT: 11" BASE: 8 3/4" x 17 1/2"

A MÄRKLIN POOL.
EARLY 20TH CENTURY.
HEIGHT: 13 1/2" BASE: 15" x 21 1/2"

By the Sea: Bath Houses, Bathing Machines and a Rare Swimmer

When this rare, early twentieth century dolls' house swimmer was discovered, in her original suit and cap, perfectly dressed for a swim, I tried not to be deterred by the absence of her bisque feet, removed, possibly, by a small brother or cousin bent on miniature mayhem.

Inasmuch as she is the only bisque dolls' house swimmer I have ever encountered, it seemed essential to display her so that her unfortunate affliction would not be visible. Burying her ankles in fish sand in a glass cracker jar[1] seemed a logical solution. At the other end she is perfect including the red fuzzy pompom on her sizeable cap.

When I located the tin bathing machine, I had reached the summit of my aquatic ambitions.

I have "a thing" about bathing machines—those vehicles which hauled their health-seeking swimmers, in privacy, into the sea. Beginning with George IV: his was of course, pulled by horses, with background music— "God Save the King." Our miniature version is actually a tin bank, but it contains all the essential features including its number (38) on the door.

The wooden bath house has not only its number (9) but a large exotic bird is silhouetted on each door. Within are wooden pegs for towels and clothing and a seat on each side. This small building has a red roof and one suspects that the ubiquitous Gottschalk may be the creator.

BATH HOUSE.
HEIGHT: 8 1/2" WIDTH: 6 1/2"

A BATHING MACHINE.
HEIGHT: 4" WIDTH: 5 1/2"

1. Jar not photographed.

Two Greenhouses

Where there are dolls' houses, there must be dolls' gardens. Although the garden pictured has been collected rather than planted, it offers some tangible evidence in support of this opinion.

One of two in the collection, the greenhouse shown has hinged glass sashes with small metal latches to prop them open in suitable weather. The benches within contain wooden pots of cloth flowers at the height of their bloom, and outside, cloth vines grow from small pots at either side of the doorway.

The other, of green painted tin with printed greenery, has a chimney and, in England, where greenhouses contain only plants requiring no artificial heat, would undoubtedly be known as a "hothouse." A young gardener's penciled labels still adhere to the brown wooden pots of wilted cloth flowers—such old fashioned plants as thistle, moss rose, and blue bell.

Two trees, white birch and apple, of an indescribable substance but a remarkable realism, were found in Germany. Not all the plants, in assorted sizes and pots, have been as well tended over the years as they might have been. One rather shaggy group has interesting clay pots, impressed with bands of pattern. The freshest of the plants, and the loveliest, are the Austrian bronzes; a holly, red with berries and an orange tree with fruit are especially beautiful. Also of Vienna bronze is a rare butterfly. This, attached to a wire, is in flight, courtesy of a magnet, and is a most exquisitely delicate butterfly indeed.

A green-painted watering can, assorted rakes, forks and spades, and a roller for the grass are pres-

Height: 5 1/2" Width: 7 1/2"

ent for the gardener's convenience; a painted iron bench[1] is provided for the stroller's comfort. There is also a most realistic metal lawn mower with wooden rollers. Although it was invented in England in 1830, this one is probably of later vintage than this garden is meant to be.

A collection of plants, by Britain's, with perforated metal beds for planting, are not pictured. These, of painted metal (in more recent years, these have been made of plastic), are in their original packages. Unwisely, perhaps, I cannot bear to remove them.

VIENNA BRONZE BUTTERFLY.
WING SPAN 3/4"

TIN HOTHOUSE.
HEIGHT: (WITH CHIMNEY) 6 1/4" WIDTH: 7"

1. This, described as a toy sofa in the 1872 Stevens & Brown catalogue, lends itself well to this purpose.

TWO GAZEBOS BY GOTTSCHALK

No book featuring the Victorian house, toy or full-size, would be complete without at least a reference to that small decorative shelter known as the gazebo. These two dolls' summer houses were made in Germany by, needless to say, Gottschalk. The larger, with climbing roses clinging to its thoroughly turned posts, is protected by a dome-shaped roof formed from the same faded, blue-striped cotton which forms the workable awning in the Gottschalk Sweet Stall shown on page 345. Within, a circular table and four chairs invite the visitor to a pitcher of lemonade or a glass of iced tea. There is an opening for an umbrella pole in the center of the round table, suggesting that Gottschalk also supplied this set as outdoor furniture, minus gazebo and plus umbrella.

The latter gazebo appears to be earlier than the smaller specimen which contains, in lieu of chairs, a pair of benches, and a table, both built-in. The roof consists of an unusual floral fabric (which defies my powers of description) and typical Gottschalk paste board trim for railings and cornices. Most of the small wood flower pots also are built-in, at the base of all four sides, and are supplied with crepe paper flowers. A glassine package with additional flowers visible but still sealed-in, accompanied the "mint-condition" gazebo, and I am reluctant to disturb it.

CENTRAL GAZEBO. HEIGHT: 14 1/2" WIDTH: 10"

The elderly couple, clearly enjoying the garden, came, rumor hath it, from a celebrated English dolls' house.[1] The lady is built into her wheelchair. The set of raffia chairs appear to be handmade, possibly from instructions in a lady's publication of the final quarter of the nineteenth century. The gazing ball was a frequent fixture of gardens of the period. The rare faux-grained Rock & Graner tin table, chairs, and circular plant stand are considerably earlier than the gazebos.

★ ★ ★

An afterthought: a rather motley painted metal gazebo should perhaps be more than an afterthought—especially in view of its presence in its original box with its original metal furniture—a table and two chairs. (Not every metal table has a checked metal tablecloth, but this one has.)

"Made in Germany" is stamped on the box, but, alas, no maker's name accompanies this information, and it is probably not by Gottschalk. While we are dealing with gazebos however, there may be some justification for offering it here.

METAL GAZEBO. HEIGHT: 10 1/4" WIDTH: 8 1/2"

1. *The Farie House*

A SEASONAL EXHIBIT

During the course of its nearly thirty years, The Washington Dolls' House & Toy Museum has observed the four seasons. The twig gazebo to be seen herewith has been shown in juxtaposition with a changing quartet of McLoughlin Bros. cardboard pop-up panels.[1] (A series copyrighted in 1884.) The winter grouping with its snowy trees in the background supplements the panels. With the arrival of Spring, green trees are substituted, the elegant glass-eyed bisque girl pushing the pram has her ermine coat removed and her companion is divested of his cap and scarf. The lady in white (a candy-box!) is moved to a more obscure part of the gazebo where the ice skates she is holding won't be visible.

1. Two of these cardboard toys are supplied for each season, enabling the viewer to see the New York firm's celebrated color lithography both open and closed.

Most importantly, the very rare pair of bisque ice skaters, their metal skates reflected on the pond, will have gone elsewhere till late Autumn. (They are the only dolls' house dolls wearing their original skates I've ever encountered.)

The gazebo itself is undoubtedly what is referred to in Britain as a "one-off"—unique and charmingly handcrafted perhaps by a gifted parent or other relative.

HEIGHT OF GAZEBO: 13 1/2"

A HOUSEBOAT FROM ANNAPOLIS

Inasmuch as Annapolis seems a very logical place to find a houseboat, and this one was discovered there, I take the liberty of labeling it "from" Annapolis.

Nothing more is known of it. It is skillfully handcrafted, possibly by one who occupied a similar houseboat, and who had time, while relaxing on the deck, to create this fully-detailed example. There are balustraded decks at either end for overlooking the Chesapeake (?), or a tributary thereof. The roof is crowned with a glazed coronet, hinged at the center, perhaps for ventilation, and additional light. This roof lifts off, and inside, there is, at each end, a flight of three steps with proper railings, leading up to the decks. There is a workable red-glazed lantern in the center which is possibly an addition.

Except for a commercially-made houseboat from the 1930's[1] and a charming modern Kashmiri example brought to me by a cousin who happened to be in Kashmir, this is the only miniature houseboat I've encountered, ever.

The crimson life-preserver, bearing the name "Meteor" and number "8," is an addition, along with the sailor in the deck chair.

The Noah's Ark which follows may be considered "A Houseboat from the Bible."

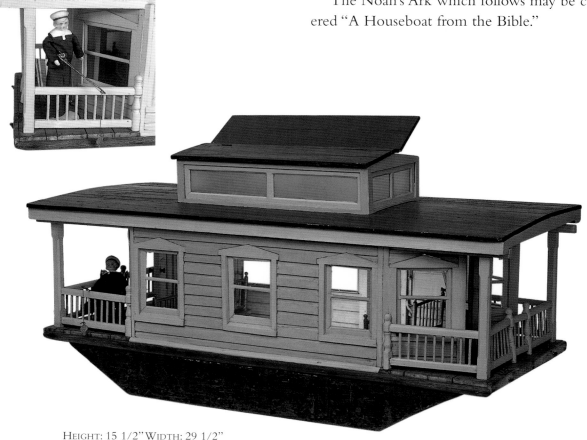

HEIGHT: 15 1/2" WIDTH: 29 1/2"

---

1. This is to be seen in *The Ultimate Dolls' House Book,* by Faith Eaton where it is identified as possibly by Triang. Unlike the realistic interior of the one pictured herewith, it is divided into two conventional dolls' house rooms.

A "Houseboat" from the Bible

Half a century ago, in the 1953 (first) edition of *A History of Dolls' Houses*, I included a Noah's Ark and attempted to justify the intrusion of what is essentially a toy: "The ark is built to dolls' house scale, and it is possible that if a neatly carved Ham or Shem or Japheth knocked on the door of a dolls' house (which has an Old Testament on the parlor table), he would be warmly received."

There are numerous Noah's Arks in the collection. One example is shown. The largest, from Sonneberg in Thuringia, has been dubbed "The Ultimate" in deference to the eighty *pairs* of creatures—grasshoppers, hyenas, anteaters, beetles, and even spiders, which inhabit it. Rarest of all is the presence of Noah and his complete family. There are Mr. and Mrs., three sons, and three daughters-in-law.

Perhaps most irresistible is the single butterfly. Its companion, I have sometimes wistfully explained, appears to have flown away.

<small>HEIGHT OF ARK: 10 1/2" WIDTH: 19"</small>

AN ELASTOLIN ZOO

The two picturesque cages illustrated are a small part of an extensive zoological garden of Elastolin, a composition sculpted by artists, pressed into molds, then, hand-painted. The results were fashioned into assemblages—Noah's Arks, safaris, farms and such, and into individual figures—military, historical, and pastoral.

In 1990 and 1991, Theriault's of Annapolis auctioned multitudinous examples from the original archive and presented them, in color, in two spledid catalogues.[1] The catalogue summary of Elastolin's history notes that these were made by "the German firm of Hausser," which had taken over in 1925, the rights to "a process perfected by the German firm of Emil Pfeiffer in the late nineteenth century." The catalogue was vague about Pfeiffer's location.

A chance purchase years ago provided a recent and exciting discovery when I was working on this material. This relates to the small figures in Edwardian dress which may be seen in the illustration. When I'd come upon them at an antiques show, I had no idea that they were of Elastolin and were made for a zoo, but I liked them and bought them. Later, because they looked "right," I displayed them as they may be seen here, in an exhibit of zoos and Noah's Arks lent to the Smithsonian's National Zoo in Washington.[2]

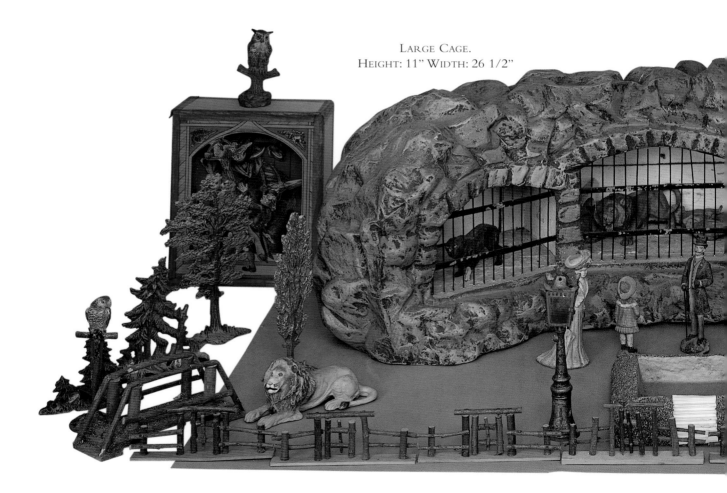

LARGE CAGE.
HEIGHT: 11" WIDTH: 26 1/2"

1. *Elastolin. Gold Horse Publishing.* Annapolis.
2. The museum lent an entire exhibit of zoos and arks to the Zoo in 1979-80.

The figures were in mint condition, and the lady and gentleman retained their original paper labels: with "E" and "P" entwined and—of special interest—"Made in Austria." Gwen White's helpful compilation of marks and labels[1] disclosed several listings for Emil Pfeiffer in Vienna beginning in 1906, with the identical trademark shown for 1916. Nora Earnshaw, in her excellent book about dolls' houses,[2] refers to Emil Pfeiffer & Successors as of "Vienna and Sonneberg," adding a town to the German attribution.

Although not all the cages and their animals can be shown here, their diversity is remarkable. Most have metal bars and wood frames and can be opened from the back. The large one pictured has dividers, separating lions, tigers, and bears.

There was also a small gratifying coincidence to note among the fences pictured on their original cards in the Elastolin catalogue. On one of them is the same log fencing to be seen in the illustration, placed there without the knowledge that this was an Elastolin product.

"In 1828, the Zoological Society of London opened its zoological gardens in Regent's Park to the public," writes David Hancocks,[3] "and the concept of housing wild animals in attractive gardens was successfully launched." Here, surely, is the ultimate toy version of the concept.

1. *Toys, Dolls, Automata: Marks & Labels.* Batsford, London, 1975
2. *Collecting Dolls' Houses and Miniatures.* William Collins Sons & Co. Ltd., 1989
3. *Animals and Architecture.* David Hancocks. Praeger Publishers, Inc. N.Y., 1971

A ZOOLOGICAL GARDEN

The toy dealer from whom I acquired this charming zoo in 1980 described it in her *Maine Antique Digest* advertisement as French. With its early chip-carved trees, which are decidedly German, I believe this beguiling toy to be as German as its trees, the latter probably from the Erzgebirge region of Saxony.

Self-contained, in a space just short of three feet by two, it is the only zoo I've ever encountered with a snake pit (dangerously shallow in appearance!). The wooden cages contain the usual "suspects"—lions, tigers, monkeys, bears, and, more surprisingly—rabbits.

There is a fish pond with "water" and a small turreted aviary. The wood fence is decorative as well as protective.

GERMAN. LATE 19TH CENTURY.
WIDTH: 32 1/2" (BASE) DEPTH: 23"

DRAMA IN MINIATURE:
THE TOY THEATER—AN INTERNATIONAL QUARTET

"The toy theater must at least be associated in any account of the microcosmic world." These words were written more than half a century ago (by me[1]) and, in the interim, I've discovered that the choice was multinational. France, Germany, the United States, and Britain all got into the act (so to speak) and examples from each have come along to prove this.

Britain's toy theaters reigned beginning in the early nineteenth century, and ranged from simple paper affairs to opulent stages with tin footlight troughs. Plays, which were presented with live actors on full-scale stages, had their scenery and cast reduced to scissor-size, and the show, after a tremendous painting and pasting, went on. There were celebrated predecessors, but the example

POLLACK'S TOY THEATER FROM ENGLAND.
HEIGHT: 18 1/2" WIDTH: 15 3/4"

1. *A History of Dolls' Houses*

illustrated is by Pollock's, a prominent name in toy theater history, and one which exists to this day.

The sheets were obtainable with and without color. The choice was immortalized in Robert Louis Stevenson's essay, "Penny Plain, Two Pence Colored." The figures with this early specimen are hand-colored, and there are oil-burning wicks. The latter, according to theater historian George Speaight in his comprehensive study,[1] "required constant attention and trimming." If that was not hazard enough, there were various kinds of chemical powders, "Red Fire" among them, to be ignited—and loud explosions. All of this, of course,

severely threatened small fingers.

★ ★ ★

Most unusual is the example from France where, in 1905, and probably before and after, there existed a toy theater play-of-the-month club! For a subscription, the participant received the scenery, the scenarios, and the performers for each production. On the elaborate proscenium arch is emblazoned *"Mon Theatre."* Seven of the monthly productions accompanied the specimen shown, and one wonders for how many months or years this modern concept continued.

★ ★ ★

GERMAN THEATER. HEIGHT: 27" WIDTH: 23"

1. *Juvenile Drama*. MacDonald & Co. Ltd, 1946.

The substantial proscenium of the German theater includes even a box for the prompter, here in the form of a ceramic shell, and with two sets of flats and side wings. These reveal the interior of a baronial mansion and the elegant street outside, with hilltop vistas in the distance, possibly of the Bavarian Alps. The cardboard actors have their names, in old German, helpfully affixed to their backs. If one were a scholar of German theater, perhaps it would be possible to identify the play by the presence of "Peter" or "Frau Elsa" and other names not easily identifiable in the German script.

★ ★ ★

The American entry is rare. Patented in 1883 by J.H. Singer of New York, it is complete with a production—properly American—of "Pocahontas." The proscenium is modest in size compared to the sizeable French and German stages, and the performers are activated by strings rather than wires, but there are soldiers and "braves" (also labeled on their bases), and of course Powhatan and Capt. John Smith, John Rolfe, and the heroine herself. There is a removable log fire for the indoor set and a teepee for the outdoor one, all accompanied by the usual side wings and red cloth curtain, the latter to be raised (on a roller) and lowered. There is also the complete scenario and a title: "*Theatre Imperial.*"

FRENCH THEATER.
HEIGHT: 29" WIDTH: 31"

SINGER THEATER, U.S.
HEIGHT: 12" WIDTH: 15"

FROM THE JAPANESE: THE HINAMATSURI

The beautiful, ritualistic doll displays which, on March third of every year for centuries past, have been the focal point of Japan's Girls' Festival, are often larger and more elaborate than this one. Some of these family treasures, handed down from generation to generation, have required a sizeable room for display, but the petite company pictured here within its own glazed case is one of the most charming examples we know.

It has, as it must, the essentials of the *Hinamatsuri*, especially the dramatis personae, with a few attractive embellishments. These are, of course, the inevitable shelves draped with red cotton cloth, with a court noble and his lady seated on the uppermost. Three lesser court ladies grace the second shelf, and a singer and four musicians with flute, drum, and tambourines are on the next. The fourth shelf supports a military and a civil dignitary, the military man with his sheaf of arrows slung upon his back. Three male servants are last, on the lowly fifth shelf between the essential blooming orange and cherry trees. Other miniature accessories, lanterns, lacquered boxes containing offerings, and tea services on low tables, are traditionally dispersed among these plump little personages in their padded brocades. Their delicate plaster faces gaze inscrutably.

MID-NINETEENTH CENTURY. HEIGHT: 18" WIDTH: 15 1/2"

PART X

The Mexican Mansion:

An Extravaganza

THE MEXICAN MANSION: EXTERIOR

It seems logical to refer to the Mexican mansion as an "extravaganza:" seven feet tall and six feet wide, it features, among other amenities, a clock tower with a workable clock, a dovecote, a glass-enclosed elevator,[1] a roof garden, and a chapel.

The splendid façade, one segment to each of the seven rooms, has some Moorish features, but it is principally French in flavor, a reflection of many full-sized structures built in Puebla and Mexico City during the mid-nineteenth-century reign of

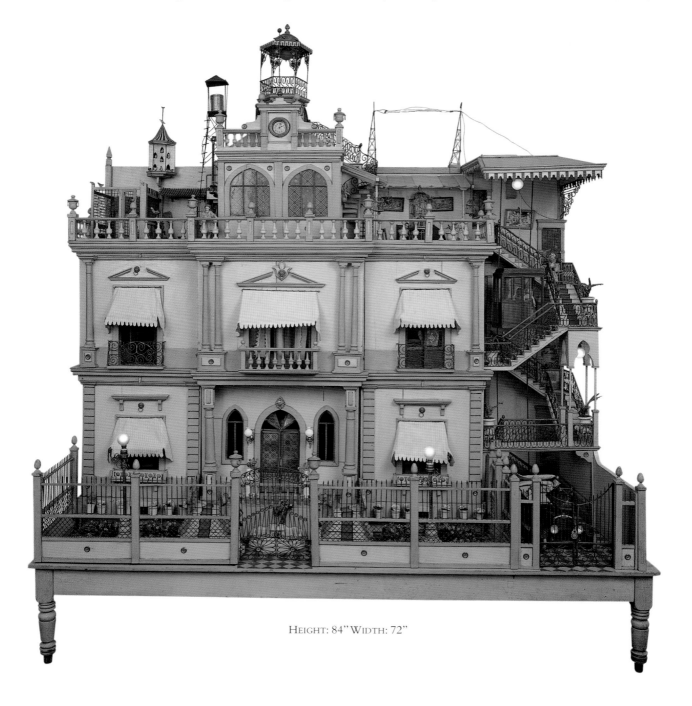

HEIGHT: 84" WIDTH: 72"

1. This worked manually when it came to the Museum. Many efforts to motorize it failed; the final one went up in smoke. Luckily no damage was done.

the French Emperor Maximillian.

The double staircase rises elegantly, on either side of a fountain, with fish pond, to the double doors. Although it seems more than a coincidence that the striped awnings, similarly-placed clock tower, window pediments, and coigning bear a striking resemblance to those of the City Hall in Puebla, the miniature building clearly is meant to be a residence rather than a public structure, and these features are probably regional rather than specific.

The unique mansion was discovered in 1976 in an antiques shop in Puebla, where it had been gathering dust for decades. A visitor to The Washington Dolls' House & Toy Museum, Mrs. Delora Simons, an American who with her husband had an export business in Puebla and lived there half the year, wrote to me upon her return to Mexico. She described the house, which was for sale. She said that the price seemed "unrealistic"

ELEVATOR
IN TRANSIT

FRONT ENTRANCE
REVEALING A BIT
OF THE GARDEN

but she added, "You might like to write about it in a book sometime." Mrs. Simons very generously extended an invitation to "fly down, be (her) guest..." I did not fly down, but Mrs. Simons sent a sheaf of snapshots along with a generous offer to deliver the house some months later when she and her husband would be in the neighborhood.

After several days of soul-searching (the price was actually all too realistic) the plunge was taken. A check was sent and the mansion was delivered some months later in the couple's small van with their eight-year old German Shepherd and her feeding dishes!

Fortunately the house is constructed in detachable sections. When the right-hand wing with its elevator and four-level winding staircase came through the door, it was possible to see at once that no mistake had been made: this was clearly a remarkable—even extraordinary—doll residence.

The history of the house, prior to the 1920's when it came to the antique shop, is shrouded in mystery. It was undoubtedly in the 'twenties that it was wired and redecorated. An imposing Jewett-Paige touring car[1] in the driveway, along with a pair of early radio towers, define the period.

An educated guess suggests that the shell of the house possibly had been imported from the continent[2] before the turn of the century, and was later—in the 'twenties—embellished in Puebla. The latter appears to have been done by a skillful worker in metal who created the fencing, the winding staircase, the gazebo which surmounts the roof, and other metallic enhancements.

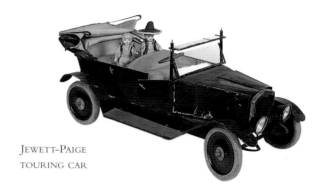

JEWETT-PAIGE
TOURING CAR

DETAIL OF FISH POND WITH "WATER"
AND GATE WITH WORKING PADLOCK

1. Thanks to James Reus, who found a reference on the internet to Jewett-Paige, these were made only in the late 'teens. The Paige company took over in the 'twenties. This may suggest an earlier date than the 'twenties for the embellishments to the Mexican House. (It is, of course, possible that the car was copied from an earlier car in the 'twenties.)
2. Commercially-made dolls' houses for export often simulated the styles of the countries to which they were sent. (See Christian Hacker "Queen Anne" on page 212.)

THE MEXICAN MANSION: INTERIOR

Although the Mexican mansion contains only seven rooms, the elaborate entrance garden below, the roof garden above and the four-level staircase-elevator wing lend it a majesty beyond mere numbers.

On the ground floor, the kitchen is dominant. Its wide "tile" range imitated in wood is a historic reminder that Puebla is a tile-making center. Also in the kitchen, there is a multiplicity of pottery jugs and bowls, in the earthen colors of their region. The

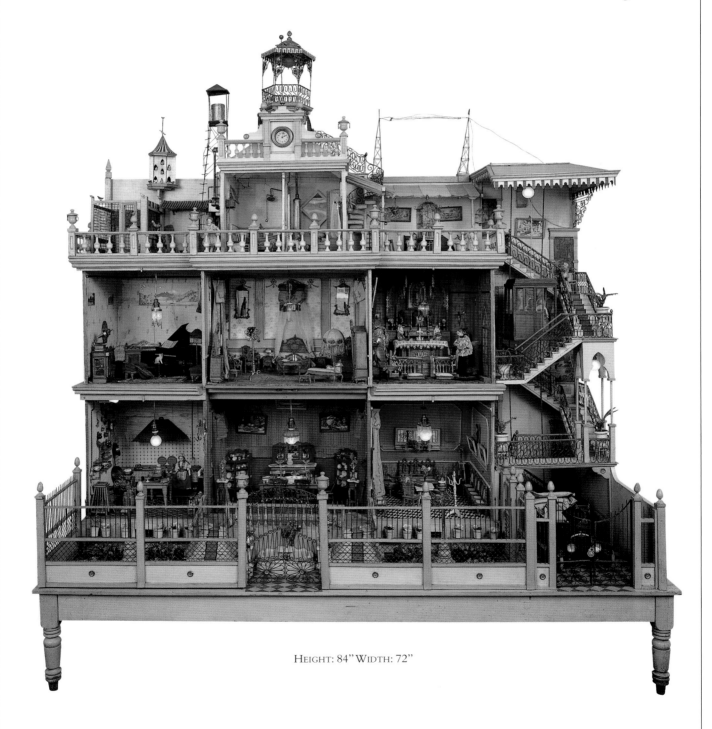

HEIGHT: 84" WIDTH: 72"

KITCHEN WITH TYPICAL PUEBLA TILE RANGE

WATER FILTER

KITCHEN WITH
MEXICAN POTTERY

drawing-room is clearly prepared to seat at least fifteen guests; there are a dozen side chairs with matching settee by the German toy company Schneegass. Such chairs were made before and after the turn of the century in the finish described in the firm's catalogue as "yellow cherry." Schneegass also manufactured the red-upholstered chairs and sofa in the music room.

The guests intended to occupy the fifteen seats in the drawing-room evidently were not invited to dinner. The dining-room contains handsome furniture, beautifully hand-crafted, but seats only six. The bedroom is elegantly supplied with pieces which appear to be made by the same hand. Each of the rooms contains an imitation "buzzer" to summon a servant and is attached to a wire reaching to the ele-

PARLOR WITH SCHNEEGASS CHAIRS

gant hand-painted ceilings of the rooms.

The chapel, in-house à la "Brideshead," is, of course, a frequent feature in affluent households in Catholic countries. With its linen-draped altar, silken-upholstered kneelers and priest in lace cassock, it is worthy of its own chapter.

Throughout this patrician residence, there are beaded chandeliers, which light with ca. 1920's bulbs, suitable pictures on the walls and a multitude of accessories. Chiffon, a frequent fabric of the period emphasizes the twentyish decor. A fringed green chiffon shade (the size of a beach umbrella) crowns the floor lamp in the bedroom. Small oval panels above the fringe are hand-painted as are the silk

MUSIC ROOM

THE ELEGANT BEDROOM

EARLY PHONOGRAPH

LAMP WITH
CHIFFON SHADE

(TRULY) GRAND PIANO

draperies. Painting on fabric, of course, is also typical of the period.

One could write, and illustrate, an entire book on the wonders of this small mansion. In 1977, the late Ann Crutcher on the editorial page of *The Washington Star,* referred to it as, "a unique structure, bigger, more elaborate, more individual than anything else of its kind in Washington and perhaps anywhere."

In the roof garden, carved doves occupy the dovecote and assorted chickens inhabit the spacious coop below. A cat presides over the music room. There are a few dolls and the priest, but a complete family is not in residence.

One would not presume to add one—or anything whatever—to this remarkable miniature household.

SEGMENT OF ROOF GARDEN

DINING ROOM WITH HAND-CRAFTED FURNITURE

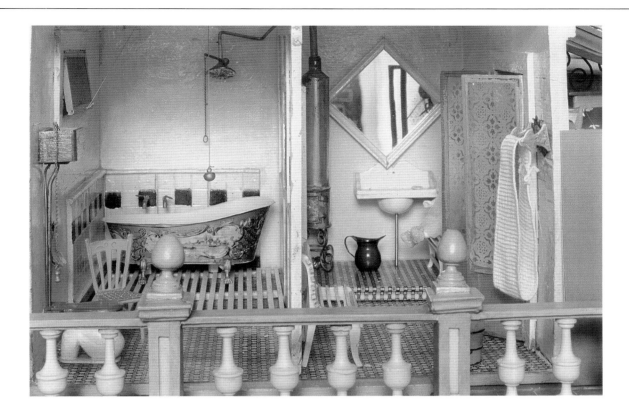

THE CHAPEL

SUBJECT INDEX
AS COMPILED BY THE AUTHOR

Abell furniture, 185-6

Ackerman, Evelyn, 106, 220, 223, 334-5, 356, 360

Adirondack Cottage, 120-1

airtwist wines, 158

album, revolving, 263

Althof, Bergmann & Company, 31-2
    catalog 294-5

Althouse, Eunice, 176, 180

American Grocery, 335

American Toy Company, 32

America's Cup, 31

Angel's Attic, 207

Annapolis, houseboat from, 400

"Annie", 25, 111

Antique & Collectible Doll Houses, 130

Antique Toy Collectors of America,
    (ATCA), 382

apartment house, 389-91

Arcade Manufacturing Co., 307, 311, 351

Art Deco, 281-2

Art Nouveau, 263, 303

Arts and Crafts, 138, 277

Asbury Park, N.J., 389-91

asphaltum, 41, 43, 62, 195, 205

Athol, Mass, 135

Au Bon Marché, 258

Au Paradis des Enfants, 233, 258

Austen, Jane, 178

Austria, 270-3

Automatic Doll Villa, 96

Baltimore, 9, 50, 57, 72-3, 123,
    schoolhouse, 373

Baltimore Bargain House, 391

Baltimore Weekly Sun, 185

Barcelona, 216

bathhouses, 393

bathing machine, 393

bathroom, rare, 76, bathroom, tin, 308,

bathroom, Arcade, 311

Bauhaus, 244, 282-3

Bayer, Dr. Lydia, 289

beach pajamas, 147-8

bedroom, 274-5, 280

beds, half-tester, 46

Bel Air House, 48-50

Benson, A.C., 334

Bethnal Green Museum, 158

bentwood, 77

Bessie Lincoln's House, 46

Beverly House, 40-1

Biedermeier, 13, 25-6, bookcase, 162

Bing roadster, 133

birdhouse, 117

Bliss, Rufus, 105, 109-21, street, 110-11, unmarked
    house, 113, bedroom, 114,
    keyhole house, 116, catalogue, 333, grocery,
    333, stable, 362-3, warehouse, 366, fortresses,
    367, church, 368, firestation, 371-2, Dollyville,
    378-9

blue sugar cones, 297

"blue-roofs", 222-27

Boblingen collection, 236-9

Bok, Edward, 58

Boothbay Harbor (Maine), 89

boudoirs, 257-8

Boule, 195

box-back houses, 100, 187-8

Boyd, Carol, 285

bristolboard carriage, 160

Britains, 395

Broughty Ferry, 383

brownstone, 22

Budd Gray house, 89, 90-3

"Bull Butcher", 322-3

bungalows, 133, 139

Burford, England, 176

butcher block, 297

butcher shop, 334, 340-1

Butler Brothers catalog, 347

butler's pantry, 61

Cairo F., of Brooklyn, 274

candy box bookcase, 66, desk, 71, 216-8

cardboard "colonials", 149

carpets, 77

Cartheuser, Carl, (Stuttgart), 336-9

Casa from Spain, 228-31

Cass Co. N.D., 135, grocery, 347

cats, 17, 25, 198, 250, 275

Cieslik-Gottschalk Archive (Marianne & Jurgen), 224, 226-7, 235, 241-3, 262-3, 278-9, 303, 328-9, 344

celluloid furniture, 208

chandelier, 10, 13, 28, 46

chapel, 418, 421

Chestnut Hill, 8

chimney sweep, 223

Chinese dining room set, 26

Christmas gardens, 22, 49, 72-3, house, 144, tree, 208, "Christmas in July", 269, Christmas room, 277

churches, 368-70

Cissna, W.A.& Co., 118, 366

clocks, 252

coin silver, 31-3

Colonial Revival, 58, 98, 145, 149

Columbian Exposition, 268

Combination Doll House, 100, grocery, 326-7

concertina table, 53, 163

confidante, 44

Connecticut, houses from, 89-93, 145

conservatory, 278-9, 284

Converse, Morton E., 110, 133-6, 304

cookbook, Nuremberg, 292

Cooper, Patty, 130

Copenhagen, 14

"copper", 164, 199

Coronation chair, 167-8

crèche figure, 289, 290, 292

Cremer's Toy Shop, 181

Crutcher, Ann, 420

Cunard, 192

Cupboard houses, 189-91

curry comb, 362

curtains, net, 79

"Dandy Toy House", 132

Deauville house, 220

dentist office, 312-313

Dibb, 49

Dollhouse Mystery, The, 37

Dolls, 9, 15-16, 54, 80, 157, 163, 166-7, 171, 178, 199, 231, 243, 257, 273, 276, 284, 343

"Dolly's Playhouse", 107

Dorling Kindersley, 206

"Dorothy Hall", 92-5

dovecote, 117, 412

Dowst Manufacturing Co., 150

draperies, original, 28

dressing table mirrors, 163

Dunham's Cocoanut House, 125-6

Dutch door, 87

Earnshaw, Nora, 403

Eastern Shore cottage, 56

Eaton, Faith, 206-7, 400

"Edison House", 81-2

"Eismachine", 300-1

El Rostro, 229

Elastolin zoo, 402-3

elevator, 412-13

Ellis, Britton & Eaton, 29, 31-3, 39

English basement, 23

English houses, 155, 161-3, 170, 188-9

Erath, Sally, 264

Ernst, Janis, 213, 215

Erzgebirge (Saxony) furniture, 164, toys, 349, 404

Essex Institute, Salem, 46

Evans & Cartwright, 167-8, 170-1, 181, 184-6

exposition chair, 39

Farie house, 397

fence, 9, 54, 85

folding house, 123, 137

fireplace with griffons, 10

fish pond, 414

flame-stitch carpet, 167

folding: screen, 54, bungalow, 122, rooms, 270

food, early, 10

Forder, Nick & Esther, 136

Fox, Muriel, 306

Francis, Field & Francis, 28-9

Franco family, 229

Frederick, house from, 17-21

French boudoirs, 257-8

French food market, 352

fret-sawed bedrooms, 259

fretwork, 55, 270-1

fruit rack, 299

Gamage's catalog, 337-9, 346

GAR Centennial canteen, 39

garage, 86

garden room, 63

gardens, houses with, 15-16, 96, 137-8, 218, 234, roof gardens, 412, 420, entrance garden, 415

Garland, Moira, 187

"Gay 'nineties" house, 66-7

Gen. Tom Thumb album, 29

general store, early, 318-19

George IV, 393

Georgian baby house, 156-8

Georgian town house, 157, 159-60, 171

Gerlach, 82, 243, 263

Gertrude's store, 325

Gertrud's house, 74-7

Gibbs Toys, filling station, 382

Giles, Ashby, 102

"Golden Oak", 214

Golliwogs, 214

Gottschalk, Moritz (of Marienberg), 220-7, transitional, 226-7, 234-5, 238-9, 240-3, 245, 260-3, 278-9, 281, 302-3, 306-7, 328-31, milliner's shop, 330-1, 334, 337, 339,

340-1, 344-6, sweetstall, 345, 356-61, caravan, 386-7, gazebo, 396-7

Graddon family, 186, 249

Grass matting, 67

Great Exhibition of 1851, 187

Green, William H., 129

Greenhouses, 394-5

Greenaway, Kate, 188

Greene, Vivien, 37, 161, 248

Greenwich, Conn., house from, 89-93

Grimm & Leeds, 132

Gröber, Carl, 317

Gross, Carl, 350

Gum tragacanth, 316-7

"gutter" houses, 130

"Gutters and Downspouts", 44, 87

Hacker (Christian), 212, 220, 233, 324-5

Haddonfield, N.J., house from, 81-2

hair-dryer, 147

half-inch house, 87

Halifax, Mass., house from, 74-7

handlung, German, early, 320-1

Hancocks, David, 403

Hanna, Mrs. John, 18

Harding, Constance, 17, Harding sisters, 56

harpsichord, 35

"hastener", 158-9

Hauser (German firm of), 402

Hazeltine's Almanac, 32

Hepner, Bessie, 297

Hersey table, 13-14

Hinamatsuri, 408

Hingham, Mass, 14

Hobbies Weekly magazine, 206-7

hooded chimney, 72-3

hooded oven, 291

Hoopes, Clara, 16

"Hospital Model Cottage", 383

hot dish carrier, 291

hot dish cover, 53

hotel, N.J., 389-91

hothouses, 394-5

"House of Mother Goose", 117

"House that Jack Built", 119

houseboat, (from Annapolis), 400

Howard, Marian, 108

Hull & Stafford, 28

Hunt sisters, 40

"indiscrète", 43-4

International Doll House News, 104, 187,
203, 206-7

International Style, 244-5

iron deer, 36

Ives R.R. Station, 380-1

Issmayer, 111

Japan's Girls' Festival, 408

Jewett-Paige touring car, 414

Jugenstil, 233

Kashmir, 400

kerosene dispenser, 321

Kestner, 26, 53, 163, 186, 189, 202

key cabinet, 13

Kilgore, 142

King Arthur's sword, 160

Kingsbury car, 89

kitchens, 60-2, 166, 170, 218, Nuremberg, 288,
Augsberg, 289, 290-3, tin, 294-5, with pantry,
298-9, 305

klismos chairs, 251

Kummerow, Lew, 386-7

ladder chair, 301

Lady Samuelson, 196

lamp, fat, 289

lamps, student, parlor & traditional, 25

Lancaster, Osbert, 67, 169

lavabo, tin, 302

Leeds Toy House, 132

Lehmann, Mr.&Mrs., 327

Leonhardt, Paul, 54

Lichten, Frances, 108, 169

lid rack, 298-9

lift-top commode, 31, lift-top house, 38

light bulbs, 82

lighting, 81-2

Lines Bros., 100, 203-5

"Livestock Express Car", 365

Locke, Felicity, 196

Log Cabin Syrup, 351

Louis XVI furniture, 221

Louis XVI parlor, 252-3, 258

macramé lambrequin, 29

Madame St. Quintin's house, 176-80, 327

Madrid sidewalk stall, 231

Maine Antique Digest, 335, 404

Maine, house from, 87-8

Mamaroneck, N.J., house from, 85

Manayunk NY, house from, 86

Mansard roof, 36

mantle garniture, 257

Marienberg, 245

Märklin, 13, 19, 21, 50, 54, 62, 102, 104, 193, 195,
212, 256-7, 269, catalog, 297, 299, 301, 338,
392

Marshall collection, 166-8

Marshall, Rev. John William Henry, 166-8

Martz, Mrs. James, 49

Mason & Parker, 134, 136

Massachusetts, houses from, 8, 11, 40, 45, 58, 74-
77, 127, 133-6

McClintock, Inez & Marshall, 268

McKim, Mead & White, 58

McLoughlin Bros., 107, 122-4, 137, 398

Mediterranean villa, 216-18

Menoni, Nancy Petrikin, 60, 156, 180

metal epergne, 54

metamorphic bed, 199

Mexican "Mansion", 412-421

Michigan, house from, 66-7, Kalamazoo, 149

mignonettes, 44, 80, 276

milliner's shop, French, 332

milliner, Gottschalk, 330-1

"miniature" (painting), 186

Minnesota, 42

Mitchell, Col. Donald, 228-31

"Model Bakery, The", 170

Moe, Mary Hamilton, 166

money drawer, 318, 320

Moorish Revival shell, 215

Moorish-style bays, 230

Morris Chair, 83

mortar and pestle, 297

"Mt. Vernon-on-the-Rhine", 240

Munn, David C., 390

Murray, Patrick, 323

"Mystery Houses", 60, 101-4, 141

Nag's Head (fretwork cottage from), 55

National Novelty Corp, 120-1, 362

National Trust for Historic Preservation, 44, 49, 54, 79

net curtains, 79

New England, houses from, 8, 11

New Hampshire house, 30-33, 38, 248

New Jersey, houses from, 81-2, 132

"New Practical Doll House, The", 127-9

New York, houses from, 23-6, 85, 144

newspaper wand, 266

newstand, German, 381

Noah's Ark, 400-01

Nuremberg, 212

Ohio, Schoolhouse from, 374

opaline tea set, 43

"Opera House", 379

"ormolu" gilded metal, 26, 35, 37, 41, 248-9, 265

outhouse, 310

Ovingdean, Sussex, 166, 168

pair of rooms, 238-9, 270-3, 278-9

Palladian villa, 187, 196

paper house, 57

Paris Salon, 253

Parker, Elinor, 14

parrots, 279

"Patent Folding House", 123

pavilion, 388

Pawtucket, R.I., 109-10

Pennsylvania, 22, Pennsylvania Cupboard House, 27-9, house from York, 56

Pennsylvania Railroad Worker's House, 83-4

"penny toy" camera, 73, toy, 80, sewing machine, 82

Perkins, Marion I., 145

Pfeiffer, Emil, 402-3

Philadelphia, 15, 141-3

Philadelphia Tin Toy Mfg. Co, 29

phonograph, 266, 419

Pia, Peter F., 267-8

piano, 14, 251, 254

piano-hinge house, 78-80

Pierce, Robert, 25-6

pincushion, 10

Planck, Ernst, 269

plate rack, 162

Platt, Senator Thomas, 23

"Playschool Pullman", 380-1

Playthings magazine, 132

Pollock's Toy Theatre, 405

porcelain shop, Japanese, 342-3

Potter, Beatrix, 269

poultry coop, 291

Pressland, David, 80, 82, 391

Prince of Wales, 167

Pringle, Agnes Gilruth, 383

provenance, houses with, 40-1, 59, 81, 89, 102, kitchen, 306-7

Providence, Rhode Island, 145

Puebla, Mexico, 412-3

Pug dog, 47, 214

Quaker dolls, 15-16

"Quaker Oats" house, 64-5

"Queen Anne Mansion", 212, 324

radiators, 67
radio, 283
radio lights, 208
Recamier sofa, 175
"Red Robin Farm", 365
"red-roofs", 242-3
Reed churches, 369
Regency town house, 157, 169
"Regional" dolls' house architecture, 45
Renaissance Revival, 255
Reus, Jim, 185, 194, 264, 324, 329, 414
Rhode Island, houses from, 109, 145-8
Rochester, N.Y., 144
Rock & Graner table, 158, 178, catalogue, 296-7, 397
"Roosevelt Stock Farm", 133, 364-5
row houses, 72-3

"Sadie", 275
salesmen's samples, 104
sandstone, 36, 156
Santa Claus Toy Manufacturing Co., 144
Satterlee, Dr. Francis Leroy, 51-4
Savory, Kenneth Cyril Barrie, 166
scale, 8, 44, 77
Schneegass, 37, 50, 64, 80, 186, 205, 214, 233, 262-3, 374, 417
Schoenhut, Albert, 110, 139-40
schoolhouses, 373-77, rooms, 375-77
Schwarz, F.A.O., 101-2, 264, 281, 309, 330, 344, 348-9, 391
Schweitzer, Babette, 174
Scientific American, 392
Seaside Villa, 112, 219-21
semi-detached houses, 62-3, 68-9
sewing machine, 202
sewn-in furniture, 219
Shackman, B., 243
shavings barrel, 21
Sheldon, Mrs., 45

shower bath, 77
shutters, workable, 48
Silber & Fleming, 100, 181-7, 196-202
silver plaques, 74
silver tea set, 31
Simon & Halbig grandmother, 47
Simon & Rivollet, 80, 208, 391
Simons, Delora, 413-14
Singer, J.H., 407
skewer racks, 291
Smith, Eleanor McCulloch, 123
Smith, Gertrude Horsey, 57
Smithsonian's National Zoo, 402-3
Sole, Eveline, 203
Somerville, Mass., "Mansion", 11-14, 51
Sotheby's , 264-5
South Jersey "Mansion", 34-7, 186, 248-9
Spain, casa from, 228-31
Spanish Mansion, 150-2
Speaight, George, 406
squirrel cages, 262, 266
St. Louis, room from, 277
stables, Gottschalk, 356-61, Bliss, 362-3, Converse, 364-5
stained glass window, 245
stanhope, 257
Stearns, Emma Owens, 8
Stevens & Brown, 9-10, 13, 31-2, 38, 40-1, 50, catalog, 294-5
Stevenson, Robert Louis, 406
Stirn & Lyon, 96-100, 326-7
store, general, early, 318-9, grocery, 321
street lamps (train), 36, 38-9
Strong (Margaret Woodbury) Museum collection, 113-14, 348
Sunday toy, 368
Sutherland Paper Company, 149
swimming pools, 392

Ta-Ka-Part Dollhouse, 131
tank, kitchen, 294-6, bathroom, 309, dentist office, 312

telephone, 263

terrestrial globe, 249

Tewkesbury, Nancy (Menoni), 180

Theriault's, 402

Thonet furniture, 77

Tiffany-Platt, 7, 23-6, 51, 331

Timpson, Anne, 158

toast rack, 10, 299

Toonerville Trolley, 147

Tootsietoy, 142, 150-2, 243

"Towgood House", 172-5

towel rack, 301

Toy & Miniature Museum of Kansas City, 187

Toy Shop Mystery, The, 317

toy stall, 316-7

toy theatres, 405-7

Treskow, Laura, 157-8, 186

Triang furniture, 208, 400

Tudor, Tasha, 256

'twenties food market, 352

Tynietoy, 92-3, mansion, 145-8

U BUILD IT Playhouse #3, The, 144

unidentified American Houses, 130

Universal German Toy Catalog, 346

unknown makers, 105-6

Upton, Florence, 214

Utrecht doll's house, 47

Venetian blinds, 169

Vernon, Amy II, 145

Victorian Gothic, 164-5

Victorian Gothic furniture, 164, 193, 195

Vienna, 270

Vienna bronzes, 202, 214, 218, 263, 269, mouse, 299, 349, 394-5

villas, 196

W.C., 231

wallpapers, 20, 53, 71

Waltershausen, 14, 20, 29, 37, 186, 195, 248

"Wampum Cottage", 42-44

Wanamaker, John, 132

Ward, Matthew, 54

Washington, D.C., house from, 59, 62-3, 68-9, 137, 281, 285

Washington Evening Star, 420

Washington, George, 241

Watt, Annie Pinkney, 102, 104

waxjack, 110, 191

Wayne Paper Company, 149

wedding, mid-Victorian, 252

Weiss, W.P., 85

White, Gwen, 403

Whitney, Zulime, 49, 59

Whitney-Reed, 120, 127-9

Whitton, Blair, 109, 379

wicker, 63

Wild, H.L., 259

window screens, 89

Windowphanie, 74, 170, 370

Woodward & Lothrop, 137

Wright, Frank Lloyd, 245

Württenberg, foodstore, 350-51

yarn winder, 32

yellow cherry, 37, 214, 417

Youth's Companion, The, 65, 268, 367, 369

Zenorini, Elizabeth, 331

Zillner, Dian, 130, 139, 149

Zimmerman, Elma, 64

zoo, Elastolin, 402-3

zoological garden, 404

Zoological Society of London, 403

SOURCE NOTES

The Ultimate Dolls' House Book by Faith Eaton, foreword by Flora Gill Jacobs, photography by Matthew Ward, Dorling Kindersley Publishing, Inc.,1994, London and New York.

Moritz Gottschalk Dollhouses, Doll Rooms, Kitchens, Stores, Furniture 1892-1931, © Verlag Marianne Cieslik, Jülich 2000, all photos © Fotoarchiv J.&M. Cieslik Publishing © Theriault's Gold Publishing 2000, Germany.

PHOTO CREDITS

Every effort has been made to credit all of the photographers whose photos are featured in this book. We sincerely regret any inadvertent omissions.

Photography © Richard C. Amt, pages: 411, 412, 413, 415, 416 (bottom), 417, 418, 419 (top), 420 (bottom), 421

Photography © Noel Barrett, page: 93

Photography © Haley Berghers, page: 106

Photography © Stanley Cypher, pages: 125, 126 (bottom left),

Photography © Flora Gill Jacobs, pages: 25 (left), 28 (top right), 29 (bottom right, 3 tin dressers), 33, 47 (bottom right), 53 (bottom left), 83 (top), 111 (top right),

Photography © Jim Reus, pages: 8 (right), 10 (all except soup tureen and early busque food), 13 (right top, center and bottom), 14 (top left), 15, 16, 19 (right: top and bottom), 21, 22, 26 (middle center), 28 (bottom left), 29 (all except bottom right, 3 tin dressers), 31 (middle and bottom), 32 (bottom right), 35 (right top, middle and bottom), 36, 37 (top right), 39, 40, 41, 43 (bottom left, center and right), 44, 46 (top right), 47 (bottom left), 49, 50 (top left), 51 (bottom left), 53 (bottom right), 54 (bottom left and right), 55, 56, 57, 58, 59, 62, 65 (left top, middle and bottom), 66 (right top and bottom), 67, 68, 71, 73 (top left), 75 (top left), 76 (right), 80 (left and right), 82 (right top and bottom), 85, 87, 88, 93 (top and bottom), 95, 100, 102 (top left and right), 103 (top right), 104, 105, 107, 110-111 (all except top right), 116 (top right), 118-119, 120 (bottom left), 121 (top right), 122, 123 (bottom), 124, 126 (top left and bottom right), 127, 128, 130, 131, 132, 133, 134, 135, 136, 137, 138, 140, 144, 147 (right top, middle and bottom), 148, 149, 152, 157 (right top and bottom), 158, 159 (left), 160, 162 (right top and bottom), 163 (left and top right), 164 (middle and right), 166, 168, 170 (right top and bottom), 174 (top right), 175, 176 (left), 177 (right), 178, 180 (right top and bottom), 184, 185, 186, 187, 188, 189, 191 (all details on right except top chair), 193 (right top and bottom), 195 (left top and bottom, right bottom), 199, 202, 205 (details), 207 (left), 208 (middle and right), 211, 212, 213 (top), 214 (bottom), 214, 215 (top), 218, 219, 220, 221 (right), 224, 225, 226, 227, 231, 22, 233, 235, 238, 239, 242, 243, 247, 248, 249, 250 (top), 251, 254 (left), 256, 258 (top), 259, 269, 275 (right top and bottom), 276, 277, 279 (top left), 280, 283 (top), 284 (left and top right), 285, 289 (top left and right), 293, 294, 295 (top and bottom left), 298, 299, 301 (top, middle right, bottom right), 302, 303, 304-305 (interior), 307 (bottom right), 308, 309, 310, 313 (bottom 321 (top left and right, bottom right), 324 (top), 328, 329 (top left and right), 331 (right top and bottom), 332, 336, 337 (two details), 339, 340-341 (interior), 343 (right top and bottom), 344, 345, 347, 348, 349, 350, 351, 352, 356, 357, 358, 359, 360 (bottom left), 363 (bottom right), 364, 365, 366, 367, 368, 369, 371, 372, 373, 374 (right), 376, 380, 381, 382 (bottom), 383, 385, 386, 387, 388, 390, 391, 392, 393, 395, 397 (right top and bottom), 398-399, 400 (top left), 401, 405, 406, 407 (top), 413, 414, 416 (top left and right), 419 (bottom left, middle and right), 420 (top),

Photography © Richard K. Robinson, pages: 42, 43 (top), 78-79, 80 (bottom), 141, 164 (left), 172, 173, 196-197, 198, 200, 201, 203, 204-205 (interior), 207 (right), 208 (left),

Photography © Matthew Ward, pages: 7, 8 (left), 9, 11,12, 13 (chair, left), 14 (bottom left and right), 17, 18-19 (interior), 20, 23 (for Dorling Kindersley Publishing, Inc.), 24 (for Dorling Kindersley Publishing, Inc.), 25 (right for Dorling Kindersley Publishing, Inc.), 26 (top center, middle right, bottom right; all for Dorling Kindersley Publishing, Inc.), 27, 28 (bottom right), 30, 31 (top right), 34, 34-35 (interior), 37 (top left), 38, 45, 46 (top left), 48, 51 (top right), 52, 53 (top left and right), 54 (top and middle), 60, 61, 63, 64, 65 (right, interior), 69, 70, 72-73, 73 (top right), 74, 75 (interior), 76 (left), 77, 81, 82 (top left), 83 (bottom), 84, 86, 89, 90-91, 92, 96, 97, 101, 102-103 (interior), 108 (for Dorling Kindersley Publishing, Inc.), 109 (for Dorling Kindersley Publishing, Inc.), 113, 116 (bottom right, for Dorling Kindersley Publishing, Inc.), 117, 121 (top left, for Dorling Kindersley Publishing, Inc.), 139 (for Dorling Kindersley Publishing, Inc.), 142-143, 145, 146-147 (interior), 150, 155, 156, 157 (left), 159 (right), 161, 162 (left), 169, 170 (left), 171 (left), 176-177 (interior), 179, 180 (left), 181, 182-183, 190-191 (interior), 192-193 (interior), 194, 206, 215 (bottom), 216-217, 222, 223 (left), 228-229, 230, 234, 236-237, 240, 241, 244, 245, 250 (bottom), 252, 253, 254 (right), 255 (for Dorling Kindersley Publishing, Inc.), 257, 258 (bottom), 260-261, 262, 263, 264, 265, 266, 270-271, 272-273, 274-275 (interior), 278-279 (interior), 281, 282-283, 287, 288-289 (interior, for Dorling Kindersley Publishing, Inc.), 290, 291, 296, 297, 300-301 (interior), 306-307 (interior), 312-313, 315, 316, 317 (top left and bottom left), 318-319 (interior), 320, 322, 324, 325, 326, 327, 330-331 (interior for Dorling Kindersley Publishing, Inc.), 334, 336-337 (interior), 341 (top right), 342-343 (interior), 355, 360-361, 363 (left top and bottom), 363, 370, 374 (left), 375 (for Dorling Kindersley Publishing, Inc.), 377 (for Dorling Kindersley Publishing, Inc.), 278-279, 394, 396-397, 400 (bottom), 402-403, 404, 407 (bottom), 408, 412, 415,

Photography © The Washington Dolls' House and Toys Museum, pages: 10 (early bisque food), 65, (base of house), 66 (left), 99, 114, 115, 116 (lower left), 163 (center), 165, 167, 171 (right), 174 (bottom right), 223 (top and bottom right), 267, 311, 333, 389